MW01222102

Challenging Neoliberalism at
Turkey's Gezi Park

SOCIAL MOVEMENTS AND TRANSFORMATION

This series tackles one of the central issues of our time: the rise of large-scale social movements and the transformation of society over the last 30 years. As global capitalism continues to affect broader segments of the world's population—workers, peasants, the self-employed, the unemployed, the poor, indigenous peoples, women, and minority ethnic groups—there is a growing mass movement by the affected populations to address the inequities engendered by the globalization process. These popular mass movements across the globe (such as labor, civil rights, women's, environmental, indigenous, and anti-corporate globalization movements) have come to form a viable and decisive force to address the consequences of the operations of the transnational corporations and the global capitalist system. The study of these social movements—their nature, social base, ideology, and strategy and tactics of mass struggle—is of paramount importance if we are to understand the nature of the forces that are struggling to bring about change in the global economy, polity, and social structure. This series aims to explore emerging movements and develop viable explanations for the kind of social transformations that are yet to come.

Series Editor:

Berch Berberoglu is Professor of Sociology and Director of Graduate Studies in Sociology at the University of Nevada, Reno.

Titles:

Social Movements in Latin America: Neoliberalism and Popular Resistance
James Petras and Henry Veltmeyer

Challenging Neoliberalism at Turkey's Gezi Park: From Private Discontent to Collective Class Action
Efe Can Gürcan and Efe Peker

Challenging Neoliberalism at Turkey's Gezi Park

From Private Discontent to Collective Class Action

Efe Can Gürcan and Efe Peker

First published in 2015 by
PALGRAVE MACMILLAN®
in the United States—a division of St. Martin's Press LLC,
175 Fifth Avenue, New York, NY 10010.

Where this book is distributed in the UK, Europe and the rest of the world,
this is by Palgrave Macmillan, a division of Macmillan Publishers Limited,
registered in England, company number 785998, of Houndmills,
Basingstoke, Hampshire RG21 6XS.

Palgrave Macmillan is the global academic imprint of the above companies
and has companies and representatives throughout the world.

Palgrave® and Macmillan® are registered trademarks in the United States,
the United Kingdom, Europe and other countries.

ISBN: 978–1–137–46901–4

Library of Congress Cataloging-in-Publication Data

Gürcan, Efe Can.
    Challenging neoliberalism at Turkey's Gezi Park : from private
discontent to collective class action / Efe Can Gürcan and Efe Peker.
        pages cm
    Includes bibliographical references and index.
    ISBN 978–1–137–46901–4 (hardcover : alk. paper)
        1. Social movements—Turkey. 2. Protest movements—Turkey.
    3. Neoliberalism—Turkey. 4. Turkey—Politics and government—1980–
    I. Title.

HN656.5.A8G87 2015
303.48′409561—dc23   2014027853

A catalogue record of the book is available from the British Library.

Design by Newgen Knowledge Works (P) Ltd., Chennai, India.

First edition: January 2015

10 9 8 7 6 5 4 3 2 1

To the memory of Berkin Elvan (15), Ali İsmail Korkmaz (19), Ethem Sarısülük (27), Abdullah Cömert (22), Mehmet Ayvalıtaş (20), Ahmet Atakan (22), Medeni Yıldırım (18), and others who were killed by the police during and after the Gezi Park Protests.

Contents

Acknowledgments

Chapter 3 is derived from the article titled "Turkey's Gezi Park Demonstrations of 2013: A Marxian Analysis of the Political Moment," published in *Socialism & Democracy* (2014, 28: 1, www.tandfonline.com). An earlier version of Chapter 2 was written as a paper titled "A Class Analytic Approach to the Gezi Park Events: Challenging the Myth of 'Middle Classes.'" This work won the Graduate Student Paper Award of the Marxist Section of the American Sociological Association (*Albert Szymanski-T.R. Young/Critical Sociology Marxist Sociology Graduate Student Paper Award*), and is featured in *Capital & Class* (2015, 39: 2, www.sagepub.com). The authors would like to thank Taylor & Francis and Sage Publications for the permissions.

Introduction: Neoliberal Globalization, State Intervention, and Collective Action

The study of the state and social movements cannot be disassociated from the particular ways in which neoliberal capitalism is organized worldwide, which is ever more true in the face of what the popular buzzword brands as a "globalizing" world. Echoing Lenin's classical work on capitalist imperialism, Berch Berberoğlu rightfully asserts that "globalization is the highest stage of imperialism that has penetrated every corner of the world" (Berberoglu 2003, 125). The association of globalization with imperialism implies that contemporary neoliberalism has resulted not from the so-called spontaneous market forces, but from a class strategy that finds its expression in "economic, political, and military violence" exerted by the capitalist states themselves (Petras and Veltmeyer 2011, 221). With the worldwide expansion of capitalism, the nationally organized capitalist state acts as the repressive-institutional arm of neoliberalism insofar as it intensifies exploitation through the expansion of cheap labor, aggressively commodifies living spaces and social relationships, and depletes natural resources (Berberoglu 2003, 127–128). Under neoliberal globalization, the state is thus of strategic importance to suppress the ever-growing social-economic contradictions of worldwide capitalist expansion at national and international levels (Berberoglu 2003, 136).

In contrast to globalist accounts that see globalization as the negation of the national state, the way capitalist societies develop relies upon the particular trajectories of reinvigorated state apparatuses that have retained their capacity to intervene

Figure I.1 Taksim Square, June 7, 2013. Photo courtesy of Mstyslav Chernov/Unframe.

in the economy, civil society, and social space (Petras 2003). As David Harvey (2005a, 7, 117) stresses, "neoliberalism cannot function without a strong state,", which is inherently undemocratic in that it reflects "the interests of private property owners, businesses, multinational corporations, and financial capital." Accordingly, it can be argued that the national state, rather than an amorphous site of "transnational activism," has presented itself as the primary terrain of a struggle that can enable genuinely foundational and structural transformation of neoliberal power dynamics. Hence the need for strong nationally organized movements that can challenge dominant classes and neoliberal states (Petras 2003, 47, 53). The transformative and emancipatory potential of popular-democratic movements depends on the political agency of class forces having attained a certain degree of leadership and cohesion in countering the advances of neoliberal development (Berberoglu 2010, 127–128). Global connections and solidarity between these disruptive movements, moreover, become paramount in an age where neoliberal globalization presents itself in geographically specific assaults on working populations.

As James Petras and Henry Veltmeyer argue, there is no ready-made formula to defeat the forces of neoliberal globalization and to rebuild society in a way that enables men and women to realize their human potential in line with egalitarian and fraternal principles (Petras and Veltmeyer 2013, 217). The coordinates for a better world rather lie in the successes and failures of individual experiments and experiences of different movements and countries with special attention paid to the ways in which the transition from "private discontent" to "collective action" can be made possible (Petras and Veltmeyer 2013, 216–217). Indeed, what is meant here by collective action is an alliance of social forces to initiate extra-parliamentary/disruptive action with the purpose of protecting communal space and social rights through the alteration of state power via frontal tactics (Petras and Veltmeyer 2011, 224). In more precise terms, the real question then becomes: "how to move from weakened, fragmented labor and social movements in retreat or on the defensive, to a position capable of launching" an offensive against various manifestations of neoliberalization (Petras and Veltmeyer 2013, 216–217)?

A myriad of factors are to be taken into account for such popular-democratic transition, which concerns the questions of (a) the correlation of structural class forces and the social class base, (b) material/objective conditions and "opportunities" in the conjunctural environment, (c) prominent organizational forms as well as organizational strategies and tactics to reinforce collective action, and (d) the symbiotic relationship between social mobilization and the articulation of political consciousness (Petras and Veltmeyer 2013, 204, 216–217). Each of these factors is inscribed in the organizational structure of the present book. Whereas the social base of a given movement speaks to its structural class background and composition, "opportunities" refer to complementary material conditions that set the conjunctural environment for collective action (Petras and Veltmeyer 2013, 216). In this book, we build on Petras and Veltmeyer's insight into mobilizing opportunities in order to contribute to a more nuanced Marxist explanation of how collective action is shaped by the political-economic and cultural-ideological conjuncture.

Organizational forms, moreover, pertain to how social solidarity, mobilization, and decision-making/participation are organized by social forces. Consensus decision-making and popular forums in the Occupy Movement is a good example for this category. In turn, strategy can be provisionally defined as class actors' choices about "targets, timings, and tactics" that dictate how to achieve movement goals and win the overall struggle, whereas tactics can be understood as the small-scale class actions and sub-goals that serve to win the individual battles of the wider struggle as it is defined by a given set of strategies (Nepstad 2011). Despite their fundamental differences, an underlying strategy of the Occupy Movement, the Arab Spring, and the Gezi Park Protests has been that of occupying public spheres and peaceful mass rallies, aiming to bypass conventional democratic tools to create new channels of social solidarity and struggle. Some of the tactics used in Gezi Park to support these strategies were the active use of social media, street and performance art, sit-ins, building barricades, flashing lights, pot-banging, etc. Our focus on organizational forms, strategies, and tactics (or shortly, "repertoires"), will be supplemented by an analysis of membership and leadership dynamics of collective action, as these dynamics are literally the "author" of organizational-strategic initiatives.

Finally, we refer to political consciousness as a crucial determinant in the emergence, spread, and sustainability of social mobilization. Taken as a shared sense of social critique of dominant class practices, the process of acquiring and developing political consciousness via social mobilization involves collective cognitive processes that challenge social systems of oppression for their injustice and illegitimacy. Re-appropriating Doug McAdam's (1982) term of "cognitive liberation," Guy Debord's concept of "détournement" (diversion), and Mikhail Bakthin's understanding of the "carnivalesque," we will contend that a distinguishing feature of Gezi Park's political consciousness was the humorous technique of "cognitive diversion," popularly known as the *Orantısız Zeka*, or Disproportionate Intelligence. Cognitive diversion overturns and exposes the incoherence and contradictions of ruling ideologies and government rhetoric through the active utilization of humor in a political context.

By definition, neoliberal globalization rests on processes of unequal and combined development, which are not only geographically specific in terms of economic relations, but they also manifest themselves in diverse forms of political arrangements and cultural/ideological configurations (Harvey 2005b, Peck and Theodore 2012). Accordingly, the social and spatial struggles against the different faces of neoliberal expansion would also vary deriving from the characteristics of the geography under discussion. It is the purpose of this study to tease out the experiments and experiences of one such disruptive movement in the particularity of Turkey, which aimed at the protection of social space and rights against the Islamically legitimated repressive neoliberal sociospatial policies of the Justice and Development Party (AKP) government, occurring in what came to be known as the Gezi Park Protests (GPPs) in June 2013. What is the social basis, class nature, and major grievances of these movements? What material/objective and subjective factors account for the emergence and persistence of such strong uprisings that have adopted not only extra-parliamentary, but also frontal tactics? How did they effect the development of leadership mechanisms and political consciousness that can potentially alter the configuration of social forces in the country? We hope that our enterprise will contribute to the understanding of the prospects and limitations of emerging popular-egalitarian alternatives to neoliberalism.

We use the term GPPs to refer to the nationwide anti-government protest cycle that erupted in Turkey on May 31, 2013, which began as a localized demonstration against the destruction of a public park at the heart of Istanbul, Gezi Park, to spark a far-reaching uprising across the country. Our understanding of the GPPs is not limited to its narrow sense that solely denotes the park and its surroundings in Istanbul. Instead, we underline the significance of "Gezi Park" as a nationally recognized and acted out symbol that triggered and reinforced anti-governmental collective action throughout June 2013 and after, as manifested in the widespread slogan, "everywhere is Taksim, everywhere is resistance." The meaning of the protests emanates from the fact that they are of unprecedented form and scale in Turkey's history. Having said that, the purpose of the book is not to provide a detailed chronological summary of the GPPs, but to theoretically tease out the structural and conjunctural foundations of the movement, along with its organizational/ leadership mechanisms, strategic and tactical repertoires, and modes of engagement with political consciousness and cognitive transformation. Our primary temporal delimitation is the approximately two-week period between Friday, May 31, 2013 and Sunday, June 16, 2013, namely the interval between the outbreak of the nationwide protests and the recapture of Gezi Park by the police. The book, nonetheless, will be in continuous dialog with the rest of Turkey's "longest summer," as well as the post-Gezi sociopolitical developments including the 12 months that followed the events.

Before dawn on May 31, 2013, the police stormed into the park to violently disperse the few hundred protesters who had been occupying the space to prevent its destruction as part of a municipal urban renewal project. By the day's end, hundreds of thousands of people throughout the country were out in the streets in a spontaneous collective response to what they perceived as the rising authoritarianism and conservatism of the AKP government. A modest urban park thus turned into a bastion and symbol of resistance against the increasingly authoritarian and socially interventionist rule of the AKP, and more specifically, Prime Minister (PM) Recep Tayyip Erdoğan.

The abrupt and spontaneous nature of the protests cannot be overemphasized. No specialist on Turkey could envisage a collective mobilization of such magnitude and versatility until the very moment it erupted. Yet when it did, it was difficult to believe that the masses had been silent for so long. Four days earlier, as the earthmovers started demolishing Gezi Park at 23:30 on Monday May 27, nothing was out of the ordinary: it was just another urban redevelopment project with relatively little public concern outside of the Taksim region. The first tweet calling people to action for the cause of Gezi Park was posted at 23:47; yet the person who wrote it could not have known that this would be the first of millions to come in the following weeks. On May 28, more and more people moved into the park with tents, books, and guitars, slowly turning it into a festival area despite the presence of bulldozers and the intermittent police attacks.

The symbolic photo of "the lady in red" frantically tear-gassed by a police officer was taken that day, which was also when people stood in front of the earthmovers to stop the demolition. On May 29, celebrating the 560th anniversary of Istanbul's conquest by the Ottomans in 1453, PM Erdoğan spoke in the grandiose ceremony that laid the foundations of the city's third bridge: "Do whatever you want in Gezi Park. We have made our decision." Taking the cue from the PM, police began burning the protesters' tents in the morning of Thursday May 30, accompanied by the extensive, reckless, and indiscriminate use of tear gas, pepper spray, and pressurized water. Yet instead of causing intimidation, police violence paradoxically brought in larger groups of protesters to the park as the weekend approached, along with raising awareness and agitation across the country. An even more violent police raid on Gezi Park and its surrounding areas was carried out before dawn on May 31, and after a day-long crackdown, all hell broke loose on that Friday evening, when hundreds of thousands took the streets in solidarity, not only in Istanbul, but across the country.

Nationwide figures are indicative of the GPPs' significance as an exceptional protest cycle in Turkey's history. According to the most conservative estimations (announced by the government), in the course of a few weeks, over 2.5 million people—labeled "a handful of marauders [çapulcu]" by the PM—filled the streets and occupied public places in 79 cities. In a survey conducted in 21 cities in June 2013, 12.1 percent of the population above the age 18 declared that they have participated in the protests (according to 2013 figures, the number of people above 18 in Turkey is approximately 50 million people) (Andy-Ar 2013, 5). Police violence caused more than 7,500 injuries and a total of 7 deaths among the protesters.[1] The police sprayed 3,000 tons of water and fired 150,000 gas bombs at the people. In addition to the deaths, 3 people remained in critical condition, 63 were severely injured, 106 suffered from severe head traumas, and 11 people lost an eye; 13.5 million tweets were shared with the supportive tags "direngeziparki, occupygezi, direnankara, direntaksim and direngezi" ("diren" means "resist" in Turkish). All this happened in less than a month.

The present book seeks to contribute to the Marxist analysis of the GPPs by focusing on its structural correlation of class forces, material-objective conditions and conjunctural opportunities, organizational forms, and articulation of political consciousness. The study opens with a theoretical engagement that exposes the deficiencies of the "new social movement" (NSM) perspective to explain social mobilization, which represents the genesis of civil society-centric, that is, classless and/or stateless approaches of left-wing globalists. The NSM perspective is used interchangeably here with the notion of the "New Left," which denotes in the specific context of this book a leftward liberal-democratic intellectual tradition that nourishes similarly from civil society centrism, cultural reductionism, post-Marxist pluralism, poststructuralism, and/or postmodernism. Having dropped the concepts of social classes, state power, imperialism, and neoliberalism, this Western "New Left" camp legitimizes capitalist-bourgeois hegemony based on an artificially counter-hegemonic language revolving around the notions of "information society," "communication revolution," "transnationalism," "corporate globalization/stateless capitalism/global corporations," "Empire," and "liberal democracy" (Petras 2003, 2001b, a). The first chapter also deals with the manifestations of the European New Left camp in Turkey, which came to be known as the "liberal Left," or what one can justifiably refer to as the "neoliberal left." Finally, the limitations and contradictions of the analysis of the GPPs by the Turkish liberal Left are discussed in light of an overall Marxist critique of NSM theories.

As an antidote to NSM perspectives, the second chapter presents a Marxist theory of class analysis building on the works of Nicos Poulantzas and Erik Olin Wright. Using that framework, we demystify the myth of "middle classes" revolving around the GPPs, which helps obscure the class dynamics of social change, by systematically analyzing the class composition and the balance of class forces in contemporary Turkey. The focal point of this chapter is the analysis of various fractions of wage-earning classes in Turkey and the ways in which their structural and organizational class capacities have evolved to lead to the GPPs under what one could call the AKP's "neoliberalism with

Islamic characteristics" (Karaman 2013). A fundamental theme throughout the book, the latter conception does not imply a "type" of neoliberalism with an essentially distinct *modus operandi*. Instead, congruent with uneven and combined development, the conception refers to the historically and geographically specific form neoliberalism has taken under the AKP government in Turkey, which presents political-economic and cultural-ideological attributes particular to this country.[2]

The third chapter ties the structural class analysis to the specific conjunctural context of the GPPs with special attention to the material/objective factors and circumstances prior to the protests. As such, this chapter provides a political economic reading of the AKP's neoliberalism in urban space and its sociocultural-ideological implications, which served as the "opportunities" that allowed the transition from private discontent to collective mobilization. Building on the preliminary discussion in Chapter 2, we devote particular attention to the analysis of the Islamic-bourgeois reorganization of political and civil society under the AKP government, its social interventionism, increasing political repression, and unaccountable Middle Eastern policy. With this in mind, we portray the economic and political-cultural conjuncture prior to the GPPs in order to trace the immediate grievances of Gezi protesters.

Chapter 4 shifts the focus to the organizational and strategic aspects of mass mobilization, namely collective leadership mechanisms of the GPPs and its various repertoires. The chapter not only examines the involvement of leading participant organizations in the protests, but also discusses how the protests' collective leadership developed and performed a vast array of strategic and tactical toolkits, generating what we call "repertoire cultivation" for group action. Engaging with a critique of the civil society-centric romanticization of "leaderless" spontaneous mobilization as a "virtuous" feature of social movements, we also argue that spontaneity is but a matter of degree, and that the GPPs expanded on concrete collective leadership mechanisms that rule out the civil society-centric "leaderlessness thesis" of the neoliberal Left. Strategic and tactical repertoires were rather cultivated through that collective leadership.

Chapter 5 expands on the subjective aspects of collective action, and offers a detailed analysis of how political conscious-ness and socio-political agency are articulated during the GPPs. That is to say, the chapter focuses on the rich variety of cogni-tive practices expressed in an innovative and humorous man-ner. This will help explain how the Gezi movement came to generate a "good sense" of social critique, establishing a moral/normative and psychological superiority over the AKP govern-ment and appropriating the streets despite police repression. We aim to reveal the ways in which the transformative potential of "cognitive diversion" in the GPPs has been maximized through *Orantısız Zeka*. Disproportionate Intelligence was used by the protesters to counter the excessive, or "disproportionate vio-lence" used by the police forces during the GPPs. This notion is commonly used to refer to the deployment of creative and humorous slogans, tweets, music, graffiti, photo captions, videos, and other forms of street and online media that chal-lenge and ridicule the various manifestations of the repressive and conservative neoliberal urban-cultural transformations in Turkey.

Our concluding chapter, finally, contextualizes the aftermath of the GPPs in contemporary Turkish politics. Here, we argue that Gezi Park was the initial catalyst to instigate a "critical juncture" in the country's sociopolitical scene, which opened a contingent period for relatively rapid transformations, the out-come of which cannot yet be determined due to the ongoing nature of the process (Mahoney 2000). In this sense, we seek to show that although the GPPs as a primary protest cycle are over, the historical process initiated by Gezi has in fact never come to an end. Morcover, based on the accumulated data in the 12 months that followed the protest cycle, the chapter identifies the emergent "path dependencies" the GPPs have created for the AKP, which have increasingly locked the government in a politi-cal trajectory that necessitates further authoritarianism and centralization of power to be able to hold on to its rule. We also show in this chapter that certain repertoires and mindsets that were cultivated in the GPPs were reactivated and utilized in this post-Gezi context to establish an enduring culture of resistance and social critique among the non-AKP population. Finally, we discuss the significance of the GPPs in the larger framework of disruptive social mobilization in the neoliberal era.

1
New Social Movement Theories and Their Discontents

The rise of neoliberalism as a global political economic project in the 1980s was parallel in time with what Ellen Meiksins
Wood (1998) calls a tendency of "retreat from class" as an
explanatory concept in social sciences. As she puts it, "the most
distinctive feature of this current is the autonomization of ideology and politics from any social basis, and more specifically,
from any class foundation", which leads to a "rejection of the
materialist analysis of social and historical processes" (Wood
1998, 2, 5). A significant repercussion of the escape from class
in academia has been the outpouring of a post-Marxist literature on the "new social movements" (or the "cultural turn")
with poststructuralist or postmodernist leanings that reject the
centrality of class analysis in the name of identity/civil society
centrism. Post-Marxist attempts put into question the analytic
relevance of social class and condemn any attempt to reclaim
its conceptual centrality as an archaic and dogmatic practice of
determinism.

This chapter is an attempt to provide a critique of new social
movement (NSM) theories. The first section is devoted to a critical presentation of the main arguments of NSM theories based
on the work of Alain Touraine, Alberto Melucci, and Manuel
Castells. The second section discusses the Turkish counterpart of the European new social movement trend, which is
known as the "(neo-)liberal Left" tradition for its post-Marxist/

poststructuralist/postmodernist tendencies as well as its emphasis on civil society centrism, essentialism/demonization of the state, and other notions that exclude social classes, imperialism, and neoliberalism. In the final section we elaborate further on our Marxist critique of NSM theories and discuss the ramifications of these perspectives for the Turkish liberal Left's response to the GPPs.

Ia. The ABCs of New Social Movement Theories

NSM theories started out as an attempt to make sense of the neoliberal restructuring of the global political economic system starting from the 1980s, which ironically amounted to adopting the very epistemological assumptions of the neoliberal *Weltanschauung*. Spearheaded by European critical social scientists, they set out to critique the top-down approach of the new generation of US-based social movements theoreticians, who assigned a secondary role to cultural factors and agency (Polletta and Jasper 2001, 286, Buechler 1995). Alain Touraine, a French sociologist, is considered to be one of the founding fathers of NSM theories (Melucci 1989). Touraine contends that the "postindustrial condition" increases the autonomy and differentiation of social actors insofar as the state cedes to be an agent of social integration (Touraine 1988, 32–33). He explains that NSMs emerged among systemic transformations that led to drastic changes in the structure of society (Touraine 1988, 25). Using a mainstream economistic language, Touraine's actor-centered approach views culture as a "stake" or "resource" that needs to be controlled and appropriated by social agents, and suggests placing culturally defined social action and agency at the center of sociological inquiry (Touraine 1988, 6–8). Accordingly, Touraine's work defines social movements as "actors, opposed to each other by relations of domination and conflict [that] have the same cultural orientations and are in contention for the social management of this culture and of the activities it produces" (Touraine 1988, 9).

Building on a critique of modernity that allegedly denies all particularisms, insists on universal values and norms, and promotes a unilinear and evolutionist understanding of history, Touraine advocates for the necessity of "liberating" social actors from social systems' structural confines by emphasizing the actors' presumed autonomy in deciding their own cultural orientations (Touraine 1988, 3–5, 10–11, 26–27). Touraine's rejection of social actors' determination by external/structural factors and social systems leads him to the conclusion that "the subject can no longer be defined in historical terms" (Touraine 1988, 40). He goes on: "societies are less and less 'in' history; they produce themselves their historical existence by their economic, political, and cultural capacity to act upon themselves and to produce their future and even their memory" (Touraine 1988, 155). According to Touraine, the biggest "capital" or "investment" of social movements is their particularistic historicity, or simply their self-consciousness defined as the "capacity of a society to construct its practices from cultural models and through conflicts and social movements" (Touraine 1988, xxiv, 8, 11–12, 41). By acquiring historicity, social movements are able to ensure unity and control upon their activities so as to create and shape social situations (Touraine 1988, 11, 26).

At first glance, Touraine's notions of social agency, particularism, and historicity seem to resonate with the GPPs in that most protesters stood up for the preservation of their secular lifestyles constrained by the AKP's social interventionist policies. These interventions included, for instance, the stigmatization and limitation of alcohol consumption, abortion, C-section, public show of affection and love, nonmarital relationships, etc. However, as the following chapters of this book reveal, such social interventionist policies cannot be dissociated from their political economic background that set the stage for cultural struggles. This, of course, is not to neglect the fact that cultural struggles also have a determinative influence over political economic processes. The main point here is to stress that a fuller appreciation of cultural-ideological struggles requires an in-depth understanding of class dynamics and the historically and geographically specific processes of neoliberal restructuring. This, however, invalidates Touraine's thesis that the actors are more and more outside of history insofar as they become purely "autonomous," that is, under-determined by the course of universal history and other material forces.

Similar to Touraine, Alberto Melucci, the scholar who coined the term "new social movement theory," builds on the assumption of "postindustrial information society" (Melucci 1996, 6). This argument advocates that the development of communication technologies gave rise to the emergence of a global media system so as to undermine class-based social conflict and analysis (Melucci 1996, 8–9). Melucci understands social movements as "complex networks among the different levels and meanings of social action" (Melucci 1996, 4). He points out that social movements' capacity for autonomous action depends on their "collective identity" defined as "an interactive process through which several individuals or groups define the meaning of their action and the field of opportunities and constraints for such an action" (Melucci 1996, 67). Social movements are then expected to forge their collective identity, acquire autonomy, and express themselves through the use of symbolic resources and communicative networks (Melucci 1996, 79, 92, 113–114). As such, Melucci proposes to conceive of inequality and power on the grounds of control over the master codes, that is, "powerful symbolic resources that frame the information" (Melucci 1996, 178–179). Melucci further claims that the real power originates in the capacity of the global media to organize the people's mind (Melucci 1996, 179).

Following Touraine's lead, Manuel Castells provides an action- and outcome-oriented definition of social movements. Social movements are "purposive collective actions whose outcome, in victory as in defeat, transforms the values and institutions of society" (Castells 2010, 3). Similar to Touraine, he suggests analyzing social movements based on three categories: the movement's "identity" ("the self-definition of the movement of what it is, on behalf of whom it speaks"), "adversary" ("the

movement's principal enemy"), and "societal goal" ("the movement's vision of the kind of social order, or social organization
it would wish to attain") (Castells 2010, 74). Castells believes
that the primary source of "purposive collective actions" is collective identity, that is "the process of construction of meaning
on the basis of a cultural attribute, or a related set of cultural
attributes, that is given priority over other sources of meaning"
(Castells 2010, 6). Furthermore, NSMs rely on social networks,
namely decentered forms of organizations that mobilize people
by producing and distributing cultural codes (Castells 2010,
362). Castells propounds that the articulation of collective identity by social movements is primarily shaped by a global condition of what he calls "informational capitalism" or "network
society," giving privilege to the primacy of communication and
media technologies (Castells 2010, 1). According to Castells,
the state's role in representing a unitary identity is seriously
challenged by globalization as it provides fertile ground for
the proliferation of plural identities as autonomous constructs.
In addition, globalization supposedly decentralizes power and
develops empowering communication and media technologies
(Castells 2010, 271–272, 300–308, 342–343).

As Melucci and Castells would agree, there is no doubt that
social media (Facebook, Twitter, etc.), alternative media, and
other new communication technologies (smart phones, com-
puters, etc.) played a significant role in the emergence and
development of the GPPs in Turkey. However, the power of
communication is only one side of the coin, and the source and
content of collective action cannot be reduced to its means of
communication. There is a myriad of other factors that are at
least as important as the existence of communication networks
and technologies. The latter does not mean anything by itself
without the existence of strong movement strategies, leadership
and membership dynamics, political consciousness, and so on.
We will seek to demonstrate in the coming chapters that the
strength of the GPPs emanated from a combination of mutually reinforcing collective action and leadership mechanisms,

including the legacy of past struggles and historical experiences as well as the active involvement of socialist parties and groups, which are casted off as "vanguardism" by most NSM scholars.

In addition, as will be shown in what follows, what the GPPs rejected was not Castell's amorphous notion of "informational capitalism," but rather the Islamically articulated and legitimated urban neoliberal political economic policies of the AKP government itself. This very fact also invalidates Castell's bold argument that the state is weakened in absolute terms and decentralized by some abstract "global forces" originating from information and technological revolutions. In fact, during the GPPs, the state came to use technological surveillance mechanisms both in the streets and on the Internet so as to arrest the social media users who supported or were directly involved in the protests. Social media and communication technologies, in this sense, are a double-edged sword in that the government also uses them to monitor the protesters more easily and spread disinformation (DigitalTrends 2013, TheGuardian 2013f, Today'sZaman 2013a). Even outside the particular context of the GPPs, it is well known that the state, as exemplified in the US government, employs social media and communication technologies to build a "centralized" intelligence database, contrary to Melucci and Castell's assertions on "information society" that decentralizes and weakens states (Damon 2013, Washington'sBlog 2013, GlobalResearch 2011). Likewise, the increasing state potential to monitor and manipulate information reveals the inaccuracy of Touraine and Melucci's overemphasis of the increasing potential of social actors to become autonomous, and independently define the meaning of their action.

1b. The Echoes of NSM Theories in Turkey: The (Neo)Liberal Left

Having its roots in the civil society centrism, essentialism/demonization of the state, and culturalism of the European New Left, the (neo-)liberal Left in Turkey constitutes a political-intellectual tradition that is represented by former Marxists, post-Marxists, liberals, poststructuralists, and postmodernists.[1] Despite a few internal disagreements on minor issues, the liberal Left seems to agree on the democratizing effects of "globalization" and trans-nationalism as well as the need to drop or trivialize the concepts of social classes, the national state (unless it is essentialized/demonized), and imperialism (Aladağ 2013). Using Wood's (1998, 7) language, the neoliberal Left perspective in Turkey can be regarded at best as "another repetition of banal and hoary right-wing social-democratic nostrums," where "the idea that capitalist democracy need only be 'extended'" for the creation of a just society lies at the heart of the analyses. Moreover, this intellectual tradition rejects "old-fashioned" notions such as US imperialism, equates anti-imperialism with chauvinistic nation-alism and putchism, and argues fiercely for Turkey's integration into the European Union (EU) for "democratization"—with nothing to say on the EU's imperialist political-cultural initia-tives (Engel-Di Mauro 2006). Reducing the whole history of the Turkish Republic to top-down authoritarianism and oppres-sion, the proponents of the liberal Left contend that Turkey is dominated by "modernist and secularist elites," who need to be overthrown by an alliance of liberal democrats and Islamists for the sake of "consolidating civil society" constrained by the all-dominating, all-encompassing state.

Tülin Öngen, a Marxist political scientist of Ankara University argues that the liberal Left has been a major constituent of the AKP's hegemonic bloc known as the "Liberal-Islamist coali-tion" since the latter's coming to power in 2002. This coalition aimed to neutralize and pacify the secular political opposition in Turkey by "colonizing people's cognitive and lively world at a rapid pace" based on an artificial counter-hegemonic dis-course (SolNews 2010). Accordingly, the liberal Left discourse draws on such euphonic notions as "civilianization" (as opposed to military dominance), "normalization," "pluralism," "identi-ties," "othering," "human rights," "freedom," the "military-bureaucratic tutelage regime," "elite rule," "status-quoism," and "anti-Kemalism." In her influential article on the blind liberal support for the AKP government, French journalist Ariane Bonzon called these liberal intellectuals "useful idiots" of the Islamists, who "played a much more important role than one would expect from their small number and electoral weight. It was through them that the AKP built their image of a post-Islamist, liberal, democratic and reformist party" (Bonzon 2013). That the AKP pragmatically—and temporarily—used the ideological support of these liberals was openly admitted by the AKP party chairman for Istanbul Aziz Babuşçu in April 2013. Babuşçu declared that unlike the first decade of the AKP rule, they would not be needing the liberals' support in their second decade, because "the Turkey that we will construct, the future that we will bring about, is not going to be a future that they will accept" (T24OnlineNews 2013b).

In what follows, we briefly outline the work of major Turkish liberal Leftist scholars, the majority of whom have published in the Anglo-Saxon academia and whose work pertain to sociological interests: Nilüfer Göle, Ferhat Kentel, Murat Belge, Ahmet İnsel, Mete Tunçay, and Baskın Oran. The rationale behind such discussion is not to provide a systematic critique of their conceptualization of the Turkish Republic, secularism, and modernism. Rather, we aim to reveal the civil society-centric, liberal democratic, and cultural reductionist essence of their New Left/NSM perspective so as to explain two points: a) why they sought to build a strategic and partially ideological alliance with Islamic neoliberalism, and b) how they accordingly failed to explain the multifaceted aspects of the GPPs.

Within the Turkish liberal Left, the scholar whose work most directly resonates with the NSM theories is Nilüfer Göle. A former student of Alain Touraine, Göle's work points to the centrality of lifestyles and aesthetic values of secularism and Islamism in Turkey. Similar to most European New Leftists employing artificially counter-hegemonic, euphonic, yet blurred notions, Göle's work is invested in "explor[ing] the plurality of cultural contexts and religious beliefs, the alternative sources of tolerance, public goods and pluralism" (Göle 2003, 18). In a repetitive and poetic fashion, Göle insists on the task of "searching for a plurality of sources of tolerance," which is "closely associated with an intellectual endeavor to go beyond the Enlightenment version of modernity" (Göle 2003, 17). She goes on to embrace Islamism as a "critique addressed to mono-civilizational definitions of modernity," where the latter is a detrimental "grand narrative" along with secularism, which obstructs the "definition of self" and the individual choice of alter-modern/Islamist lifestyles (Göle 2003, 19, 21, 24).

Parallel to Göle and Touraine's appeal to pluralism, individual autonomy, and unconstrained social agency, Ferhat Kentel offers an "alternative" reading of modern Turkey that puts in the foreground the "polarization between religion and secularism" rather than that of social classes, in the name of pluralism, individualism, autonomization, and liberal democracy (Kentel 1998, 1, 5). Kentel goes so far as to assert that the Islamic individual as the catalyst for a new alternative and autonomous expression has become an eligible candidate for a "new 'Left' as an actor of democracy" (Kentel 1998, 14). Indeed, Kentel also believes that "new types of communities replace the nation that is no longer able to satisfy these subjects" insofar as the borders allegedly disappear (Kentel 2011, 61). The references to Göle and Kentel serve to reveal the rationale behind the idea of the Turkish liberal Left to strategically and ideologically ally with Islamism.

Establishing the centrality of a dichotomy between "authoritarian secularism" and "democratic Islamism," which portrays the latter as the natural ally and agent of the New Left, many liberal Leftists conclude that Turkey's problems are not class-related, or have anything to do with neoliberal capitalism. Instead, they are caused entirely by a lack of "liberal democracy" or an "excess of secularism" complemented by a vague problematic of "cultural oppression" and "othering." Regarding the case of Turkish "despotic modernism," Göle asserts that secularism has supposedly turned into an elitist "fetish of modernity," which in turn made modernity function as a fetish in itself (Göle 2002, 184). According to Göle's eclectic framework that rather carelessly combines Touraine, Clifford Geertz, Erving Goffman, Cornelius Costoriadis, Henri Lefebvre, and Pierre Bourdieu, the foundation and development of the Republic created nothing but a state ruled by loosely and superficially defined secular/despotic "elites." This conceptualization leaves no room for a political economic analysis that accounts for the ways in which different classes create the conditions for the waging of cultural struggles. Göle portrays elites as "social groups such as intellectuals and the technical intelligentsia (engineers and technicians) which, through secular and modern education, have acquired a 'cultural capital'" (Göle 1997, 46–47). This translates into the sphere of the Turkish liberal Leftist politics such that the liberal Left can (or should) well unite with Islamists, who represent the popular and oppressed "periphery" against the representatives of the dominating "center," promoting top-down/elitist modernism, secularism, and "Jacobinism"—instead of capitalism itself.[2]

Murat Belge is another major figure of the Turkish liberal Left, whose intellectual evolution originates from a post-Althusserian stance on new social movement theories. In his book *Socialism, Turkey, and the Future*, Belge openly contrasts class movements with new social movements (feminisms, ecologists, anti-war movements, etc.) by criticizing the "class-reductionism" of Marxism (as cited and quoted in Aladağ 2013, 136, 139–140). According to Belge's New Left account, the most important problem in contemporary Turkey is the crisis of democracy and the despotic rule of Kemalist elites and institutions (Belge 2009). In parallel, Turkish socialism's emphasis on anti-imperialism and class struggle does nothing but further intensify this crisis by also propagating chauvinistic-nationalist ideas as well as militarism. Like other liberal Leftists, Belge contends that Turkey's accession into the EU can play a crucial role in overcoming the "crisis of democracy." Accordingly, he disapproves of the anti-imperialist position of many Turkish socialists vis-à-vis the

EU. Using an NSM-inspired tone, Belge does not refrain from arguing that "socialists have much to learn from the Islamic AKP" and they would be better off focusing on "'issue-based' movements or civic groupings" so as to "infuse the principles and the values of pluralism" (Belge 2009, 19–20). Elsewhere, he goes on to explicitly insist that "Turkey needs a kind of 'Muslim Democratic Party,'" by applauding the rise of the AKP in the name of the country's democratization—or "normalization" (Belge 2002). With regard to the question of allying with Islamists and the AKP, Belge summarizes his position as "struggling side by side for a common goal" (Belge 2008, par. 9, as quoted in Aladağ 2013, 247).

Belge's discourse on normalization finds its echo in Ahmet İnsel's work, which argues that the rise of the AKP "created an unexpected possibility of exit from the authoritarian regime established after the military coup of September 12, 1980" (İnsel 2003, 293). Interestingly enough, İnsel praises American style neo-conservatism, and applauds the AKP as the "authentic version of the American-style liberal-conservative development that had partially started with Özal" (İnsel 2003, 294). Creating a false dichotomy between the military coup of 1980 and the right-wing conservative tradition of Özal/AKP, İnsel ignores the fact that the latter is in fact the offshoot of September 12, which set the foundations for a neoliberal society legitimated by Turkish-Islamic conservatism—strategies embraced and energetically promoted by Erdoğan's government (Cosar and Yucesan-Ozdemir 2012, Uzgel and Duru 2010).

In direct connection to İnsel's eulogy of Islamism, Mete Tunçay of Bilgi University, another major figure of the liberal Left, purports that Turkey needs "neo-Ottomanism." Tunçay argues for Turkey's reorganization in ethnic and religious lines in the name of pluralism and democracy, and the Turkish Left would be better off rejecting all of the values of the Republic in the name of dropping dogmatism (AkşamDailyNews 2012, YeniŞafakDailyNews 2007). In accordance with the New Left arguments by Belge, İnsel, and Tunçay, Baskın Oran boldly concludes that Turkey would not turn into an Islamist state even with the rise of Islamist movement (Oran 2001, 41–42), thus adding to the vast liberal Left literature that casts off any criticism of the AKP's Islamist advances as "elite-modernist anxieties."

A majority of liberal Leftist figures in Turkey have some kind of familiarity with and even former adherence to the work of Antonio Gramsci and Louis Althusser, especially when it comes to employing buzzwords such as hegemony, historical bloc, the state, and ideology. Paradoxically however, many of them have taken active part in the AKP's hegemonic initiatives such as the support for the 2010 referendum for a new constitution, the Abant Platform, and the Wise People Commission. In 2010, the AKP held a referendum for a package of constitutional amendments that served the strengthening of the executive over the judiciary, where the liberal Left intellectual bloc in Turkey provided the AKP package with active support with the slogan of "Yes, but not enough! [*Yetmez ama Evet!*]" Furthermore, the Abant Platform is a collective platform founded in 1998 by the Gülenist movement, the most influential Islamist move-ment in Turkey both economically and politically, as will be touched upon in the following chapters. The platform consti-tutes an alliance of Islamist and liberal leftist intellectuals who function to generate new political-cultural strategies to advance the AKP's—and more particularly the Gülenist fraction's—hegemony (Nişancı 2013, 132). In addition to the "Young Civilians [*Genç Siviller*]," a pro-AKP liberal youth organiza-tion, major liberal Leftist figures such as Kentel, Tunçay, and Mehmet Altan have assumed leading positions in the Platform. Similarly in 2013, the AKP government formed a "Wise People Commission" to regulate the negotiation process with the Kurdistan Workers' Party (PKK) and to establish a pact that would advance the hegemonic agenda of the government. This committee included famous liberal Leftists such as Belge, Oran, Fuat Keyman, Etyen Mahçupyan, and Oral Çalışlar. The sec-tion below continues our efforts to critically analyze European

NSM theories in dialog with the limitations of the Turkish liberal Left in their response to the GPPs.

Ic. NSM Theories and "Misreading" the GPPs

As for the overall critique of NSM theories, one could argue that Touraine's actor-centered work has an ahistorical understanding of autonomy and particularism of agency that is assumed to be independent from any structure and is therefore replete with a myriad of contradictions and complexities. On the one hand, striving to avoid any kind of "totalizing" claim, Touraine argues that agency is to be conceived outside of history, and that it produces its own individual historicity and cultural models independent of any social structure (Touraine 1988, 40, 155). On the other hand, in a way to contradict his own "actor-centered" and "anti-structuralist" paradigm, he paradoxically maintains that the conditions for the proliferation of autonomous and plural movements have been created by large-scale systemic changes that result from the shift from industrialism toward a so-called postindustrial or hyperindustrial society (Touraine 1988, 25, 33, 111).

Furthermore, Touraine promotes a sharply dichotomizing approach to civil and political societies. He assumes "an increasingly complete separation of civil society, with its social movements, from the political system and the state" (Touraine 1988, 152). He thus openly argues that "one must separate more and more the analysis of the State from that of civil society" (Touraine 1988, 114). In parallel, Touraine (1988, 32) also contends that the state has given up its role as an agent for the integration of social actors, which echoes Kentel's previously mentioned arguments about the disappearance of borders and nation-states. This is a highly misleading statement, however, which contradicts the realities of the neoliberal era advanced by strong states (Panitch 1994, Panitch and Gindin 2012). In the third chapter, we transcend the "statelessness" thesis with our notion of the "political-cultural fix" carried out by the Turkish

state in the framework of "neoliberalism with Islamic characteristics." Therefore, our conceptualization establishes direct
ties to world history and political economy without neglecting
the significance of cultural struggles and local peculiarities.

Analogous to Melucci and Castells' obsession on the "power"
of media and cultural codes, Touraine (1988, 104) also fixates
on the increasing importance of information and knowledge.
However, one can argue that information and knowledge were
never regarded as less crucial under Taylorist and Fordist practices than in the post-Fordist/neoliberal era. A similar complex-
ity is found in Castell's work, which seems to overestimate the
decentralization of state power and decreasing state capacity. He
indicates a so-called shift from the "oppressive 'Big Brother'" to
"a myriad of well-wishing 'little sisters'" (Castells 2010, 271,
301–302). As mentioned earlier, the emergence of the "security state" in the United States and other Western countries
after the 9/11 events invalidates Castells' "little sisters" thesis
(Hallsworth and Lea 2011, Bennett 2011). In addition, Castells
projects an overly optimistic view about the empowering potential of new information technologies, which leads him to exag-
gerate the effects of the Zapatistas' use of Internet and media
to create a spirit of global solidarity and legitimacy. Despite
Castell's assertions on the Internet and "information age," there
is no empirical evidence to demonstrate that the sociopolitical
ramifications of new media technologies for social organizing
have been greater than those of the invention of the printing
press, electricity, and telephone, and the development of national
postal systems, and so on, which have all contributed to massive
social changes in human history. Moreover, the state's manipulation and utilization of new communication technologies for
intensified security, surveillance, and social control mechanisms
are overlooked in the "information age" account.

Many other complexities remain noticeable in the NSM literature due to its rejection of class politics without any substantial reasoning (Laclau 1985, 27, 29–30, 41–42, Laclau and
Mouffe 2001, 1–5, 177). Most importantly, the discourse and

cultural reductionism of most NSM theories contributes to a fuzzy image of society and cultural change by "treat[ing] texts an object of analysis itself" rather than employing them "as a window into human experience" (Russell and Gery 1998, 595). Instead, we argue that a mere focus on discourse analysis and identity-building processes cannot offer more than a superficial treatment of cultural factors in mobilization. Discourse constitutes only a partial and even misleading indicator to the same extent that identity stands as a poorly defined and shallowly operationalized category.

As Eric Wolf puts it, to understand how power mechanisms function in the field of culture not only requires an understanding of how individual groups construct meanings, but also a consideration of tactical and organizational aspects of power with regard to culture, and a more rigorous grasp of the "whys and wherefores" of human interactions and lifestyles with socioeconomic realities (Wolf 2001, 384, 386). Both Touraine's notion of historicity and Laclau and Mouffe's identity-centrism give way to some sort of "anthropological nativism" that conceives of societies as isolated entities devoid of any ties to world history and class politics (Wolf 2001, 385). In other words, instead of limiting one's analysis to descriptive images that simply praise anthropological particularities, the researcher should expose the underlying world—historical and class-related structures conditioning cultural meanings, symbols, and conflicts.

In the specific context of the GPPs, the complexities of the NSM- or New Left-informed arguments find their fullest expression in the analysis of the protests by the Turkish liberal Left. For some, the reaction of Halil Berktay, an important liberal figure, came as a shock. Berktay not only insisted that police repression in the GPPs was a myth, but also accused the protesters, arguing that for them, "almost everything was about provoking the police," and that the "aggression and violence initiatives came from the protesters" (Berktay 2013). A similarly tragic response came from Baskın Oran, who held the Taksim Solidarity Platform and other socialist organizations responsible for the death of

Gezi protesters and countless other injuries (Oran 2013). Etyen Mahçupyan, another pro-government liberal, referred to the GPPs as the manifestation of "pathetic politics of adolescence," maintaining that the popular occupation of the park and the declared demands of the Taksim Solidarity Platform are illegitimate, authoritarian, and undemocratic (Today'sZaman 2013c). A common denominator in Berktay, Oran, and Mahçupyan's statements is their roots in civil society centric New Left/NSM tendencies, as they accused political organizations and leadership of playing the evil "vanguard" to manipulate the "youth." This approach found echo in most liberal left interpretations.

Moreover, arguments for the ending or containment of the protests were advocated by many liberal leftists. Fuat Keyman, for instance, looked at the events from the government's point of view instead of the protesters, arguing that "the AK Party could have treated them as an opportunity" (Keyman 2013a). Elswehere, Keyman advised "the youth," "as a father, as a professor," to go back home and end the protests, pointing to the government's tasks to use its hegemonic tools such as the Wise People Commission (Keyman 2013b). In a similar fashion, the Gülenist Abant Platform, whose Board of Trustees includes liberal leftists such as Levent Köker, Mete Tuncay, Mehmet Altan, and Ferhat Kentel, publicly called for the termination of the GPPs in the name of preserving "democratic stability." The platform declared that the protests quickly went beyond a "democratic and humanistic framework," that the ballot box was the only legitimate means to change a government, and that bringing an end to these protests is an "ethical and humanitarian responsibility" (T24OnlineNews 2013a). Oya Baydar joined the chorus by propounding that those who reject to end the protests are the ones "who cannot accept the normalization of the country and cannot dare continuing the democratic struggle in a normalized environment." If the protests do not stop, she added, it will lose its legitimacy completely (T24OnlineNews 2013d).

Many other liberal leftists, although seemingly sympathetic toward the GPPs, actively downplayed the movement's radical political scope in a civil society centric and culturally reductionist vocabulary. Kentel, for instance, argued that the GPPs correspond to "not economic, but a life-style based" protest, constituting "Turkey's first genuine civil society movement" (HaberTurkNews 2013b). Ahmet İnsel, on his part, vaguely called the GPPs an upheaval of "dignity" based on lifestyles and identities. Understating the disruptive potential of the GPPs, İnsel argued that in this "cultural" and "libertarian" struggle, "the legitimacy of the regime is not being questioned." Accordingly, the movement was not necessarily against the AKP, but only against the PM Erdoğan's condescending attitude and assertions (RadikalDailyNews 2013f). Oral Çalışlar likewise argued that Gezi brought together those who lost their "privileges" under the AKP government, and those whose lifestyles were threatened by the "conservative faction" within the AKP (RadikalDailyNews 2013d). Besides the evident cultural reductionism, the common point in İnsel and Çalışlar's accounts, which was also shared by other representatives of the liberal left tradition, is to offer an overly fragmented perspective of the AKP that neglects the consistency of this party's Islamic-neoliberal advances in the last decade. Such distortion does not only "misread" the AKP's excessive police violence and conservative impositions on society as contingent upon personal/voluntarist factors (such as the PM, conservative factions, etc.). It also serves to vindicate the authors' long-term active/passive support for the AKP through ascribing this party an abrupt and unforeseeable "authoritarian turn."

Nilüfer Göle, finally, held that the GPPs represented a "citizenship rehearsal" acted out by an apolitical "public agency," and that the movement's "public" aspects must be separated from its "political" ones, as "the protesters are not organized into a political force" (Göle 2013b, a). In a patronizing tone, Göle advised this "youth movement" to remain apolitical, for "if it inserts itself into a political movement, it will, in fact, distance itself from democracy" and lose its inherent "innocence" (Göle 2013a). Why being political is undemocratic is unexplained in

Göle's analysis. In reality, this normative dichotomy between "innocence" and "politics" served the government initiatives to divide the movement along "good" and "bad" protesters. Accordingly, the "well-intentioned" protesters should be "without flags/banners" (*flamasız Gezi*), that is, remain outside of politics to preserve their "innocence," whereas anyone involved in a political organization (parties, unions, etc.) were regarded as sectarian opportunists seeking to profit from the Gezi spirit.

These ideas were repeated by many of the authors discussed. In line with Berktay, Oran, and Mahçupyan's statements discussed earlier, Baydar, for instance, wrote that Gezi Park created an opportunity for coup-d'état seekers to manipulate social opposition; and Çalışlar denounced those who saw Gezi as a "political power struggle," thus alienating the "youth" (RadikalDailyNews 2013d, T24OnlineNews 2013c). Overall, the constant reference to the "youth" as an "apolitical," "naïve," "romantic," and "innocent" grouping ultimately became a condescending tool for the (neo-)liberal Left to imply the GPPs' lack of direction and/or susceptibility to manipulation. Our theoretical perspective rests on the rejection of an irreconcilable opposition between "spontaneity" and "leadership," holding that the two are dialectically intertwined. Contrary to these New Left accounts, it is one of the major arguments of this book that the GPPs, albeit spontaneous, were collectively organized and acted out, and were inherently political protests with a class basis. A fuller understanding of the GPPs requires a balanced study of political, economic, and cultural-ideological factors, which will be our task in what follows.

Reprise and Review

In this chapter, we have seen that NSM theories rely on a superficial and ill-operationalized definition of culture and cultural change in the name of prioritizing (or, more precisely, romanticizing) social agency and social movement autonomy. Despite their "totalizing" claim for a so-called postindustrial society and information age, social agency and cultural change are paradoxically conceived outside of world history and any ties to deep-rooted systemic causes. Political-ideological factors are completely ruled out in order to legitimize a kind of culturalist idealization. In other words, their heavily descriptive account blended with an impervious obsession with semiotics prevents them from explaining the "whys and wherefores" of social and cultural change as well as the particular ways in which neoliberalism and class politics influence social agency. Based on a civil society-centric framework that imposes a superficial dichotomy between civil society and the state, NSM theories also present a distorted image of the capitalist state as allegedly being dismantled or decentralized so as to give up its role of the repressive "Big Brother" and its ever existing hegemonic ties to civil society. Unsurprisingly, the aforementioned limitations of this perspective find their shape in the Turkish branch of the New Left tradition, which offers an incomplete and even distorted account of the GPPs.

As an alternative to NSM theories, the following chapter presents a framework for a Marxist class analysis informed by the works of Nicos Poulantzas and Erik Olin Wright. Poulantzas and Wright's work can provide crucial insights into the development of a rigorous analytical and empirical model of collective class action in a way to supersede the vague framework of NSM theories. The enterprise of this book is to supplement Poulantzas and Wright's work with James Petras and Henry Veltmeyer's contributions to social movement theory, as they are presented in our research questions.

2

Debunking the Myth of "Middle Classes": The Class-Structural Background of the Gpps

Since the eruption of the protests on May 31, 2013, the class con-figuration of the Gpps occupied the forefront of discussions in both leftist and mainstream media. The debate revolved around whether the Gpps could be reduced to an instinctual and fast-waning reaction of the educated/secularist elite/middle classes, or if they represent an instance of persisting/foundational mobiliza-tion of wage-earning classes. In reference to this debate, we hold that a class-analytic lens to assess the involvement of classes and class fractions is particularly useful in illuminating the nature and orientation of social mobilization (Borras Jr, Edelman, and Kay 2008, 25). This chapter thus opens with a theoretical dis-cussion on Marxist class theory as developed in the works of Poulantzas and Wright. Based on that framework, the second section of the chapter develops a critique of mainstream middle-class accounts of the Gpps through a political economic analysis of Turkish wage-earning classes in light of empirical data. In turn, the last section shifts the focus from the objective loca-tions of wage-earning classes and takes on an analysis of their ideological-political location in relation to "neoliberalism with Islamic characteristics" in the specificity of Turkey, which inter-relates closely with their organizational class capacities.

Immediate mainstream accounts in June 2013 contended to brand the Gpps as an uprising of "middle classes" concerned almost exclusively about secularism. Paul Mason from the *BBC* portrayed the Gezi events as the revolt of "secular middle classes" albeit the participation of a minority of urban poor youth (Mason 2013). *The Economist* echoed by stating that "the young middle class…chafes against the religious conservatism of the prime minister" (TheEconomist 2013c). In a similar manner, the *Washington Post* spoke of "the summer of middle-class discontent" in response to "the encroaching power of Islam" (Faiola and Moura 2013). The *New York Times* joined the chorus to call the protesters the "educated haves who are in some ways the principal beneficiaries of the regimes they now reject" (Keller 2013), and the *Wall Street Journal* depicted the protesters as "the 'white' secular elite" that eat "gourmet pizza," who are against the "'Black Turks,' a more pious lower class" (Bohn and Bayrasli 2013).

The "middle class" account was also used as a strategic tool of labeling by the government circles in Turkey in two ways: to underline the AKP's political and economic successes in supposedly raising the expectations of middle classes, and/ or to discredit the protesters as a well-off elite (that is argued to have no respect for religion). The AKP's deputy chairman Süleyman Soylu, for instance, held that middle-class membership in Turkey supposedly reached 43.5 million (59 percent of the population) thanks to the economic growth achieved under the AKP government, which explains the middle-class influence in Turkish politics (Erandaç 2013). The pro-government *Anadolu Agency*, similarly, linked the protests to Turkey's being an "emergent power" and a "regional force," but unlike the concurrent mass mobilization in Brazil in June 2013, protests here "are not based on social injustices" given its middle-class character (TGRTNews 2013). In order to discredit the protestors as privileged middle classes, the PM Erdoğan himself referred to them as a whisky-sipping, Bosphorus-gazing elite; a minority "upper-crust…imposing their ways on the country" (BBCTurkish 2013, StarNews 2013). He also insisted, despite lack of evidence, that they "drank beer in mosques" or "harassed women with headscarves" to highlight their "irreligiousness," which were both eventually proven to be fabricated government propaganda (HürriyetDailyNews 2013h, RadikalDailyNews 2014d). Many pro-government intellectuals followed his lead by framing the protesters as the secular "white Turks" of the "center" reclaiming their privileged status after the AKP displaced their political domination in favor of the "periphery" in the last decade, although still helping the former prosper economically (Haber7News 2013a, SabahNews 2013a). In the words of the pro-government liberal Etyen Mahçupyan, "indeed, at the very heart of the incidents is the reaction by secular groups to the 'lack of power' they feel in the face of being banished from the political center" (Today'sZaman 2013c).

An academic elaboration of these ideas came from the French sociologist Loïc Wacquant as he visited Turkey in January 2014 to give a talk on the GPPs at Boğaziçi University, Istanbul. Wacquant's argument is summarized in the following quote: "In Gezi we saw a fraction of the Istanbul population, the new cultural bourgeoisie of intellectuals, urban professionals, the urban middle class rising to assert the rights of cultural capital...We see bearers of cultural capital, the new cultural bourgeoisie of the city rising, and in a sense protesting this and wanting to propose a different use of the construction of the city" (cited in Göker 2014). Wacquant's geographic blindness, which reduces the scope of the GPPs to Istanbul—and even to the Park itself—to neglect the millions who took to the streets across the country, is a central problem that distorts the rest of his analysis. Relatedly, his culturally defined designation of "elite middle classes," very much in line with the European New Left/NSM perspectives discussed in Chapter 1, remains indifferent to the disruptive nature of the protests. The counter-hegemonic expressions of the movement against neoliberal economic, political, and ideological domination in the country are consequently overlooked. Unsurprisingly, Wacquant's reasoning leads him to the conclusion that this "new bourgeois" movement was utterly exclusionary vis-à-vis lower classes to actively prevent their integration into the sphere of collective mobilization. A quick look at the poor neighborhoods that actively fought the police for weeks, and the modest background of the protesters killed in Istanbul, Ankara, Hatay, and Eskişehir suggests a very different empirical reality. Yet the deficiency of Wacquant's interpretation is theoretical as much as empirical. As Saraçoğlu (2014) notes, in addition to equating the GPPs to the park and to the demands of a "cultural elite," Wacquant's automatic derivation of the movement's political scope and meaning from its members' assumed position in social stratification echoes rational choice determinism. In result, the evident counter-hegemonic potentialities of the GPPs against neoliberal forces not only remain unexplained in Wacquant's perspective, but they are consciously ignored to the extent that they do not fit his culturalist framework.

The common denominator of all these "middle-class" references is their taking of the term as given without providing any definition for it, let alone offering tools for its empirical operationalization. Such lack of elaboration is partly due to the journalistic and politically motivated nature of the abovementioned sources (except for Wacquant's), yet this makes the constant repetition of the term "middle classes" an all the more problematic truism for the analysis of the events. In consideration of the inadequate theoretical and empirical depth of class discussions around the GPPs, we argue that instead of the so-called middle classes, it was an alliance of various wage-earning class fractions that has been the catalyst for the GPPs. This alliance was led by service sector employees and the educated youth, and comprised white and blue-collar workers. Neoliberalism here appears as a key process in debunking the myth of middle classes and revealing the class nature of the protests.

In its most general terms, we refer to "neoliberalism" as a theory of political economic practices, which holds that "human well-being can best be advanced by liberating individual entrepreneurial freedoms and skills within an institutional framework characterized by strong private property rights, free markets, and free trade" (Harvey 2005a, 2). Having emerged as a response to capitalism's political and economic crisis of the 1970s, neoliberalism is primarily a political project initiated in the 1980s to reconstitute the circumstances of capital accumulation and to reinstate the power of economic elites (Harvey 2005a, 19). Indeed, a rigorous grasp of neoliberal practices requires the taking into account of the particularities of uneven geographies and the varying ways in which the states adapt "variegated" policy frameworks shaped by the given balance of class forces and cultural configurations (Peck and Theodore 2012). In this chapter, we are particularly concerned with the Turkish case in which neoliberalization goes hand in hand with a process of proletarianization and an Islamic reconfiguration of society. In order to show the extent to which Turkish neoliberalism contributes to proletarianization, we engage with data on unemployment, youth unemployment, part-time work, decreasing levels of unionization, the informal sector, the expansion of wage labor, micro-debt, life satisfaction, job security, etc. We then deal with how this process of proletarianization is politically and ideologically maintained so as to reproduce neoliberalism and class incapacities based on Islamic codes. This constitutes the gist of what we call "neoliberalism with Islamic characteristics" in Turkey, which will be further discussed in Chapter 3.

Going back to the GPPs, there have been two interrelated major factors that explain why specifically wage-earning working-class fractions took the lead in the uprisings against the AKP's neoliberal project. First, the economic conditions as well as the structural and organizational capacities of most segments of working classes have been severely undermined under neoliberalization. Regardless of income levels, working-class fractions share increasingly precarious economic realities, where elevated productivity and exploitation rates are met with heightened job insecurity and consumer debt to maintain a decent life, accompanied by low unionization and high unemployment levels. Second, although this reflects the situation of working classes nationwide, political and ideological alliances specific to Turkish neoliberalism rendered the relatively more educated and secularly oriented wage-earning fractions more prominent in the uprisings. The AKP-centered Islamic-neoliberal power bloc placed an important segment of the working classes in a politico-ideologically subordinate position through culturally legitimized paternalistic labor relationships, conservative trade unionism, religious-clientelist aid networks and other ideological state apparatuses. The free articulation of class grievances was thus more likely for the secularly oriented fractions that are relatively free from these influences yet still suffering from exploitation, precariousness, and indebtedness. Moreover, AKP's intensified authoritarianism and conservatism that expanded social interventionism and exclusion based on its own cultural-ideological standards further threatened the life space and life chances of these latter fractions. A combination of these economic, political, and cultural-ideological grievances culminated into the GPPs. The GPPs, therefore, cannot be reduced to a "middle class" or a purely ideological "secularist" uprising of the "cultural bourgeoisie." It is, however, a mostly secular class reaction against neoliberal authoritarianism and proletarianization with Islamic politico-ideological characteristics in Turkey.

2a. Bringing the Class Back in: A Marxist Framework

The processural aspect of class formation presents itself as one of the most important challenges of contemporary Marxist theories of class, which has been partly dealt by Poulantzas (political-ideological relations, class power, and power bloc) and Wright (contradictory class locations, class consciousness, and class capacity). Poulantzas defines social classes as "groupings of social agents" identified principally by their place in the "production process" as well as by their location in "political and ideological relations" (Poulantzas 1975a, 14–15). Poulantzas thus contends that economic position is not the sole criterion to assess class structures, but class relations also rely heavily on political and ideological factors. We believe that such emphasis is crucial for the analysis of the GPPs, especially when it comes to the question of why secularly oriented wage-earning classes instead of traditional working-class movements (i.e. industrial proletariat and manual laborers) played a significant role during the protests.

Another important merit of Poulantzas's work is to have pointed to the need to take into account the structural and subjective locations of "class fractions" for a more nuanced class analysis. Accordingly, Poulantzas argues that class structures are made up of a number of fractions or strata. What he calls "autonomous fractions" refers to social ensembles of the same class that are capable of acting as relatively independent units on the basis of their place in the production process and political-ideological relations. Poulantzas distinguishes, for instance, among commercial, industrial, and financial fractions of the bourgeoisie (Poulantzas 1975b, 84–85). Other well-known examples of class fractions are "working-class aristocracy" and "petty bourgeoisie" (Poulantzas 1975a, 15–16, 270, 1975b, 84). This nuanced framework for the analysis of social classes problematizes the utilization of generic concepts such as "middle classes," which has turned into a truism for the GPPs. As Poulantzas puts it: "the transformations which capitalist societies are…undergoing are supposed to have given rise to a vast 'intermediate class' which comprises all social groups except the bourgeoisie and proletariat and which, by virtue of its numerical weight, provides the real pillar upholding modern societies. As has been noted, we are here faced with several classes: there is no justification at present for claiming that these intermediate classes are fused into a single class" (Poulantzas 2008, 194). In the case of Turkey, class fractioning in the economic and political-ideological level is important in understanding not only the increasing role of the educated and secularly oriented segments of wage-earning classes, but also the strong influence of the Islamic segments of Turkish bourgeoisie and different variants of Islamist-capitalist ideology over the country's entire class structure.

Wright proposes a more sophisticated theory of social class based on a critical and expanded reading of Poulantzas' work.

Wright's main objection to Poulantzas is that the latter offers rigid criteria for distinguishing workers from the bourgeoisie. Poulantzas argues that any laborer who is not in the "productive sector" (i.e. manual labor) belongs to the petty bourgeoisie, and managers are necessarily part of the bourgeoisie regardless of "contradictory class locations" (Wright 1978, 35, 61). On the contrary, depending on the economic, political, and ideological specificities of a social formation, Wright propounds that "unproductive" wage workers such as service sector and white-color employees, technicians, supervisors, civil servants, and so on may as well be included in the fractions of the working class. This calls for a wider definition of working classes, which also applies to the case of contemporary Turkey. Accordingly, "the working class, even if defined narrowly, remains the largest class location in the class structure of…capitalist countries, and, if it is extended to include those contradictory locations closest to it, then it constitutes a substantial majority of the labor force" (Wright 1997, 54).

We hold that Wright's critique of Poulantzas' superficial distinction between productive/unproductive and manual/mental labor is all the more valid in contemporary societies where service sector dominates as a category of wage employment. The exploitation, precariousness, and common life chances of non-blue collar wage earners render them as a fraction of working classes. Wright's larger definition of working classes is relevant to the case of Turkey where the service and the informal sectors constitute a significant portion of the working force. The shared destiny of such various wage-earning fractions in capitalist societies is captured in the Marxist parlance by the term "proletarianization." Wright and Singelmann define proletarianization as an underlying tendency in capitalist societies whereby work is "becoming more routinized and degraded, with less autonomy and responsibility for the worker," which goes hand in hand with "the complex process by which non-working-class locations are destroyed or transformed and working-class locations created" (Wright and Singelmann 1982, 176, 183). It has been documented that the Turkish work force has been going through an intensive process of proletarianization since the 1980s (Kaya 2008). Kaya holds that, as a long-term phenomenon in the country, "proletarianization occurred through a transition from Turkey's agrarian tradition, a relative decline of the public sector, and an expansion of classes who sell their labor without workplace authority" (Kaya 2008, 161). Accordingly, Kaya reveals that the share of agricultural employment in the total workforce declined from 53.6 percent in 1980 to 29 percent in 2005, whereas the share of service employment sector rose from 25.9 percent to 46 percent in the same interval (Kaya 2008). As far as proletarianization in Turkey is concerned, our analysis will draw attention to the boosting role of precarious work and unemployment as well as the rise of a working-class segment made up of clerks, service and sales workers, and unqualified employees as the core of Turkish working class.

The alliance of class fractions takes on a greater significance when social groups of "contradictory class locations" (Wright 2005, 8–10) are included in the picture, which "represents positions which are torn between the basic contradictory class relations of capitalist society" (Wright 1978, 62). That is to say there are many class fractions between the bourgeoisie and the proletariat that share attributes of the class locations above and below them, which would include groups such as managers and supervisors, semi-autonomous employees, and small employers (Wright 1978, 63). This nuanced picture renders politico-ideological struggle crucial in the establishment of various class alliances, given that class positions are not fixed rigidly to particular class ideologies. The active participation of white-collar groups to the GPPs to protest neoliberal practices demonstrates that flexibility. What Wright calls "ideological class formations" highlights this point, which holds that "a map of the ways in which class-linked organizations of different ideological and political profiles penetrate different parts of the class structure would provide a basic description of the pattern of class formation" (Wright 1997, 222). Accordingly, our analysis will begin the discussion on the political and ideological underpinnings of the GPPs in the third section—to be continued in Chapter 3— which contributed to the alliance of service sector, white-collar and blue-collar workers, as well as students and educated youth.

Lastly, Wright's arguments on class capacities should be briefly addressed. For class consciousness and class formation to emerge, social agents need to establish diverse social relations that link themselves within a common class location. This constitutes the core of "class capacities." Wright identifies two kinds of class capacities, namely "structural" and "organizational" capacities. Structural capacities concern the capabilities to ensure the unity of class agents shaped in a particular ensemble of social relations. A classic example of structural (in)capacity would be the evolution of capitalism toward the creation of job hierarchies to undermine the unity of the working class (Wright 1978). In Turkey, structural class capacities are undermined by the precarization of work, indebtedness, and jobless growth. Organizational capacities simply refer to the conscious organization of the members of a class, and involve the organizational structure of such spheres as trade unionism, party politics, and neighborhood mobilization (Wright 1978). We will discuss that the organizational class capacities of the traditional working class in Turkey are undermined by the dominance of paternalistic labor relations and Islamic legitimation practices, which supplement the disciplining mechanisms of neoliberal markets with extra-economic tools such as pro-government and/or Islamic media and educational institutions. In the absence of a structurally unified traditional working class, the young and relatively educated sectors of the expanding wage earning fractions came into prominence thanks to the relative autonomy of their politico-ideological and organizational resources from the AKP's hegemony.

2b. Beyond the Amorphous "Middle Classes" Thesis

As soon as the GPPs broke out in June 2013, two immediate objections to mainstream "middle class" perspectives came from Korkut Boratav, a renowned Turkish Marxist economist, and Mustafa Kemal Coşkun of Ankara University. Boratav and Coşkun cautioned against the use of the term "middle classes" given its lack of explanatory power (SendikaNews 2013c, RadikalDailyNews 2013e). Putting forward that the GPPs constitute an inherently class-based collective action "against predatory capitalism,…the bourgeoisie, and its state," Boratav provided an alternative explanation:

> When we look at the triggering incident, the start of the Taksim project,…there is a matured class reaction: highly qualified and educated workers, together with their future class comrades (students), and with the inclusion of professionals; confronting…a massive urban plundering attempt by the…bourgeoisie and the political power unified with it. (SendikaNews 2013c)

According to Boratav, students and the educated youth, who were among the driving forces in the GPPs, cannot be automatically branded as "middle-class" actors in consideration of their class roots. Their class characters are to be further explored in view of their future class trajectories (SendikaNews 2013c). Boratav went on to assert that the qualified constituents of the service sector are also to be considered in the status of subordinate wageworkers, due to increasing proletarianization. Many educated wageworkers increasingly find themselves in the ranks of unqualified service sector jobs such as salesclerks, caretakers, secretaries, more precisely "office, sales, security personnel and staff members":

> The productiveness of their branches of activity…does not alter our point of discussion. As wage-laborers, they either create surplus value directly for their employers or engage in a labor activity that enables their employers to…expropriate surplus value…from different business sectors. And, in the broadest sense, they are the elements of real or reserve labor armies. In short, objectively in today's conditions, their existence…belongs to the working-class to constitute an important proportion of that class. (SendikaNews 2013c)

Similarly, Coşkun criticized the salience of terms such as "youth" and "middle classes" as the leading agents of the Gezi Park events. He underlined that "youth" is not an explanatory concept without a close examination of its socioeconomic and political constituents (RadikalDailyNews 2013e). Coşkun went on to hold that the young protesters' "efficient use of social media, high cultural capital, and development of new resistance methods are not indicators of their middle class background" (RadikalDailyNews 2013e). Coşkun, instead, argued that the protests brought together various fractions of wage-earning classes. This includes the unqualified fractions that work in "part-time, temporary, volatile, low-paid" jobs, as well as upper level industrial workers and "well-educated, foreign language speaking" fractions that are relatively better paid (RadikalDailyNews 2013e). Students and the unemployed, who were actively involved in the protests, are the class comrades of these groups. Theoretically speaking, Wright clarifies the situation of these groups as follows: "The class locations of students...must be defined by the class location into which they will move upon the completion of their studies...It is the fundamental class interests of such trajectories...which defines their class location," which is also valid for "the reserve army of the unemployed" (Wright 1978, 92–93). It is relevant to note here that according to a survey conducted by GENAR in the Taksim region in June 2013 (as the protests were ongoing), 53.8 percent of the protesters declared to be wage-earners, whereas 24.1 percent stated that they were students, and 10.8 percent unemployed (GENAR 2013). These figures were recorded as 52 percent, 37 percent, 6 percent, respectively, in KONDA's research carried out around the same days (KONDA 2013).

The commonality of all these wage-earning class fractions that took the lead during the GPPs is their increasingly precarious position with no trade union protection under neoliberalism (Özugurlu 2011, Aydin 2013, Burkev 2013). In Turkey, only 9.2 percent of the work force is unionized, which corresponds to 1,001,671 people (Kılıç 2013). Moreover, the undermining of

the organizational capacities of working classes is closely inter-
linked with the decline of their structural capacities due to four
major factors: unemployment (which was 9.2 percent in 2012
according to ILO), privatization, sub-contracting/outsourc-
ing, and contract manufacturing (Koç 2010, 2009, ILO 2013).
These take place in the background of Turkey's "jobless-growth
pattern" in the last decade, where "rapid rates of growth were
accompanied by high rates of unemployment and low participation rates" (Yeldan 2009, 3). In this context, a major tendency
that contributes to the undermining of Turkish working-class'
structural capacity is the precarization of work to the extent
that "growing numbers of people are traveling vendors, small
retailers, or craftspeople" occupied with a "nomadic activity"
(Yücesan-Ozdemir 2012, 133). The extent to which the precariousness of work is expanding can also be assessed by the drastic
increase in part-time employment from 6.6 percent in 2002 to
11.7 percent in 2011 (OECD 2013b).

In order to unveil the factors that cause lower levels of structural class capacities for the Turkish working class, it is possible
to provide a rough estimation of the size of the informal sector by calculating the sum of the self-employed and the unpaid
family worker. According to the available data, between 2004
and 2012, the average percentages of own account (or self-
employed) workers and unpaid family workers are respectively
21.1 percent and 13.8 percent, which equals to an average informal sector size of 34.8 percent of total employment in the same
interval (TurkStat 2013c). It goes without saying that such high
level of informality is a major factor that hinders the structural
class capacity of the Turkish working class. The figures demonstrate that at least a third of the total workforce in Turkey is
informally employed, and stands as disorganized and isolated
from the rest of the working population.

It is worth exploring the composition of wageworkers and
service sector employees for they constitute the main catalyst of
the GPPs. TurkStat's Household Labor Force Survey estimates
that 51 percent of the labor force contributes to the service

sector, whereas the contribution of the industrial, construction, and agricultural sectors are respectively 19 percent, 6.3 percent, and 22.4 percent (TurkStat 2013b). Another set of findings of the same survey indicates that employers constitute only 4.8 percent of the work force, whereas 19.2 percent, 64.3 percent, and 11.7 percent are respectively own account workers, wage workers, and unpaid family workers (TurkStat 2013c). World Bank data on Turkey, moreover, illustrate that wage labor has expanded in the country between 2002 and 2011 from 49.8 percent to 61.7 percent (WorldBank 2013).

A major grievance of wage labor in Turkey is the growing levels of consumer indebtedness, especially through credit cards, housing, and other types of microcredit and personal loans. In a study by Karaçimen (2014, 163), it has been documented that "since 2003, there has been a rapid increase in household sector borrowing from financial institutions. As a proportion of Turkey's gross domestic product...the total of consumer loans and credit card debt increased sharply from 1.8 per cent in 2002 to 18.7 per cent in 2012...Strikingly, household debt reached 49 per cent of disposable personal income in 2012, implying around a seven-fold increase since the end of 2003." According to the author, these numbers speak to a historically unique tendency in Turkey caused by extreme neoliberal financialization in the last decade. Likewise, *Bloomberg Businessweek* reports that more than 30 percent of Turkish people's daily expenses are made via credit cards with interest rates as high as 29 percent, which explains the alarming increase in credit card debt recorded as 23 percent in 2010 and 20 percent in 2011 (Matlack and Bryant 2011). There is "an estimated 3.7 million delinquent cardholders, and 2.5 million others who make only their required minimum monthly payments, which are generally less than half the balance" (Matlack and Bryant 2011). Consequently, the Bank revenue coming from commission on credit fees and transactions increased by 332 percent between 2003 and 2013. The number of credit cards under scrutiny reached more than 1.5 million with a debt of around 3.6 billion TL (VatanDailyNews 2013).

These figures of skyrocketing indebtedness are an indicator that wage-earning classes depend more and more on a vicious circle of debt mechanisms to maintain a decent livelihood.

Moreover, according to OECD's Better Life Index, which seeks to measure well-being rates in OECD countries, Turkish society's living conditions have considerably low rankings in almost every field, which undermines the validity of the affluent middle-class thesis in Turkey. Life satisfaction rate in Turkey, for instance, is 5.3 out of 10, which is below the OECD average of 6.6, ranking 33rd among 36 countries. Turkey ranks the very last among 36 countries in the ratings for job security and employment, work–life balance, and housing. With regard to employment, the index mentions that "people in Turkey work 1,877 hours a year, more than the OECD average of 1,776 hours," and "around 46% of employees work very long hours, much higher than the OECD average of 9%." Lastly, Turkey is among the last five countries in terms of income levels, education quality, and environment, and ranks 30th for social inequality (OECD 2013a). These statistics speak directly to the grievances of wage-earning classes.

For descriptive purposes, which would facilitate the portrayal of wage-earning class fractions, it is worth briefly discussing the data about the percentage distribution of employees and their average monthly gross wage in Turkish Liras (TRY). Professionals represent the highest monthly average gross earning (2,683 TRY) next to legislators, senior officials, and managers (3,710 TRY). According to the latest figures of TurkStat, the annual average gross earning of technicians and associate professionals, clerks, service sales workers, and elementary (unqualified) occupations is respectively 1,873, 1,596, 1,099, and 1,015 TRY (TurkStat 2010). The same figures also indicate that clerks, service and sales workers, and unqualified employees constitute the core of Turkish working class (43.1 percent of total employees), having a representation of 13.4 percent, 14.3 percent, and 15.4 percent, respectively. The ratio of clerks, service and sales workers, and unqualified employees was recorded as 35.9 percent in 2006, suggesting a gradual rise in this segment of the working class in Turkey. Among technicians and associate professionals, only 1.4 percent has a privileged position in terms of both authority and wage disparity, which amounts to a difference of 668 TRY. Greater disparity of authority and wage is however observed in clerks (TurkStat 2010). Overall, a majority of clerks, service and sales workers constitute various fractions of the working class, as opposed to the so-called middle classes, a term that is carelessly used to denote any group that is between the uppermost and lowermost segments of society.

Considering the role of students in the GPPs, it would also be worthy of taking a glance at the composition of the youth. Turkey is one of the countries that have the highest youth population with a rate of 16.8 percent, exceeding the United States (14.1 percent) and exceeded by Brazil (17.2 percent), and Mexico (18.3 percent) (TurkStat 2012). However, the schooling rate in higher education for the youth between the age of 18 and 22 is only 35 percent. It is striking to note that, according to TurkStat data, youth unemployment between the years 2004 and 2012 held an average of 20.3 percent (suggesting that in the youth population, 1 in every 5 is unemployed), and was recorded as 17.5 percent for the year 2012 (TurkStat 2013a). The assessment of World Bank data between 1991 and 2008 makes possible the assumption that nowadays unemployment of those with "tertiary education," a category that was active during the GPPs, tend to assume an important aspect of unemployment. Accordingly, in the last two decades, the share of tertiary education unemployment among the total unemployed population in Turkey rose from 4.9 percent in 1991 to 9.6 percent in 2000, and to 13.9 percent in 2008 (WorldBank 2013).

If one takes into account Boratav's previously discussed argument that the educated youth feels uneasy about high levels of unemployment and being confined to unqualified jobs, one could understand the reason the educated youth led the GPPs. That such economic grievances were not explicitly addressed by the youth in the protest wave does not contradict the class character of the movement, nor does it justify approaching the GPPs in purely culturalist terms. Burkev mentions that the Turkish youth "can hardly go on with their daily lives without depending on the support of their parents. Yet they do not accept themselves as a member of the proletarian class. They mostly do not think and behave with respect to classical proletarian patterns" (Burkev 2013), which was a factor that strengthened the myth of the "middle classes" in mainstream analyses. However, as Eken (2014, 431) puts it, "from the perspective of the question of agency, this must be called a 'proletarian' movement: it is the revolt of those for whom life has become an oppressive term of survival."

Overall, the data discussed in this section speak to the invalidity of the mainstream arguments that categorizes a myriad of working-class fractions under the so-called middle classes. Moreover, the data point to a long-term tendency of proletarianization of the Turkish labor force rather than the growth of an affluent class. Although the structural capacity of the Turkish working class to act in unity is undermined by several factors, the young and relatively educated segments of wage-earning fractions had the advantage to mobilize against the government thanks to their politico-ideological and organizational resources critical toward the AKP's hegemony. This, nevertheless, does not in any way make them the "cultural bourgeoisie/elite." The next section will elaborate on this argument to reveal how structural class (in)capacities find their counterpart in organizational ones in consideration of the political and ideological dispositions of working-class fractions.

2c. Political-Ideological Disposition of Working Classes in Turkey

The assessments so far serve as an answer to how people are objectively located in terms of production processes. The analysis of fractions reveals that a loose portrayal of wageworkers and service sector employees as "middle classes" cannot deliver an accurate explanation of class structures. Instead, an alliance of wage-earning fractions is visible in the GPPs, which was led by service sector employees, educated youth, and white- and blue-collar groups. That the relatively qualified wageworkers contributed largely to the protests should not come as a surprise. As Poulantzas writes, when it comes to social services, precarious working conditions, and job security, "middle-level-salaried workers are, by their nature, particularly sensitive to the objectives of a struggle in these domains; the base of their alliance with the working class is therefore considerably extended" (Poulantzas, 2008: 318). In Turkey, critical white-collar initiatives such as *Plaza Eylem Platformu* and *Uyanma Saati* have already been addressing concerns of routinization, alienation, and precariousness of work, which can be viewed among the constituents of proletarianization (PlazaEylemPlatformu 2013, UyanmaSaati 2013).

We contend that a political-ideologically informed class analysis is required to further explain the prominence of such alliance of class fractions, and particularly the largely secular orientation of the protests. Our focus thus shifts to how people subjectively locate themselves in relation to extra-economic factors. As previously mentioned, Poulantzas holds that politics and ideology play an important role in understanding the class dynamics of a given social formation. He puts forth that "we are not faced...on the one hand with an economic 'structure' that alone defines class places, and on the other hand with a class struggle extending to the political and ideological domain...From the start structural class determination involves economic, political and ideological class struggle, and these struggles are all expressed in the form of class positions in the conjuncture" (Poulantzas 1975a, 16). The rise of the aforementioned class fractions, therefore, cannot be reduced to mere economic concerns caused by intensive neoliberalization and proletarianization. This is also related to the particular ways in which neoliberalism is reproduced in Turkey through politico-ideological domination and subordination exercised by various state apparatuses under the AKP government (Poulantzas 1975a, 17, 21, 25).

In the case of Turkish neoliberalism, the authoritarian social and spatial engineering of the government along Islamist lines was a central politico-ideological element that agitated class grievances. The GPPs, therefore, were not simply an ideologically motivated "secularist" movement, but a secularly oriented class reaction to Islamically legitimated neoliberalism in the particularity of Turkey. Slavoj Žižek touched upon this aspect of the protest:

> It is crucial that we don't see the Turkish protests merely as a secular civil society rising up against an authoritarian Islamist regime supported by a silent Muslim majority. What complicates the picture is the protests' anti-capitalist thrust: protesters intuitively sense that free-market fundamentalism and fundamentalist Islam are not mutually exclusive. The privatisation of public space by an Islamist government shows that the two forms of fundamentalism can work hand in hand. (Žižek 2013)

Parallel with this perspective, AKP's Islamic neoliberalism can be understood "as an example of how … political Islam adjusted to neoliberal restructuring project within the process of globalization" marked by a strong "articulation of identity-based feelings of exclusion for different political projects" (Bedirhanoğlu and Yalman 2010, 110, 112). The bourgeois-Islamic reorganization of political and civil society under the AKP government served to refashion Turkish society in line with the market logic by legitimizing neoliberalism through Islamic-conservative codes (Tuğal 2011, Blad and Koçer 2012). One of the underlying objectives of the neoliberal project under the AKP era has been to veil class-based politics by atomizing working classes along politico-ideological lines (BağımsızSosyalBilimciler 2009, 28–29, 33, Koç 2010, 432). Accordingly, organizational capacities of the Turkish working class have been severely undermined by the politics of identity, which are "putting an end to class-based politics" (Yalman 2012, 23). Within this rhetoric, "the abolition of class distinctions and the emergence of an Islamic type of solidarity … guarantee social 'peace and tranquility' and in this way incorporate the masses in the neoliberal program" (Moudouros 2014, 185).

The expansion of culturally legitimized paternalistic labor practices, conservative trade unions, and Islamic social aid networks have been crucial components of the AKP's "neoliberalism with Islamic characteristics." In parallel with the rise of political Islam and what can be loosely conceptualized as "Muslim bourgeoisies" since the 1980s, sentiments of gratitude and paternalistic relationships between capitalists and workers have been promoted to erode class antagonisms (Buğra 2002, 1998). The concept "Islamic/Muslim bourgeoisies" is used here not as a geographically distinct class fraction located in Anatolia (as opposed to Istanbul), but it rather refers to those class fractions that are politically and ideologically engaged, in an organic fashion, "to the project of Islamic society" spearheaded by the AKP government (Sönmez 2010, 180). This is to imply neither the existence of inherently monolithic "Muslim" and "secular" class fractions, nor a necessary antagonism between them, especially given that both the "secular" circles of TÜSIAD and the "Islamic" business organizations such as MÜSIAD and TUSKON have been largely supported, and prospered under the AKP government (Sönmez 2010, 181). For our purposes in this chapter, the antagonizing internal divisions among the neoliberal-Islamic power bloc in Turkey, particularly between the AKP government and the Gülen Movement since December 2013, will not be the central concern. Instead, we deem the conceptualization of "Muslim bourgeoisies" as significant in indicating those class fractions that are actively involved in the AKP's neoliberal transformation of society along conservative-Islamic lines, as well as the relevant ideological strategies they utilize vis-à-vis labor, which has had consequences for the structure and capacities of the working classes in Turkey.

The Islamic ideological component is well documented to contribute to the expansion of flexible, non-unionized, informal, and paternalistic work relations in Turkey (Durak 2011). "In this Islamic context of industrial relations, mutual trust replaces the need for a formal labor code and labor unions," where strikes, for instance "clearly, do not form a part of Islamic labor market" (Buğra 2002, 195). Given that "harmony and peace as opposed to conflict and controversy is what Islam preaches," class struggle is despised in this mentality, and must be replaced by "feelings of solidarity...in a cultural frame of reference where Islam significantly contributes to the establishment of a shared understanding" (Buğra 1998, 529, 533). These ideals are echoed in the articulations of the US-based Islamic cleric Fethullah Gülen, who exerts considerable influence over conservative capital and labor organizations in Turkey: "The boss is on the side of the worker....Like a family member, he provides the worker with food when he eats himself;...with clothing when he dresses himself up, and he does not impose on the worker a task that is beyond his own capacity" (as quoted in Yıldırım 2010).

The predominance of paternalistic labor relations is heavily felt also in the growing strength of conservative and pro-AKP trade unionism. The most organized trade union in the public sector is the conservative Confederation of Public Servants' Trade Unions (Memur-Sen) with 707,652 members, as compared to its leftward counterpart Confederation of Public Workers' Unions (KESK) with 237,180 members (HaberlerNews 2013). Similarly, the religious/conservative and pro-AKP trade unions of the private sector represent the largest trade unions in the country, with Türk-İş (around 702,000 members) and Hak-İş (around 166,000 members), outweighing the leftward DİSK (around 100,000) (SendikaNews 2013d). According to the mainstream *Milliyet Daily Newspaper*, the rising strength of such conservative/religious trade unions as Hak-İş and Memur-Sen is closely linked to the power of the AKP government, under which Memur-Sen, Hak-İş and Türk-İş's membership base boosted in the last decade by 650 percent, 40 percent and 16 percent, respectively; in comparison with a 14 percent rise at DİSK and a 14 percent decline at KESK (Senol and Metin 2013). Conservative trade unionism greatly contributes to the reproduction of paternalistic labor relationships through the emphasis of "social cohesion...rather than class conflict...in full conformity with Islam" (Buğra 2002, 199). In addition to the rise of conservative trade unionism, it must be added that Turkish trade unionism as a whole suffers from a loss of legitimacy due to severe corruption and political defeats, which further undermine the organizational capacities of working classes (Koç 2010, 2009).

To further clarify "neoliberalism with Islamic characteristics" in Turkey, the rise of "Muslim bourgeoisies" should also be elaborated on. Islamist capitalist class fractions, although clearcut distinctions may be misleading, can be understood as "newly growing domestic capital groups engaged in aggressive strategies of accumulation and looking for state support in their vigorous project of further growth and integration with the world market" (Ercan and Oğuz 2006, 652). In this regard, the Association of Independent Industrialists and Businessmen (MÜSİAD founded in 1990, 6500 members) and the Turkish Confederation of Businessmen and Industrialists (TUSKON founded in 2005, 33,260 members) must be highlighted. Establishing an organic relationship with the AKP government, MÜSİAD mobilizes its financial and human resources to support the former, whereas the former provides the latter with state support (Başkan 2010). Such organic relationship with the state is also evident in the case of TUSKON, despite the recently emerging frictions between the government and the US-headquartered Gülen movement that controls TUSKON itself. "Although not formed by the state, [the TUSKON] works closely with state institutions, sharing many functions with DEİK [Foreign Economic Relations Board of Turkey] regarding Turkey's foreign business relations" (Tür 2011, 592). It is interesting to note that in June 2013, during the GPPs, conservative trade union confederations Hak-İş, Türk-İş, and Memur-Sen joined the conservative business associations MÜSİAD and TUSKON (along with others) to publish a full-page message in several newspapers, calling on protesters to end the GPPs. The message argued that the government "responded positively to the...concerns of citizens," and that anybody pro-testing after this would be contributing to harming "Turkey's power and image," as well as "stability and economic growth" (AnadoluAjans 2013). The unification of Islamic business and labor against the GPPs demonstrates their shared allegiance to the AKP government.

Relatedly, another contributor to the incapacitation of a segment of Turkish working classes is the AKP's multilayered populist/clientelist social aid networks that function through the combined efforts of the central government, local-municipal authorities, and religious brotherhoods. Karaman (2013, 3421–2) notes that "these aids are organized in such a way to empower the Islamic communities and the AKP as a whole," and they "cannot be thought separate from the Islamic moral phi-losophy of the AKP itself." Consequently, "state-administered social assistance delivered in the appearance of alms creates a relationship of indebtedness" that prevent the development of critical perspectives toward the government and/or the mar-ket, where Islam plays a passivizing cultural-ideological role in preaching docility, obedience, and gratitude. Through the AKP's sustained and socially entrenched Islamic-patronage net-works, a significant portion of the working classes in Turkey are made ultimately reliant on the government for subsistence, as they are locked in a mechanism of dependence that would prove extremely risky and costly to abandon. Combined with cultur-ally legitimized paternalistic relations of labor exploitation and conservative trade unions, therefore, these aid networks further constrain the emergence of progressive politics of citizenship based on claiming "rights."

In terms of cultural-ideological life, moreover, the grow-ing economic and hegemonic strength of "Muslim bourgeoi-sies" came to generate distinct tastes and consumer choices (Gümüşcü 2010), which was accompanied by their significantly increased hegemonic control of various segments of civil soci-ety through the establishment of mosques, schools, universities, training centers, and student residences (Doğan 2010, 297). The development of Islamic capitalist fractions' organic ties with the state expanded the Islamist hegemony via the proliferation of the media power, private high schools, and universities (Sharon-Krespin 2009). Hand in hand with the rise of Muslim bourgeoisies went the AKP's increasing monopolization of the state apparatus and reshaping of civil society via state repression, which rendered Islamic-neoliberal authoritarianism all the more a central issue in the eyes of secularly oriented class fractions. This is represented, as the next chapter will demonstrate at length, in the significant decline in civil liberties and political rights for non-AKP groups, extreme measures of media censorship, skyrocketing imprisonment rates, and massive court cases against various opposition groups (*Ergenekon*, *Balyoz*, and *KCK*), Islamic "social interventionism" and concomitant restrictions on secular lifestyles, and so on.

We thus argue that the Islamic character of neoliberalism in Turkey made it more likely for secularly oriented educated youth, wageworkers, and service sector employees to take the lead in the protests. Relatively free from the AKP's politico-ideological subordination of labor (namely through paternalistic work relations, conservative trade unionism, and Islamic aid networks), these groups were able to openly react against neoliberal practices as well as their political and ideological manifestations in the AKP-led power bloc. Secondly, another reason that aggravated the grievances of secular wage-earning class fractions was the AKP's increasing social and spatial engineering personified in the Islamic authoritarianism of PM Erdoğan (discussed further in Chapter 3). Secularly inclined educated youth, wageworkers, and social sector employees realized that the consolidation of "neoliberalism with Islamic characteristics" in Turkey was not only detrimental to them economically, but also particularly restrictive on their lifestyles and cultural choices, which significantly contributed to the GPPs.

Gezi Park, therefore, represents the culmination of these economic, political, and ideological-cultural grievances. Demolishing a public park through urban restructuring to build yet another shopping mall, military barracks, and the PM's vow to construct another mosque in Taksim were symbolic of the neoliberal-Islamic engineering of society and space under the AKP government, which added to the augmented economic grievances of proletarianization and precariousness experienced by various wage-earning class fractions. In one word, "peoples' reaction to the general process of proletarianization in Turkey turns out to be a secular reaction because the associated neoliberal policies have been carried out by 'the...Islamic AKP'" (Burkev 2013).

Reprise and Review

This chapter sought to demonstrate that the class background of the GPPs could not be simply reduced to an amorphous category of "middle classes," or to a purely ideological "secularism-centered" uprising. A heavy reliance on the term "middle classes" to understand the GPPs serves to blur the intensification of class struggles under the Islamic neoliberal project imposed by the AKP government. Instead, resting on the works of Poulantzas and Wright, we argued that Gezi Park brings together an alliance of various wage-earning class fractions sharing the common destiny of decreased class capacities and life-chances, and increased precariousness, exploitation, and proletarianization. Keeping in mind that class relations are as much political and ideological as they are economic, we put further stress on these aspects of the class struggle. Accordingly, shifting the focus to "class capacities," we advanced that the subordination of large segments of working classes through paternalistic work relations, conservative trade unionism, and Islamic-clientelist networks created a supportive environment for the free articulation of class grievances for the secularly oriented educated youth, relatively qualified wage workers, and service sector employees. Also, the AKP's authoritarian social and spatial interventionism based on an Islamic worldview made these secular class fractions more sensitive to the perils of neoliberalism, and mobilized their organizational class capacities. This is the main reason the GPPs may appear to be a "secularist middle class revolt" from the surface, although its deeper roots lie in a combination of economic, political, and ideological factors to tackle "neoliberalism with Islamic characteristics." The next chapter elaborates on the various aspects of AKP's Islamic-neoliberal authoritarianism and social interventionism as a crucial cultural-conjunctural factor for the GPPs.

3

"Neoliberalism with Islamic Characteristics": Political, Economic, and Cultural Conjuncture of the GPPs

Having discussed the structural class foundations of the GPPs, we now build on the previous chapter by providing a systematic understanding of the conjunctural "opportunities" that triggered the events (Petras and Veltmeyer 2013, 216). Political-economic and cultural-ideological opportunities can be broadly understood as the more immediate material/objective factors that implicitly or explicitly lead to collective action, or in more precise terms, to the process by which private discontents of social actors start escalating into social mobilization. It is important to stress that "cultural factors" constitute an underlying component of political-economic-ideological opportunities of class action insofar as they filter the ways in which neoliberal policies are implemented. Neoliberal restructuration policies are not adopted as they are prescribed by hegemonic international institutions in a top-down fashion (Gill 2011). There is no "one size fits all" formula, because of the need to adjust neoliberalism to the geographical and cultural peculiarities of a given location for a more successful political legitimation (Peck and Theodore 2012). We thus use the term "neoliberalism with Islamic characteristics" to refer to its particular political, economic, and cultural-ideological manifestations in the geography of Turkey (Karaman 2013).

We argue that three sets of conjunctural opportunities have been crucial in the emergence and development of the GPPs through the agency of secularly oriented wage earning class fractions. The first concerns the transformation of urban and cultural space along Islamic-neoliberal lines, the second is the AKP's accompanying Islamic social interventionism and political repression personified in the figure of PM Erdoğan, and the third is the government's adventurous Syrian policy to set off a crisis of legitimacy. Accordingly, in the first section, we analyze the political-economic restructuring of urban space in Turkey through Harvey's concept of "spatial fix." In the second section, we suggest supplementing the notion of "spatial fix" with what we call the "political-cultural fix" (PCF) in order to underline capitalism's need to rely on the political-cultural readjustment of society in parallel with the neoliberal adjustment of the economy. It is in this section that we discuss how neoliberal urban restructuring in Turkey hinges on Islamism and neo-Ottomanism to ensure ideological legitimacy and coherence. The third section, in turn, sheds light on the AKP's Islamically motivated "social interventionism" to further transform society through moralistic impositions, coupled with politico-judicial repression that seeks to overpower popular opposition and grievances. The final section examines the role of Turkey's opaque, unaccountable, and Sunni-Islamically biased foreign policy on Syria, and the "Reyhanlı Bombings" in creating a social distress that contributed to mobilization prior to the GPPs. All these factors served as "opportunities" to bring secularly oriented wage-earning class fractions to the fore of the movement against "neoliberalism with Islamic characteristics."

3a. The Political-Economic Restructuring of Urban Space

The political-economic and cultural-ideological factors leading to the GPPs are rooted in the rise in power of the AKP as an Islamist neoliberal political party, which consolidated its power since 2002. The AKP government can be seen as a by-product of the economic crisis of 2001, during which Turkish neoliberalism was going through a severe crisis of hegemony (Yaşlı 2013, 9). In Ziya Öniş's terms, the 2001 economic crisis, during which "a major collapse of output and employment occurred," had far-reaching impacts on Turkish society and politics in that "domestic political actors and notably the parties that constituted the incumbent coalition government emerged as the main targets for criticism" (Öniş 2006, 1, 6). In this sense, it is possible to argue that the foundation of the AKP was a direct response to the implications of the 2001 crisis, which set out to reestablish neoliberal hegemony through merging it with political Islam (Öniş 2006, Çavdar 2013, Boratav 2011). As Karaman (2013, 3416) underlines, "upon assuming office, the AKP strictly adhered to the IMF-supervised crisis management program that had begun in April 2001...The IMF-crafted anti-inflationary, debt-management program mandated checks on spending for public services and social reforms. The compliant AKP quickly implemented policies cutting public spending, controlling wages, significantly rolling back agricultural subsidies and privatizing state-owned enterprises, as well as natural resources."

According to Fatih Yaşlı, the AKP government served not only to advance neoliberalism but also to create the necessary conditions for its hegemonic expansion based on Islamic conservatism (Yaşlı 2013). As such, Yaşlı points to the crucial role of political opportunities and "social interventionist" policies of the government in indirectly providing the fertile ground for the eruption of the GPPs (Yaşlı 2013, 11–13). What we call "social interventionism" refers to AKP's efforts to establish political and ideological domination along Islamic lines via the diffusion and imposition of a conservative-neoliberal *Weltanschauung* in all state institutions and segments of civil society. This refers not only to the government's interference with lifestyles to exert Islamic-moralistic control over society, but also the larger transformation of social-urban space in the framework of Islamically embedded, legitimated, and reinforced neoliberalism.

In understanding Turkish neoliberalism within the context of the GPPs, our primary focus is on neoliberal urban policies as they pertain to the grievances of the urban wage-earning class fractions. The Turkish case of urban neoliberalism under the AKP speaks directly to Harvey's theorization of "spatial fix." Harvey's concept of "spatial fix" seeks to understand the political economic aspects of capitalism's geographical specificities. Spatial fix underlines that the crisis-prone internal contradictions of capitalism can only be "solved," or rather deferred, through the geographical expansion of capital to produce and commodify new spaces (Harvey 2003). The term "fix" has a double meaning in this context. On the one hand, "fix" means "a certain portion of...capital is literally fixed in and on the land in some physical form" to open up new areas for investment. On the other hand, "fix" is "a metaphor for a particular kind of solution to capitalist crises through temporal deferral and geographical expansion" (Harvey 2003, 115). Harvey goes on to assert that spatial fix is both economic and political (Harvey 2003, 44), given that "building a new landscape...accommodate[s] both the endless accumulation of capital and the endless accumulation of political power" (Harvey 2003, 135).

One of the main pillars of AKP government since 2002 has been the massive reorganization of space along neoliberal lines through infrastructural investments, construction projects, and the wholesale restructuring of urban landscapes. The AKP's "spatial fix" invests predominantly in land at the municipal and national levels with the purpose of deferring accumulation crises. The grandiose government project, Canal Istanbul, which envisages the construction of a 45-kilometer long, 150-meter wide artificial waterway between the Marmara Sea and the Black Sea by 2023, costing more than $10 billion, is the zenith of this "accumulation by construction" mentality. This project is also extended to the virtual construction of a new city within Istanbul, an airport, a seaport, and a number of recreational areas. The building of new highways and a third bridge in the Bosphorus further exemplify the AKP government's attempt to ensure the stability and expansion of capitalist accumulation. Rent-seeking and speculative construction initiatives constitute the backbone of AKP's political economy, the influence of which undermines agricultural and industrial sectors as foundations for economic development (Dorsay 2013, 240, Kahraman 2013, 38–39, 46, Sönmez 2013, 18, 136).[1] The centrality of spatial fix for the AKP is also demonstrated in their long-term projections on 2023, the centenary of the Republic of Turkey. The party's official 2023 vision propagates numerous colossal projects: by 2023, the objective is to build 11,000 kilometers of additional railway, 15,000 kilometers of divided highway, at least three nuclear power plants, hydro-electric centrals, and one of the largest ports in the world (BusinessTurkeyToday 2013).

According to data from Turkstat, the number of permits for the construction of new buildings rose from 43.4 thousand in 2002 to 75.5 thousand in 2004, to 106.7 thousand in 2006, and to 116.5 thousand in 2013. In terms of square meters, the new land opened to construction in 2002 was 36.2 million m^2, 69.8 million m^2 in 2004, 122.9 million m^2 in 2006, and 168.2 million m^2 in 2013 (TurkStat 2014b). Comparing these figures with the decade prior to the AKP years further reveals the zeal for construction. Between 1992–2002, an average of 71.1 million m^2 of new land was annually opened to construction, whereas between 2003–2013 the annual average rose to 117.8 m^2, which demonstrates a rise of 66 percent (TurkStat 2014b, a).

With regard to the AKP's "spatial fix," the Housing Development Administration of Turkey, TOKI, reinvigorated in the 2000s, stands out "as the single most important player in urban regeneration in Turkey" (Lovering and Türkmen 2011, 78–79). Considered one of the most controversial institutions of the AKP years because of its lack of transparency and regulation, TOKI came to displace the urban poor toward new housing units that are unaffordable in the long run and to commodify urban spaces that were previously occupied by squatters (Lovering and Türkmen 2011, 82, Sönmez 2013, 144). As an influential governing body, TOKI administered the construction of 621.911

housing units in 81 cities comprising 800 districts since 2003. As the TOKI website proudly declares, this number of housing units is equivalent to the creation of 23 new cities populated by 100,000 residents each. In total, TOKI-led projects amount to a massive investment of 62.9 billion TRY through 5,149 public bids. The housing projects, moreover, are accompanied by 502 commercial centers, 493 mosques, 341 police stations, 954 school buildings, 525 gymnasiums, and 16 stadiums (TOKI 2014). These numbers represent a conscious political economic project based on construction, as 14 laws were passed between 2002 and 2008 to particularly enlarge TOKI's field of activity and financial resources (Balaban 2011, 24). To create demand for housing, moreover, Law No. 5582, commonly known as the "mortgage law," was passed in 2007, which enabled banks to offer long-term real estate loans with low interest rates. As will be discussed in the next section, the strategic importance of TOKI emanates also from the fact that it serves as the mainstay for the consolidation of "Muslim bourgeoisies" organically connected to the AKP government (Karaman 2013). Similarly, the widespread construction of shopping malls throughout Turkey has been another major driving force of the neoliberal spatial fix in the last decade, leading to a spectacular transformation of the leisure of urban people and the erosion of small shopkeeping (Erkip 2005). The year 2005 is considered to be a landmark in the spread of shopping malls, after which their number increased from 106 in 2005 to 263 in 2010 and is expected to reach 347 in 2014 (HürriyetDailyNews 2012a). The total investment in shopping malls has reached $40 billion, generating a turnover of 50–60 billion TRY.

In a report published in November 2013, the Union of Chambers of Turkish Engineers and Architects (TMMOB) showed that the AKP's prioritization of neoliberal "spatial fix" in designing top-down urban policies across the country is likely to trigger social and environmental crises (TMMOB 2013). The document demonstrated that the Ministry of Environment and Urban Planning, which replaced the Ministry of Public Works and Housing in 2011, has been embellished with new and extraordinary authorities to facilitate the neoliberal plundering of cities. Amendment of the Law No. 2863 in 2011, for instance, transferred the management of protected areas with cultural and natural significance directly to the ministry, thus paving the way for their demolishment for construction projects. These include national and natural parks, protected areas, wetlands, and so on, which applies to the case of Gezi as an urban public park. Rangelands across the country, moreover, were also opened to construction with the amendment of the Law No. 3194, allowing the state to rent these lands out to private companies. These sets of legislation are in addition to a number of decree laws silently passed and implemented by the government with no democratic accountability. It is also emphasized in the TMMOB document that urban areas in Turkey are extremely vulnerable against natural disasters, given the complete lack of planning in policymaking. All in all, the Chamber underlines that under the AKP government, "the notion of public interest was discarded" from urban policymaking. Instead, the latter is "made subject to deregulation, privatization, commercialization," and non-planning became the rule of the game in every city of Turkey, which are "surrendered to rent-seeking projects" (TMMOB 2013, 5). The opportunities arising out of the AKP's political-economic spatio-temporal fix found their immediate expression in popular slogans that underlined the rent-seeking urban renewal projects of the government. These will be discussed in Chapter 5.

The AKP's insistence on the renovation of the Taksim region, including Gezi Park, can be seen as the quintessential expression of its larger motive for "accumulation by construction." It was in September 2011 that the municipality of Istanbul resolved to initiate the "Taksim Square Pedestrianization Project." In January 2013, the Regional Board for Preservation of Cultural Assets in Istanbul voted against the project on historical grounds, holding that Gezi Park has a significant place "in the collective memory of Istanbul's residents." The decision, however, did not stop the government: in February 2013, the AKP-led High Council for Preservation of Cultural and Natural Assets reversed the regional board's judgment to give the green light to the redevelopment project. Unsurprisingly, the main contractor for the multimillion-dollar project, Kalyon Group (owned by Orhan Cemal Kalyoncu), is known to have close ties with the government and the PM Erdoğan.[2] The next section discusses how spatial expansion of capital in Turkish neoliberalism goes hand in hand with the AKP's promotion of Islamic/neo-Ottomanist culture and symbolism.

3b. The Political-Cultural Restructuring of Urban Space

TOKI, Canal Istanbul, the Third Bridge, shopping malls, highways, and the AKP's other rent-seeking major national and urban projects can be considered as prime examples of neoliberal spatial fix, as understood by Harvey. However, such an economic framework cannot fully account for the political-cultural peculiarities of urban geographies. Harvey's notion of spatio-temporal fix pays no systematic attention to the linkages between the economic and political/extra-economic aspects of the reproduction of the capitalist system (Jessop 2004b, a). Jessop rather points to the role of "socially constituted spatio-temporal boundaries" or "social arrangements" that help defer or displace the contradictions of capitalism via the hegemonic alteration of the "social significance" of place and space based on the temporality of memory and cultural identity through educational and other kind of institutional activities (Jessop 2008, 8, 47, 86, 104, 113, 134).

We argue that it is possible to build on Harvey's notion of spatio-temporal fix by distinguishing between "political-economic fix" that is specifically concerned with the temporal overcoming of the crisis of capital accumulation and "political-cultural fix" (PCF) that is particularly related to the political cohesion, expansion, and sustainability of capitalist political regimes, as they pertain to the articulation of cultural and hegemonic struggles unique to a given geography. In one way or another, capitalist political regimes need to rely on a political-cultural readjustment of society in order to keep up with neoliberal adjustment of the economy. In this sense, PCF constitutes an effort that is not only confined to the field of economy and the aim of capital accumulation, but also encompasses the transformation of a nation's "memory" and culture through spatial reconstruction and re-symbolization. In the particular case of Turkish neoliberalism, the AKP's rent-seeking urban redevelopment is embedded in an Islamist-Ottomanist urban/cultural symbolism and ideology, which seeks to dissolve and replace the secular-republican representations of history, identity, and memory. The TMMOB report stresses: "the closure of Haydarpaşa Train Station, the underpass built in front of Ankara Train Station, the demolition of Ankara Gas Factory, or the building of a shopping mall to replace Gezi Park...exemplify the destruction of urban identity as well urban memory" (TMMOB 2013, 20). In the words of Eken (2014, 430), "the Gezi protests rejected precisely this cultural regime of memory as an instrument of legitimation of the current political power."

Lovering and Turkmen demonstrate that the implementation of the neoliberal agenda in Turkey, which has reached unprecedented levels under the AKP government, went hand in hand with the "tightening [of political-cultural hegemonic] control over the media and educational appointments" (Lovering and Türkmen 2011, 78). This laid the groundwork for the AKP government to transform people's "common sense" and everyday culture, through the "Islamic takeover of the city" with a neoliberal and neo-Ottomanist thrust (Lovering and Türkmen 2011, 81, Karaman 2013). The AKP's blend of neo-Ottomanism with Islamic ideology imposes on the city what Serkan Öngel, the head of the DISK Research Department, calls a "conquest mentality" (Öngel 2013). Here, neo-Ottomanism broadly refers to a political-Islamic hegemonic project that aspires to eradicate the Kemalist-Republican interpretation of national culture, history, and politics by replacing it with a modern but nostalgic and traditionalist re-interpretation of the Ottoman legacy in a way to erode secularism, civic nationalism, and the idea of progress as the building blocks of the Republic (Çolak 2006). Neo-Ottomanism also has severe implications for Turkish foreign policy, which aspires to create a "greater Turkey" that acts like an "empire" and "global leader" in the world arena in line with Sunni Islamic principles (Çolak 2006). Critiquing neo-Ottomanism, Öngel (2013) points to the AKP's efforts to restructure people's perception and memory of Istanbul from the city of the Republic to a city built on the legacy of the Ottoman conquest of 1453. Öngel finds it symbolic that the demolition of Gezi Park by the government started in the wake of May 29, the 560th anniversary of Istanbul's conquest by the Ottomans. Mouduros (2014, 188) confirms that under the AKP rule, "Islam's harmonization with neoliberalism...has ended up being a political 'obsession' of rebuilding the entire Istanbul and converting it into a symbol of the new Turkish 'global profile'" hinging on an imperial design.

One of the most immediate implications of the Islamic takeover of urban spaces is the increase in the number of mosques across the country. According to the latest official data from the Directorate of Religious Affairs, the number of mosques has increased from 75,369 in 2001 to 84,684 in 2012 (Diyanet 2012). The AKP government considered the construction of mosques as an opportunity to express its neo-Ottomanist thrust and hegemonic impact on the masses' cultural-historical memory, as clearly observed in the construction of the Mimar Sinan Mosque in Ataşehir, a district in the Anatolian part of Istanbul. As "a near replica of the fabulous 16th century Selimiye Mosque in Edirne," the mosque has become a "power symbol of the AKP government" (DünyaNews 2013). An even more grandiose mosque project was initiated on Istanbul's Çamlıca Hill, an archeological site with no legal justification for a construction project. For the PM Erdoğan, however, Islamic symbolism mattered more, who declared that "this giant mosque in Çamlıca was designed so as to be visible from all parts of Istanbul." According to İhsan Eliaçık, a Muslim critic of AKP's neoliberal policies, Çamlıca "reflects Erdoğan's desire to build a 'Sultan mosque' in Istanbul just like Suleiman the Magnificent and Mehmet the Conqueror did" (HürriyetDailyNews 2012c). Relatedly, the municipality of Üsküdar declared that the project was not just about building a mosque, but about reinvigorating the *külliye* tradition of the Ottoman Empire (Haber7News 2013b).[3]

Sunni Islamic-Ottomanist symbolism also presents itself in the naming of AKP-led construction and infrastructure projects. Istanbul's Third Bridge, for instance, was named after the Ottoman Sultan Selim I, who is responsible for the widespread massacre of the Alevi population in the sixteenth century. The Sunni-Islamic bias in the choice of name greatly offended the Alevi community (BloombergNews 2013), the largest religious minority in the country. In Ankara as well, Seljuk sultans' names (such as Sultan Alparslan, İzzettin Keykavus, Aleaddin Keykubat, etc.) were given to numerous small-scale bridges and tunnels, particularly in left-wing districts. Among the four dozen public universities opened since 2003, moreover, many were given names that carry Islamic-historical significance such as Sheik Edebali, Yıldırım Beyazıt, Mehmet Akif Ersoy, Necmettin Erbakan, Katip Çelebi, and so on. (These are in addition to Recep Tayyip Erdoğan University and Abdullah Gül University, named after the PM and the President.) The choice of such names is evidently not out of a neutral respect for history, but it represents a deliberate attempt to bolster the Islamic heritage to underpin the AKP-led neo-Ottomanism. As Gramsci underscores, even street names, among other things, "operate as factors or elements in the struggle over hegemony" (Morton 2007, 92).[4] In the case of Turkey, besides "restricting public space" neoliberalism "at the same time...highlights the pursuit of the political power to imprint, 'spatially and visually,' its ideological hegemony" (Moudouros 2014, 189).

The PCF of Turkish neoliberalism under the AKP government can also be found in TOKI projects and the renovation of Taksim, the site of Gezi Park. While serving as a cultural-hegemonic tool to expand the market logic of neoliberalism and to create a misleading image of the AKP government as the protector of the urban poor, TOKI also contributed to the proliferation of AKP-led Islamic capitalists insofar as most of its contractors are both related to the AKP's conservative-Islamic circles and are founded during the AKP era (Karaman 2013, Sönmez 2013, 20, 144). This is where Harvey's "political-economic fix" (capital accumulation) and our "political-cultural fix" (cultural-ideological accumulation) are articulated simultaneously with a strong cadence: The three largest TOKI realty corporations (Emlak Konut, Torunlar, Sinpaş) are indeed organically tied to the AKP government, with Emlak Konut having more than a third of TOKI assets (Sönmez 2013, 136–138). Despite the claim to provide the poor segments of society with social housing, the largest 25 TOKI projects in Istanbul serve to distribute the rent of previously public lands to firms that build luxury housing and shopping malls. It is thus no coincidence that no public information is available as to TOKI's financial accounts and resources including profits/losses, staff, and investments (Sönmez 2013, 144–147).[5] As Moudouros (2014, 189) notes, "the current Islamic bourgeoisie and the business elite of Turkey are integral to the investments and partnerships... in large shopping malls, luxurious hotels and modern residential complexes. On the other hand, urban transformation is a key element in reshaping space, in controlling this reshaping and in the reproduction of the ideological model through which the AKP envisions society."

As such, the Gezi protests were related to the question of drastic urban renewal under the AKP government, championing the commodification of urban spaces, the lack of accountability, and the destruction of green spaces. The ideal of "Islamizing" Taksim's landscape, which has long haunted the Turkish right, is placed in a neoliberal framework by the AKP in a way to create a political opportunity for the GPPs. As Birge Yıldırım (2012) suggests, public squares have been among the symbols of

the Kemalist Republic. They were part of the Republic's secularist struggle to eliminate the urban fabric of the Ottoman past.
Taksim Square and Gezi Park, as symbols of secularism and
progress, were planned as urban spaces that would make the
celebration of the new republic permeate into the daily lives of
the newly branded "Turkish citizens," along with solving the
problems of urban transportation, hygiene/ecology, and aes-
thetics (Yıldırım 2012, Baykan and Hatuka 2010).

Besides being a symbol of the Republic, Taksim Square also
constitutes a symbolic space for the Turkish left, especially for
the celebration of May Day. The Square signifies government
repression for most Turkish leftists, and it is registered in collective memory as the site of the 1977 May Day Events, which
tragically ended with gunshots, bombings, mass panic, and
34 deaths. Since 2007, the thirtieth anniversary of this bloody
event, the restriction on May Day demonstrations in Taksim
by the AKP government has been a major source of contention
and controversy, which led to excessive police violence (Baykan
and Hatuka 2010). The concept "disproportionate violence,"
which became commonplace in the GPPs, was first used to
denote the widespread police brutality during the May Days of
2007 onward. Unable to contain the social resistance, the AKP
was forced to declare May Day an official holiday in 2009, and
sought to trim its disruptive potential by calling it "Labor and
Solidarity Day." Still, major clashes between the protesters and
the police continued every year mainly due to the latter's provocation of the former. One month prior to the GPPs, finally,
the government reacted to May Day 2013 demonstrations by
shutting down all public transportation and closing two of its
major bridges in an attempt to slow demonstrator commute to
the square. Indeed, while police fought demonstrators attempt-
ing to make their way to the square, tourists were left stranded
downtown and missed flights because of the enormous ban on
transportation throughout the city. Given this background, the
consistent May Day mobilization of the Left since 2007 can be
seen as part of the prelude to the GPPs.

In addition to such embedded meanings, Taksim Square has also been subject to severe cultural controversies that engaged a broader public with the AKP government's attempts to build a mosque in the square. "The building of such a mosque is a decades-old hope of Turkey's Islamists," and for those who are opposed to the aggressive Islamization of urban spaces, it can only "symbolize the power of the Islamists over Taksim as well as the whole country." This was epitomized in Erdoğan's words: "A mosque will be built in Taksim...I do not need permission from the main opposition and a few looters" (NewYorkTimes 2013). These concerns were exacerbated by the government project to rebuild the historic Topçu Barracks, a symbol of the Ottoman past, built by the Sultan Abdulhamid I (eighteenth century), and its insistence on demolishing the Atatürk Cultural Center (AKM), a secular cultural symbol hosting a concert venue and opera/ballet house—which is currently evacuated. In this regard, it is no coincidence that the Gezi protesters re-appropriated the AKM and turned it into a strategic symbol of resistance by occupying its building and decorating it with giant flags and banners. Above all, the protesters strongly resisted the construction of military barracks and/or shopping mall at the expense of Gezi Park.

Another emblematic instance of PCF under the AKP rule is the demolition of the *Emek Movie Theater* so as to turn it into an entertainment and shopping area. Serving as a centerpiece of Istanbul's prestigious international film festival, *Emek* dates from the early republican era and used to be a major symbol of the Republic and modern art. Its demolition in 2013 aroused the angst of secular and leftist sectors and intelligentsia, and was accompanied by sonorous public criticism and protests. In addition, the small İnci Patisserie (historically famous for its delicious profiterole) was closed in lieu of reconstructing yet another mall in the Taksim area, which was later moved to Mis Street, a symbolic space of the Gezi resistance thanks to the Street's shopkeepers providing the protesters with active support. Protesters contested the police headiness at the time in an attempt to stop them from shutting down the century old establishment. Another source of massive contention has been the ban of outdoor seating in bars and restaurants by the AKP-run municipalities, along with severe limitations on and stigmatization toward the consumption of alcohol. The relevant law of 2013 "prohibits retail sales between 10pm and 6am, bans all alcohol advertising and promotion, and stops new shops and bars from opening within 100 meters of schools and mosques" (TheGuardian 2013c, TheEconomist 2013a).

In sum, the AKP's Taksim Project is closely related to the conservative elimination of Taksim's historic urban fabric as the center of entertainment, leisure, and alcohol consumption. Regarding the AKP's struggle with entertainment and alcohol, it is no coincidence that the protests erupted in the Taksim area with the slogans of "we are all looters and drunkards" in the aftermath of the announcement of AKP's alcohol laws (more on slogans in Chapter 5). A similar kind of controversy arose out of the prohibition of alcohol during the domestic flights of the Turkish Airlines (THY) and the banning of red lipstick and nail polish for flight attendants for they appeal to sexuality. These attempts backfired and the airline administration had to postpone its ban on the color red as severe criticisms echoed the public opinion (TheEconomistBlog 2013). It is relevant to note that THY workers, who have been on a long-term strike since 2012, provided active support to the GPPs with their participation to the protests by wearing Guy Hawkes masks (SözcüDailyNews 2013).

For the AKP, therefore, redeveloping the Taksim area is representative of more than "accumulation by construction," as there are also high cultural stakes embedded in the region for Islamists. The demolition of the AKM, Emek Theater, and Gezi Park as well as imposing severe conservative restrictions on the city's modern loci indicates the AKP's wholesale assault on the secular-republican urban fabric, lifestyles, and memory. Instead, building a mosque, neo-Ottoman military barracks, and a shopping mall in Taksim through the micromanagement of the PM himself is greatly symbolic in physically embodying

Islamic-neoliberal authoritarianism, which has been intensifying in Turkey during the last decade.

3c. State Repression and Islamic Social Interventionism

Indeed, the Islamic sociospatial interventionism of the AKP government has deeper roots in the restructuring of the state apparatus in the 2000s so as to ensure the sustainability of "neoliberalism with Islamic characteristics." In this sense, one could argue that Turkey is fast becoming a security state with an Islamic disposition. In 2013, the security apparatus of the Turkish state (including the General Directorate of Security, the General Command of Gendarmerie, the Councillorship of the National Intelligence Organization, and the Command of Coastal Security) received a gigantic budget of 22 billion TRY. Similarly, the budget of the Directorate of Religious Affairs increased from 0.55 billion TRY in 2002 (when AKP came to power) to 1.3 billion in 2006 and 4.6 billion in 2013, exceeding that of 11 major ministries, including the Ministries of Interior, Health, and Economy.

The rise of AKP's authoritarianism also revealed itself in their initiative to change Turkey's system of government from parliamentary to a presidential regime with autocratic tendencies. Public opinion was divided into two hostile camps: those who support the AKP government, and those who are concerned about the PM's ambitions to declare himself a neo-Sultan through the "introduction of a powerful presidential system guaranteeing his hold on power for the next two decades" (Aybet and Başkan 2011, 19–20). As underlined in *Foreign Policy*, "over the last decade the AKP has built an informal, powerful, coalition of party-affiliated businessmen and media outlets whose livelihoods depend on the political order that Erdoğan is constructing. Those who resist do so at their own risk" (Cook and Koplow 2013).

There is no question that the AKP's Islamic and security-oriented state capacity led to a considerable decline in freedom, civil liberties, and political rights (FreedomHouse 2013). According to the Freedom House,[6] at the time the AKP government came to power, the freedom, civil liberties, and political rights ratings were respectively 4.5, 5, and 4, which declined to 3.5, 4, and 3 in 2013. This decline is mainly due to the lack of an independent judiciary, of free self-expression and of academic freedom, censorship, and to the "pretrial detention of thousands of individuals...in campaigns that many believe to be politically motivated." Increasing authoritarianism is also reflected in skyrocketing imprisonment rates. When the AKP "came to power in 2002, there were 59,429 prisoners in Turkey. In just six years, the AKP nearly doubled the prison population to 103,000, which rose to 132,000 in 2012, breaking a record in Turkey" (Buğlalılar 2012). It is thus not surprising that the prevailing slogans of the GPPs expressed the need for democracy and freedom: "down with the AKP dictatorship," "shoulder to shoulder against fascism," and so on.

Judicial oppression has been a major issue in the assessment by Freedom House. In their second term of office after the 2007 elections, the AKP initiated massive court cases such as *Ergenekon*, *Balyoz*, and *KCK* to launch a full-scale war against various groups of opposition. Thousands of politicians, activists, businessmen, journalists, and intellectuals were arrested in the process without regard to evidence or even "any legal charge," whose only commonality was their critical stance toward AKP (FreedomHouse 2012a, b, HürriyetDailyNews 2013n). The *Ergenekon* case started in 2008 to allegedly expose an ultra-nationalist-secularist terrorist organization that aims to overthrow the AKP government by creating social chaos. Instead of relying on credible evidence and a transparent trial process, the case turned into a widespread witch-hunt targeting influential anti-AKP groups. Such political arbitrariness served to intimidate the opposition and threatened the basic rights and freedoms of non-AKP supporters in the country.[7] *Ergenekon* has been followed by the *Balyoz* (Sledgehammer) case, under which hundreds of anti-AKP military officials have been jailed, accused of plotting a coup (Tisdall 2012). That both of these cases rested on a vast array of sloppily fabricated data has been proven with overwhelming evidence. In the words of Dani Rodrik, who, along with Pınar Doğan, contributed greatly to exposing the inconsistencies of these forged documents, "the Ergenekon/Sledgehammer investigations have been riddled with severe problems from the outset. It is impossible to square the systematic violation of due process and of evidentiary standards observed in these trials with the rule of law" (Rodrik 2011, 100). Lastly, the case against the PKK-related Kurdish organization KCK (Group of Communities in Kurdistan) was prone to similar concerns of judicial oppression, violation of human rights, prolonged detention periods, and prevention of the suspects' access to evidence against them (HumanRightsWatch 2011b). These cases, the first two of which were supported wholeheartedly by the (neo-)liberal Left in the name of "democratization," not only led to general unrest among the non-AKP population, but they were also utilized to pit Turkish and Kurdish nationalist groups against each other to consolidate the AKP's authoritarian rule.

Another major public concern was government phone tapping. Phone tapping of politicians, activists, journalists, intellectuals, and even ordinary citizens has become one of the most heated issues for Turkish public opinion. According to the US Country Reports on Human Rights Practices issued in 2012, in Turkey, "widespread use of eavesdropping bugs and wiretapping had a chilling effect on freedom of expression and encouraged self-censorship at home as well as in professional environments. There were numerous reports by individuals and public figures alleging that their telephones were illegally tapped without a court order" (USDepartmentofState 2012, 17). This has added to the public debate on the "media autocracy that the AKP administration has created" by exerting political and economic pressures on the mainstream media, and by actively supporting the growth of Islamic-oriented media corporations (Akser and Baybars-Hawks 2012, 305). Media ownership patterns have shifted drastically in favor of AKP-friendly corporations that took over such conglomerates as the *Uzan* and *Ciner* groups. The same picture is visible in newspapers: "excluding the Islamist television and radio stations, newspapers such as *Zaman, Sabah, Yeni Şafak, Türkiye, Star, Bugün, Vakit*, and *Taraf* all have AKP and/or Gülen-affiliated ownership. By circulation, such papers represent at least 40 percent of all newspaper sales in Turkey" (Sharon-Krespin 2009). Parallel with these developments, many columnists critical of the AKP were laid off by the mainstream media, which could not resist pressures from the government, and a record number of journalists were imprisoned. In the year 2013, Turkey ranked number one in the world in journalist imprisonment rates (with 40 journalists), outpacing countries such as Iran and China (TheGuardian 2013a). Moreover, there have been severe Internet bans on websites such as YouTube, file-sharing websites, and even pornographic websites. According to the NGO *EngelliWeb*, the total number of blocked websites in Turkey rose from 7,834 in 2010 to 15,148 in 2011, 23,619 in 2012, and 39,506 in 2013 (EngelliWeb 2014).

On December 28, 2011, the AKP's unaccountable rule, authoritarianism, and media censorship became all the more visible in what is known as the Uludere Massacre. That night, Turkish warplanes bombed Kurdish citizens from the town of Uludere (Roboski in Kurdish), who were crossing Turkey from Iraq. The strike killed 34 people, most of whom were teenagers, who were smuggling cigarettes and diesel oil packed on mules— a practice well known by security forces in the region. The next morning, as the horrible news from Uludere shook Facebook, Twitter, and other social media, mainstream television channels and newspaper websites remained completely silent for 16 hours until the government made an official declaration. As Ayşenur Arslan, an experienced journalist on CNN Turk, took personal initiative to give the viewers highlights about Uludere, the editor-in-chief is reported to have stormed in the newsroom and intimidatingly instructed her through the headphones to stop reporting on the event (EvrenselNews 2013). Regarding the massacre, the government did not demonstrate any sign of accountability over the incident, and to this day, no civil or military official was held responsible for the killings. This was unlike some of the survivors of the bombings, who were prosecuted due to smuggling activities. During 2012, several demonstrations were held in Diyarbakır, Istanbul, and Ankara to protest the AKP regarding Uludere. In response, Erdoğan accused Kurdish politicians, arguing that they were "'necrophiles' seeking political gain and that journalists were servants of their cause." Instead of investigating the massacre, he sought to shift attention away from it by abruptly announcing his plans to ban abortion and C-section, saying that "every abortion is an Uludere" (TheEconomist 2012b).

The insistence on abortion and C-section was part of the government's larger and systematic Islamic social interventionism toward lifestyles, which directly contributed to the GPPs in June 2013. Women have, not surprisingly, been at the center of the government's Islamic social engineering, where their social existence has been conceived mostly in the framework of familial and maternal functions. Fittingly, the "Ministry for Women and Family," an already problematic appellation from a women's rights perspective, was replaced in 2011 by the "Ministry of Family and Social Policies," thus shifting the focus completely away from women as a separate policy issue. According to Human Rights Watch, this was a major backward step for women's rights, as the new ministerial configuration "signals a reduced emphasis on women's rights, and efforts to promote the rights to non-discrimination and freedom from violence will suffer" (HumanRightsWatch 2011a). Positioning himself as a paternalistic figure, Erdoğan kept arguing that each family should have at least three children: "One or two children mean bankruptcy. Three children mean we are not improving but not receding either. So, I repeat, at least three children are necessary in each family" (TurkishWeekly 2013). Although statistics suggest that the murder rate of women in Turkey increased by 1,400 percent between 2002 and 2009 (VOANews 2011), according to Erdoğan and Minister Fatma

Şahin, the media blows violence against women out of proportion.[8] Other misogynic declarations of the AKP members have been bitterly inscribed in public memory. Erdoğan, for instance, declared in 2010 that he does not "believe in the equality of men and women." During the debate on abortion, moreover, the AKP's controversial mayor of Ankara, Melih Gökçek, uttered that "if a woman is raped, then she should die, not the child"; which was complemented by the remarks of the AKP MP Ayhan Sefer Üstün, who stated that "rapists are more innocent than those who abort their babies."

People's long accumulated concerns about Erdoğan's authoritarianism and AKP's social interventionism took on a greater influence as the PM publicly stigmatized alcohol consumption by targeting people who "drink until they wheeze and sneeze." In turn, Bülent Arınç, the deputy prime minister, asserted that "life is not just about sex and booze." Erdoğan's call to make *ayran* (a non-alcoholic beverage made with yogurt) the national drink so as to delegitimize *rakı* (a Turkish alcoholic beverage made of grape and anise) was met with a humorous yet critical response on social media, whereas his not so implicit reference to the secular founders of the Republic as "a few drunkards" deeply offended the nationalist population (TheGuardian 2013d). Parallel with moralistic restrictions on abortion, C-Section and alcohol, which aroused the anger of thousands of people, State Minister Aliye Kavaf asserted publicly that "homosexuality is a disease," and in May 2013, the AKP rejected the opposition's proposal to include gay rights in the constitution, because "homosexuality is abnormal" (LGBTNewsInTurkey 2013).

Non-believers were particularly targeted by the AKP government. Adding to the PM's controversial remark that his party "wants to raise a religious youth" as opposed to a "sniffer or atheist" generation, other AKP members declared publicly that "no benefit can come to society from atheists," and that "atheists must be destroyed" (HürriyetDailyNews 2013l). In line with these statements, Fazıl Say, an internationally renowned Turkish pianist, was sentenced to 10 months in prison for blasphemy because of his retweet of a verse by the eleventh-century Persian poet Omar Khayyám. This was followed shortly by the sentencing of Sevan Nişanyan, an intellectual and linguist of Armenian origin, to imprisonment due to blogging about Islam and the Prophet Mohamed (CNNWorld 2013). Accompanying the clampdown on atheism, the Directorate of Religious Affairs (*Diyanet*) was revitalized as an ideological state apparatus in the last decade to promote the expansion of Sunni Islam in the structures of everyday life. In addition to its increasingly massive budget discussed earlier, the institution began playing a central role in the matters of family, health, and social services (Peker 2013). *Diyanet* also serves as an organ of religious legitimation for the AKP's socially interventionist policies. When the government sought to ban abortion in 2012, for instance, Diyanet declared that "abortion is murder" (BloombergNews 2012). The government's overhauling of the primary education system along religious lines in 2012 was another major concern, which, according to one AKP deputy, creates the occasion "to turn all schools into Imam Hatip schools" based on Islamized curricula (VOANews 2012). In addition to the already existing obligatory religious education (introduced by the military in 1982), the law also added "Quranic Studies," "Life of *Our* Prophet Muhammed," and "Basic Religious Knowledge" in the national curriculum as new elective courses (Reuters 2012).

A few days before the June uprising, on May 25, 2013, a sensational protest occurred in a subway station in Ankara against public transit employees interfering with couples' behaviors. During what is known as the "kissing protest," around 200 people got together and began kissing in public, who were in turn attacked by Islamists. The interference of conservative transit employees with couples and single women has become a common pattern, with several incidents having occurred also on buses, where bus drivers assaulted women wearing mini-skirts and couples sitting arm in arm. In result, citizens coming from a diverse array of backgrounds (gays, environmentalists, feminists, Armenians, socialists, anarchists, Turkish and Kurdish nationalists, and atheists) felt threatened by the government's judicial oppression and social interventionism that seeks to dictate what the national-religious values are and how individuals should (or should not) behave in their private lives (TheEconomist 2013d). Within this context, the protesters resolutely reacted against the Islamic social interventionism of the AKP government, which contributed to the further escalation of the GPPs. Graffiti such as "public morality, whose morality?" "don't make war, make love with me, Tayyip," or "would you like three more kids like us?"and so on reflected that public reaction.

3d. Turkey's Aggression to Syria as a Trigger of the GPPs

The AKP government's foreign policy initiatives, particularly those in the Middle East, constitute an additional enabling variable for the conjunctural opportunities leading to the GPPs. The AKP government has long provided both financial and logistical support for the Sunni extremist challengers to President Bashar al-Assad in Syria. The Al-Qaeda/Salafist movement has become the main beneficiary of Turkey's support and hospitality for the opposition groups, and they have been actively armed and trained by the Turkish government since the beginning of the conflict (Al-Monitor 2013e, TheTelegraph 2012). They are welcomed by the Turkish government in thousands, and they were constantly involved in quarrels with the locals of Hatay, the southern province of Turkey bordering Syria. The Salafists explicitly articulate Turkey's official support to them in their daily confrontation with local people. Refusing to pay for services they get from local businesses, many Salafists invoked the government protection they received, saying "it is Prime Minister Erdoğan who brought us here, he would be the one to pay the bill," or backing up threats by saying "or else we will call Recep" (HürriyetDailyNews 2012b).

According to *The Economist*, the flow of refugees increased at a rapid pace, reaching 4,000 people a day (TheEconomist

2012a). Moreover, it is reported that contrary to Turkish government figures (which indicate 42,000 asylum seekers) there are at least 40,000 more "guests" in the area who are unofficially settled in individual houses, each inhabited by groups of 10–15 people, serving as cells linked to organizations such as Al-Qaeda. The inhabitants of Hatay explicitly express their fear of those groups who disturb the public order, having been involved in a total of 157 incidents in which 360 Syrians have been sued (HürriyetDailyNews 2012b). Turkish military and other state officials do nothing to prevent the border breach by such terrorist groups. On the contrary, they facilitate their infiltration by partially removing the barbed wires on the borders, and reports indicate that officials are providing shuttles and ambulance services to these groups in Turkey (SolNews 2012). Moreover, at least 50 people with Turkish citizenship have joined the fight against President Assad's regime, a large majority of whom were trained in Afghanistan. Among them are volunteers who previously fought in Bosnia, Chechnya, and Iraq, and who were involved with Al-Qaeda bombings of HSBC, the British Consulate General, and many synagogues in Turkey (RadikalDailyNews 2012).

Directly speaking to the conjunctural political opportunities leading to the Gezi mobilization, local concerns have gained a nationwide character and reached their pinnacle with the infamous car bombings in the town of Reyhanlı, Hatay. The repercussions of the bombings, leading to at least 50 deaths and 140 injuries, were strongly felt in the rest of the country to erode the government's legitimacy. Besides being one of the major triggers of the GPPs (Vurucu 2013, 16), the eruption of people's anger against the AKP government following the Reyhanlı bombings can be considered a turning point in contemporary Turkish politics. With government controlling the media and business, almost any voice of dissent was censored, and the crime escaped scrutiny. A court order was passed to officially prohibit the press from talking about or investigating the bombings, which led to serious doubts regarding spoliation of evidence by the Turkish government. The government's attempt to blame Assad's regime for the bombings found little credibility in Turkish public opinion, which instead faulted the government's adventurist policy in Syria. The result was widespread mass protests throughout the country and a sensational protest during a soccer game days before the GPPs, which called on the government to resign. This massive public reaction signaled a transformation of people's perception from a "republic of fear" (dominated by the AKP) into a "republic of protest," uniting various groups against the AKP to create an opportunity for mobilization. In the words of a Gezi slogan, "The Republic of Fear has collapsed!" Thus, the AKP's reckless politics in Syria, by suddenly destroying the credibility of the government, was another central element that added to the political opportunities leading to the GPPs. As Mahdi Darius Nazemroaya of the *The Centre for Research on Globalization* indicates, the mobilization "in Taksim Square represents a rejection of Erdoğan's stillborn neo-Ottoman regional policy—which at its core serves the crony business interests that Erdoğan and the AKP represent—by the Turkish people" (Nazemroaya 2013).

Reprise and Review

This chapter has argued that the GPPs cannot be fully understood without addressing the political-economic transformations of urban space in view of the political-cultural peculiarities and practices of Turkish neoliberalism. Both political-economic and cultural-ideological factors have played a central role in configuring the conjunctural environment of the GPPs, shaped by not only Turkey's aggression to Syria and the Reyhanlı Bombings, but also by the demolition of Gezi Park, *Emek Movie Theater,* and *Atatürk Cultural Center,* the stigmatization of alcohol consumption, public show of affection and abortion, the PM's three kids "suggestion" and other paternalistic and authoritarian remarks of government officials, and the imprisonment of dissident artists and intellectuals, and so on. The case of "neoliberalism with Islamic characteristics" in Turkey speaks to the fact that neoliberalism is a geographically variegated phenomenon that plays on the existing cultural framework and polarizations of a given polity. Its particular manifestation in Turkey spearheaded by the AKP government merges neoliberal policies with an Islamist politico-cultural agenda to complement aggressive capital accumulation processes with ultra-conservative/neo-Ottomanist "social interventionism" that dominates urban space and individual lives. Building on Harvey's "spatial-temporal fix" that denotes political and economic accumulation of power and capital, our conceptualization of "political-cultural fix" sought to demonstrate that this process is accompanied by "political-cultural accumulation" to transform society's mind, memory, and active perception of the world along neoliberal lines. The GPPs, in this sense, was a powerful response against this Islamic-neoliberal *Weltanschauung*, the counter-hegemonic expressions of which will be outlined in Chapter 5. How such response was organized and acted out is discussed in the next chapter.

4

Organizational-Strategic Aspects of the GPPs: Leadership and Resistance Repertoires

The main objective of this chapter is to shed light on the leadership formation processes and resistance strategies/tactics (repertoires) that were acted out in the GPPs. We understand leadership as a collective construction as opposed to being individually driven, which also allows us to transcend the dichotomy between "spontaneity" and "leadership"—one of the central discussions regarding the nature of the GPPs. Rather than being a "real person" or "concrete individual," leadership is of a collective character as an "organism, a complex element of society in which a collective will...begins to take concrete form" (Gramsci 2000, 240). We go on to argue that spontaneity is a matter of degree rather than a mere state of "leaderlessness" (Gramsci 2012, 196). As Gramsci clarifies, spontaneous collective action tends to contain "multiple elements of 'conscious leadership'" although "no one of them is predominant" (Gramsci 2012, 196–197). Leadership can thus be defined as an organized collection of institutional bodies and collective activities that determine organizational forms and the formulation of strategies and tactics, or simply the deployment of resistance repertoires. As such, it can be traced to the modes of "within-movement participation," "decision-making," and "alliance-building" (Otero 1999).

Our interpretation of the GPPs seeks to demonstrate that collective leadership has been an important component of spontaneous mobilization in shaping the organizational forms and resistance repertoires of wage-earning class fractions during the events. In response to mainstream accounts of the GPPs that romanticized spontaneity (as "apolitical" and "innocent") while demonizing organized leadership (as an opportunistic search for political gain), we intend to document that the dynamics of spontaneity and leadership were closely intertwined in the development and organization of the movement and its resistance repertoires.

We use the concept of "repertoires" as the arsenal of tools, strategies, and tactics employed in disruptive/extra-parliamentary collective mobilization such as the GPPs.[1] Bringing together a range of wage-earning class fractions, the GPPs utilized a myriad of repertoires that were intimately linked with the movement's organizational forms. Additionally, we propose a new framework to explain the emergence and development of resistance repertoires through the concept of "repertoire cultivation." We define repertoire cultivation as the development, accumulation, and sophistication of specific sets of knowhow and capabilities, namely tactics and strategies of resistance, in the very process of mass mobilization. The process of cultivation occurs in the following categories: (a) repertoire refinement, (b) repertoire transfer, (c) repertoire expansion, and (d) repertoire generation.

Repertoire refinement refers to the enhancement of already existing repertoires to increase their capacity for resistance. *Repertoire transfer* indicates the reutilization of certain repertoires from a different time or place to adapt and apply them to the circumstances at hand. This may happen through repertoire "redeployment," which is the reinvigoration of—not necessarily political—past abilities developed in a given community for novel situations; or through repertoire "emulation," which means borrowing tools of resistance from outside of the protest cycle. *Repertoire expansion* is the widening of a repertoire's sphere of influence as it is assumed and practiced by a larger group of people. Lastly, *repertoire generation* produces new repertoires for social mobilization through innovation. What is to underline about repertoire cultivation (as well as its four elements of refinement, transfer, expansion, and generation) is that it is born in the actuality of collective action as social interaction and solidarity intensifies to boost creativity in the face of various offensives made by political regimes.

The versatility and magnitude of the resistance strategies and tactics used in the GPPs provides ample material to demonstrate how repertoire cultivation works. In a matter of only two weeks, various types of know-how and capabilities were collectively cultivated to resist the government's physical and psychological advances to halt the movement. In terms of repertoire refinement, the capacity of already existing repertoires such as street protests and online social networking has been significantly heightened with the enrichment of related sets of knowledge and competencies. What to do when exposed to different types of tear gas, how to build barricades in the face of a police attack, which back alleys to take (political street smarts), how to assemble a critical mass in a matter of hours, how to follow and authenticate information on social media, and so on are but a few examples of the refinement process we will discuss.

Regarding repertoire transfer, certain familiar tools and capabilities were redeployed, and some others were emulated partly from outside. Collectively banging pots and pans in balconies at a given time was a dormant type of civil protest in Turkey since 1997, which was redeployed in the GPPs. Moreover, the collective experiences gained in the May Day Protests since 2007, Republican Rallies of 2007, the TEKEL Resistance of 2010, protests against Internet bans and the AKP's various judicial oppressions played into the organizational repertoires of the GPPs. Similarly, certain extra-political capabilities, such as the collective street action experience of soccer fan clubs (like *Çarşı*); or the communication networks (like *Ekşi Sözlük*, Facebook, and Twitter) were redeployed for the purpose of political organization and meaning creation. For the case of Facebook and Twitter, transfer through emulation was also an important factor. The central role these sites played during the Arab Spring was very well known to Turkish activists, which facilitated its utilization for organizational purposes. More significantly in terms of emulation, certain repertoires of the Occupy Movement such as sit-in and civil resistance contributed greatly to the Gezi Park protesters' mindset. This also demonstrates that repertoire transfer and refinement are not mutually exclusive, and repertoire transfer through emulation can well contribute to enhancing and refining already existing mobilization capacities.

Repertoire expansion was one of the most evident aspects of the GPPs, as it introduced an unprecedented number of people to various tools and strategies of collective action. Countrywide protests enabled the popularization of resistance-related knowhow and capabilities to large masses that had little or no background of involvement in such practices. For instance, according to a survey conducted on the site of Gezi Park in June 2013, 44.4 percent of the protesters declared that they had never participated in a protest, rally, or a sit-in before (KONDA 2013, 16). Larger masses were thus recruited to social mobilization, and internalized/contributed to the accumulation of repertoires. Lastly, it was unsurprising that a combination of refinement, transfer, and expansion would generate new tricks in the resistance toolbox. What is known as the "standing man" (a type of civil resistance defined by the pure act of standing still in public places) was one such result of repertoire generation. Another one was the establishment of people's forums in other public parks to provide spaces of democratic discussion and collective action. These will be elaborated further in what follows.

The chapter is divided into three sections. The first section discusses the underlying member integration and involvement processes of the GPPs in order to make sense of the dialectics of spontaneity and leadership. The second section identifies the leading organizations that assumed pivotal roles during the

GPPs, as well as the role of communication networks such as the social media. In dialog with these organizational forms, the final section expands on the cultivation of resistance repertoires in the GPPs, which not only built on past experiences, but also incorporated innovative tactics and strategies into the collective action toolkit and vocabulary in the country. We believe that the cultivation and spread of resistance repertoires may be one of the most enduring effects of the GPPs in Turkey, as they are inscribed in public memory and culture, and they can easily be reactivated as political opportunity manifests itself.

4a. Member Integration and Involvement

The previous chapters discussed the structural sociopolitical background and the conjunctural opportunities that provided the context for the GPPs. Member integration/involvement in the GPPs was built on these foundations, which drew its strength from the alliance of class fractions discussed in Chapter 2, and from the spontaneous externalization of popular grievances summarized in Chapter 3. The survey data collected by social researchers about the protesters in the first two weeks of June 2013, although mostly limited to the park and its surroundings, may be helpful in drawing a more detailed picture of the membership composition and the collective claims voiced in the GPPs. Selected data from four such studies will be presented here, namely from the research and consultancy companies KONDA (2013), GENAR (2013), and MetroPOLL (2013), as well as a study carried out by Bilgi University (Bilgiç and Kafkaslı 2013).[2] The average age of the protesters was 28 according to KONDA. MetroPOLL similarly recorded that 69.8 percent of the protesters were between the ages 20 and 29, and Bilgi University noted that 63.6 percent was between 19 and 30, which all suggest that the youth were predominant in the protests. With regard to gender, active participation of women stood out as an important factor. KONDA found that 50.9 percent of the protesters were women, which was 44 percent in

MetroPOLL's study. As mentioned earlier, KONDA registered that 44.4 percent of the protesters declared having never joined a protest, rally, or sit-in before Gezi Park. This figure was 46.3 percent in Bilgi University's study, and went as high as 70.4 percent in MetroPOLL's survey. Given that the latter study was conducted four days after KONDA's survey and a week after Bilgi University's, it may be possible to deduce that as days passed, more and more people, who had not been in a protest before, joined as newcomers to Gezi Park.

Social media and friend networks played a significant role in the recruitment process. KONDA's data demonstrate that 69 percent of the protesters first heard about the protests through social media, whereas 15.4 percent was familiarized by friends and acquaintances, 8.6 percent through news websites, and 7 percent through TV (the average age of the 7 percent who heard about the events from TV was 40, which is much higher than the overall average age). Moreover, 84 percent declared that they have shared posts about the events on social media, which further confirms the latter's importance in the GPPs. Parallel with low levels of prior involvement in street protests, low party-political membership rates have also been noted among the protesters. KONDA shows that 79 percent of the pro-testers was never a member of any political party, association, platform, or civil society organization. It is equally striking that 93.6 percent claim that they do not represent any political insti-tution and simply joined the protests as "ordinary citizens." In MetroPOLL's study, likewise, 50.6 percent said they did not feel close to any political party, which was as high as 70 percent in Bilgi University's research. Their ideological tendencies as well showed variations in different studies, where socialism (27.6 per-cent in MetroPOLL, 12.4 percent in GENAR), anti-authoritar-ianism (15 percent, 19 percent), and Atatürkism (11 percent, 33.5 percent) were among the popular choices.

As for the reason of their participation in the protests and their collective claims, a fairly diversified set of answers was registered, although a commonality can be found on the principal concerns

regarding freedoms, democracy, authoritarianism, social interventionism, and police violence. The KONDA research suggests that 58.1 percent of interviewed protesters participated in
the events because they thought that freedoms were restricted
in Turkey. Of those who referred to themselves as "ordinary
citizens," 73 percent decided to come because of excessive
police violence; 37.2 percent declared that they were particularly opposed to the AKP and its policies; whereas 30.3 percent
reacted against the PM Erdoğan's statements and paternalistic
attitude. In GENAR's study, 58 percent of the participants stated
that the PM Erdoğan was the real reason of the protests, and in
another question, 46.4 percent said they joined the movement in
solidarity to support other protesters. In MetroPOLL's survey,
32.8 percent indicated "demands of democracy and freedom" as
the cause of the protests, whereas 23.8 percent referred to "an
accumulation of grievances against the government." According
to Bilgi University, similarly, 86 percent of the protesters
"strongly agreed" that "the imposition of a certain lifestyle" by
the government was a major cause of the protests. Additionally,
91.4 percent cited "disproportionate police violence against the
protesters," and 92.4 percent referred to the PM's authoritarian
attitude, and 91.1 percent to restrictions on freedoms and violation of democracy. With reference to collective claims, about
52 percent demanded "freedoms" and wanted to "put and end
to violation of rights" (KONDA 2013); 43 percent prioritized
"freedom of expression" as a claim, whereas 36.6 percent and
27.1 percent demanded the release of detained citizens and preserving Gezi Park as it is, respectively (MetroPOLL 2013). In
various questions, 96.7 percent "strongly agreed" that police
violence should stop (and 94.3 percent demanded an apology
for the police violence); 79.3 percent desired the PM to resign,
and 92.2 percent wanted the non-AKP voters' voices to be heard
(Bilgiç and Kafkaslı 2013).

   The numbers, although not definitive by any means, suggest
that popular masses of diverse backgrounds were triggered by
their "private discontent" with the AKP government's excesses,

and they took to the streets to become part of a spontaneous initiative of "collective action" to resist against such arbitrariness and to claim various sociospatial rights (Petras and Veltmeyer 2013, 216–217). In lack of high levels of prior political participation, friendship, neighborhood, and workplace networks played an important role in motivating member integration and involvement, which was sustained mostly via face-to-face relations, telephone communication, as well as Facebook and Twitter. Police violence and PM Erdoğan's disdainful statements against the protesters only served to continuously boost membership recruitment and created further solidarity among the masses. In this environment, popular participation led to a rapidly emerging sense of belonging to an alternative, highly diverse, and lively ethical community, as we will further discuss in the next chapter. As such, demonstrations quickly became part of people's everyday routine, which attracted higher participation outside of work hours throughout June 2013. The police thus paid special attention to advance in the morning or late at night, while public participation was relatively lower.

Integrated with the spontaneous reaction of masses, a more cohesive and organized membership component came from previously established political/activist networks, especially as the Gezi Park sit-in escalated into nationwide demonstrations on May 31. These networks include leftward political parties, major national trade unions, mass organizations, and intellectual and student circles. The most visible among them that added to the spontaneous collectivity were the Communist Party of Turkey (TKP), Workers' Party (IP), Socialist Democracy Party (SDP), and to some extent Republican People's Party (CHP). Those who refrained from supporting the protests officially were the Peace and Democracy Party (BDP), the leading Kurdish party with 29 MPs and about 100 municipalities, and the Nationalist Action Party (MHP), the third party in the parliament as the advocate of right-wing Turkish nationalism. Many members and supporters of these political parties, however, participated individually. MP Sırrı Süreyya Önder of the BDP, for instance, was actively present in the park since the beginning of the events and stood in front of earthmovers to prevent demolition. As for the trade union actors, the Confederation of Revolutionary Trade Unions of Turkey (DISK) and the Confederation of Public Workers' Unions (KESK) officially participated in the events, along with doctors' and engineers/architects' organizations such as the Turkish Medical Association (TTB) and the Union of Chambers of Turkish Engineers and Architects (TMMOB). Other relatively cohesive membership elements originated from progressive communities of dissent and subcultures, including but not limited to Taksim Solidarity Platform (TDP), which was established against the government's urban renewal projects, the Youth Union of Turkey (TGB), People's Houses (*Halkevleri*), Anti-Capitalist Muslims, various feminist groups (such as Socialist-Feminist Collective, Women's Coalition), LGBT movements (such as KAOS GL, LGBT Bloc), as well as soccer fan clubs (*Çarşı* of Beşiktaş FC in particular along with Fenerbahçe, and Galatasaray fans). Online militant support, moreover, came from the highly active Marxist-Leninist computer hacker group RedHack.

Social media played a momentous part in providing a strong basis for communication networks that integrated spontaneous masses with collective leadership mechanisms. The centrality of social media in the protests was validated by the KONDA research cited earlier. The strength of social media and the Internet has proved to be so irritating for the AKP that PM Erdoğan did not restrain from verbally assaulting new communication technologies: "There is a trouble called Twitter. The height of lies, exaggeration is there. The thing that is called social media: To me, it is the nuisance of society" (RadikalDailyNews 2013b). Social media tools that contributed to the political and cultural diffusion of protest movements included Facebook, Twitter, *Ekşi Sözlük* (eksisozluk.com) and Zaytung (http:// www.zaytung.com).

Facebook is extremely popular in Turkey. According to global social media statistics, Turkey ranks seventh in the world for the number of Facebook accounts in 2012, which is more than 30 million users, 86 percent of whom belonging to the 16–44 age group (Socialbakers 2013b). Especially given the limited mainstream media coverage of events, the networking site was the primary source for raising consciousness among friends through the sharing of related videos, photos, captions, posts, comments, articles, and other materials. Twitter, which has a smaller social base of 9.6 million in Turkey (Webrazzi 2013), was also actively used for news sharing and for live updates from protest zones. The difference of Twitter is that it facilitates the sharing of information more publicly than Facebook (which rests more on friends from real life). In the 15 between May 31 and June 14, 13.5 million tweets about the resistance was sent with tags such as #direngezi (resist Gezi), #occupygezi, and #direnankara (resist Ankara) (CNN-TURK 2013). In the face of media censorship, Facebook and Twitter served not only as the main news source on Gezi Park, but at the same time a venue through which active participation and involvement in the movement became possible. They created virtual communities to underpin various forms of collective action and leadership, interaction, meaning creation, and solidarity among the protesters. It goes without saying that the increasing use of social media and online communication is based on a drastic rise in the number of Internet subscribers in Turkey. According to figures from TurkStat, the total number of subscribers increased from 8.8 million in 2009 and 14.4 million in 2010 to 22.4 million in 2011, 27.6 million in 2012, and 32.6 million in 2013 (TurkStat 2013e).

The indirect contribution of *Ekşi Sözlük* and *Zaytung* to the GPPs has been to enable collective meaning creation that critically engages with the government through the use of humor and satire. *Ekşi Sözlük* (Sour Dictionary, created in 1999) is a Turkish hypertext dictionary built up on user contribution, considered as "one of the biggest online communities in Turkey with over 400,000 registered users." Its counterpart in North America is Urban Dictionary (http://www.urbandictionary.com)

with an important distinction that *Ekşi Sözlük* plays a much more active role in "communicating disputed political contents" (Wikipedia 2013) so as to shape the everyday political and cultural life for many. Founded in 2010, *Zaytung* (derived from the German word *Zeitung*, i.e. newspaper) is a highly popular Turkish satirical news website that runs with the motto "honest, objective and immoral news." Its North American counterpart is The Onion News (http://www.theonion.com). *Zaytung* has helped the creation of shared meanings, jokes, and solidarity around the authoritarian advances of the government, some of which will be exemplified in the next chapter. Compared to Facebook and Twitter, however, the role of *Ekşi Sözlük* and *Zaytung* has been at best of secondary importance with regard to political and cultural diffusion.

4b. A Focus on the Leading Organizations of the GPPs

The constituents of the cohesive membership core of the Gezi movement were briefly mentioned in the previous section. This section provides further details on their profile and involvement. It is possible to argue that collective leadership structures during the GPPs assumed a highly decentralized, non-hierarchical, and diversified character in conformity with the spontaneity of protests. As the movement took a nationwide character on May 31, 2013, collective leadership merged with spontaneity to create a novel and colorful dynamic. The protests featured soccer fan clubs (particularly, *Çarşı*), online activism of RedHack, national trade union centers such as DISK and KESK, left-leaning political parties such as the Communist Party of Turkey (TKP), Workers' Party (İP), and some militants members, PMs and the youth of the left-of-center Republican People's Party (CHP). As mentioned, certain groups affiliated with Kurdish nationalism (BDP) and with right-wing Turkish nationalism (MHP) participated in the protests as well, although their party organizations hesitated to get involved. Indeed, smaller political parties such as the Socialist Democracy Party (SDP), Freedom and Solidarity Party (ÖDP), and leftist/popular organizations like Youth Union of Turkey (TGB), Anti-Capitalist Muslims, People's Houses, Atatürk Thought Association (ADD), Socialist Feminist Collective (SFK), Women's Coalition, LGBT groups like KAOS-GL, LGBT Bloc, and environmentalists joined the events in a vigorous fashion. These were also supplemented by the individual participation of certain prominent public figures (such as actors/actresses, musicians, artists, writers, etc.), which added to the movement's dynamism. "Actors and actresses like Mehmet Ali Alabora, Halit Ergenç, Bergüzal Korel and Erdal Beşikçioğlu who are quite popular with their TV series or programs made calls for more participation, posted photographs from the resistance on their Twitter accounts ('it's not just a park issue, don't you get it?')" (Buğlalılar 2013).

What is to note as a unique characteristic of the GPPs is the unlikely alliance and solidarity established among a diversity of groups. A week prior to the protests, the idea of bringing together such multitude of ideologies would be dismissed by any specialist on Turkey. The protest cycle took everybody by surprise. Groups with strong Kurdish and Turkish nationalist tendencies, secularists, and devoted Islamists, Feminist-LGBT communities and groups with patriarchal mentalities, fans of antagonistic soccer clubs, various class fractions, and so on unexpectedly joined together against the authoritarianism of the AKP, and its leader in particular. We hold that the political significance and strength of the GPPs stem largely from those unlikely alliances. These alliances not only opened up the possibility of communication, empathy, and solidarity between groups that were at best indifferent to each other, but they also produced rich and variegated processes of meaning creation and repertoire cultivation throughout the movement.

We will limit our analysis to the most visible and influential actors of collective leadership that took part in the events. Considered to be a highly politicized group with socialist and anarchist tendencies, Çarşı (a left-leaning soccer fan club represented by Beşiktaş fans) has been the most engaged soccer fan club during the GPPs and played a major role in bringing together the football fans of the four major and "irreconcilable" soccer clubs (*Beşiktaş, Galatasaray, Fenerbahçe*, and *Trabzonspor*) during the protests (HürriyetDailyNews 2013m, FoxNews 2013). Besides contributing to the creation of a more inclusive sphere of protest that smoothed previous social, political, and cultural differences and quarrels of different societal sectors, *Çarşı*'s physical presence and active participation served to ignite the protests relying on their prior accumulation of experience in slogan shouting, chanting, and confronting police forces. *Çarşı*'s militant role also gave way to the spread of urban legends on which the Gezi park membership drew, among which are the hijacking of a bulldozer that was used to break through police lines as well as an alleged hijacking of a police panzer (TOMA), which was later humorously advertised online "for sale" ("An underused TOMA that was taken from our dearest state two days ago is now for sale") (SolNews 2013b). In the second week of the protests, as some members of the group were arrested, *Çarşı* published an open declaration to the government: "We remind you that *Çarşı* is the rebellious spirit in all those who participated in the uprising against injustices; it cannot be reduced to physical bodies" (ForzaBeşiktaş 2013).

RedHack, a socialist online hacker group founded in 1997, has been very influential in mobilizing the people since the beginning of the protests. In line with their motto "hak yersen hack yersin" (you'll be hacked for your injustices), the group is known for bringing down government websites and leaking official documents that expose political corruption and irregularities. In May 2012, for instance, the group hacked the Turkish Airlines website in solidarity with the long-lasting worker strike, and in May 2013, they leaked documents to indicate government negligence in Reyhanlı bombings and hacked the governor's website (MilliyetDailyNews 2013c). The group's online activism had already earned them legitimacy and respect within leftist circles, yet the GPPs placed RedHack in a more significant position in collective leadership. This is demonstrated in the increase in their Twitter follower basis. On May 30, 2013, a day before nationwide protests began, RedHack had 216,795 followers. By June 23, 2013, this number was almost tripled to reach 630,732 (Socialbakers 2013a). In addition to providing important news and strategic guidance throughout the protests, RedHack hacked several government websites such as the Parliament TV to give the protests online support. On June 7, 2013, the anonymous leader of RedHack gave a four-hour interview on HalkTV (through an untraceable audio Skype connection), which was widely shared on social media. In this motivational speech, RedHack's leader affirmed: "as the people, we will keep peacefully voicing our demands of freedom and we will take what is ours...Let me give the government a sad piece of news: they think the Gezi resistance is over, but this is just the beginning" (EkşiSözlük 2013a).

Major national trade union centers such as DISK and KESK mobilized their mass organizations through the declaration of two general strikes in two weeks. Founded in 1967, DİSK is an umbrella organization of 19 trade unions; whereas KESK, founded in 1995, contains 11. The first general strike in the current protest cycle was on June 4–5, following the outbreak of events, and the second was on June 17 after the police violently recaptured Gezi Park (NTVMSNBC 2013b). Turkish Medical Association (TTB) and The Union of Chambers of Turkish Engineers and Architects (TMMOB), which are among the largest professional organizations in the country, also participated in the general strike. The joint declaration issued by these four organizations held that "a government tyrannizing its own people has lost its legitimacy," and that they would not "surrender to the fascism of the AKP" (SendikaNews 2013a). In another joint statement, they called the government to "release all unlawfully detained citizens" from the protests, and condemned police violence that resulted in the death of four people (KESK 2013).

TKP and İP exhibited a very active participation particularly in Istanbul and Ankara, not just by their physical involvement, but also by the way they enabled a more organized mobilization based on their past experiences. Many of their slogans, particularly TKP's *Boyun Eğme* ("Do not comply/bow") and İP's *Mustafa Kemal'in Askerleriyiz* ("We are Mustafa Kemal's soldiers") were widely adopted by the crowds (the latter slogan also faced within-movement criticism, as we will discuss in Chapter 5). Their dynamic youth potential and media power were also among the underlying factors that added to the propagation of the GPPs. İP's TV channel *Ulusal Kanal* (National Channel) and daily newspaper *Aydınlık* (Clarity) proved to be an important resource for social mobilization and political consciousness. *Aydınlık* boasts a national circulation of around 74.000 with a broad readership from socialist, nationalist, and populist backgrounds (MedyaTava 2013). *Ulusal Kanal's* national ratings moved up from 263rd position in May 2013 to 124th in June 2013 (CanliTV 2013). Moreover, many young members of İP joined the protests under the banner of the Youth Union of Turkey (TGB), a youth organization that is particularly organized in university student clubs and societies, and relies on a heterogeneous membership base with nationalist, socialist, and populist backgrounds. TKP is considered to have the strongest and most dynamic youth base among socialist parties in Turkey. Their newspaper (*soL*, or "The Left"), which reached a circulation of around 20,000 in June 2013, exerted a tremendous impact in the mobilization of leftist circles as the largest socialist/communist newspaper alongside its influential online news portal (http://haber.sol.org.tr) (MedyaTava 2013). The party has published frequent declarations during the GPPs to call people to the streets, one of which stated that "let us not accept to live under the orders of the dictator. If we give in today, tomorrow we will not even be able to go out in the streets" (SolNews 2013d). ÖDP, likewise, gave active support to the GPPs, especially with its popular newspaper *Birgün* (circulation around 15,000 in June 2013). *Birgün's* satirical headlines during the GPPs were widely shared and discussed on social media as well, thus contributing to the movement solidarity and morale (BirgünDailyNewspaper 2014).

Being the main opposition party, CHP joined the protests with its youth organization and a small number of militant MPs, some of whom were even injured by the police. A major contribution of CHP came from its TV channel *Halk TV* (People TV), which provided 24-hour live broadcasting of the events reaching millions of people. In the face of mainstream media's blackout of the GPPs, *Halk TV* became the go-to television channel for many, and their national ratings moved up from 46th position in May 2013 to 19th in June 2013 (CanliTV 2013). Anti-Capitalist Muslims, moreover, a pious activist group critical of the AKP's instrumental use of Islam for underpinning neoliberal policies, were actively present in the GPPs. The group, although small in size, played a much larger role in creating bonds between secularly and religiously oriented protesters based on mutual respect and understanding. They took active part in the collective leadership mechanism of the protests, and were warmly welcomed by secular groups as they united for the common enemy of Islamic capitalism (TheEconomist 2013b).

Taksim Solidarity Platform (TDP) constituted the core of the collective leadership mobilization centered around Gezi Park. Established in 2012 as a grassroots movement started by neighborhood residents, the TDP evolved into an umbrella organization that embraces more than 120 organizations including leftist political parties, professional associations, trade unions, environmentalist, and feminists and LGBT movements (TaksimSolidarityPlatform 2013). On June 5, 2013, TDP outlined its claims to the government as follows:

- Taksim Gezi Park will not be re-developed under the name of Artillery Barracks or any other project; an official statement on the cancellation of the current project must be made; and the attempts to demolish Ataturk Cultural Centre must stop.
- Dismissal (from their post) of every official responsible for the thousands of injured people and three deaths—starting with the governors and the police chiefs of Istanbul, Ankara, Adana, and Hatay, as well as everyone who prevented the exercise of the most basic democratic rights of the people, including those who gave

orders for violent repression, as well as enforced or implemented these orders. Furthermore, the use of tear gas bombs and other similar materials must be prohibited.

- Immediate release of detained citizens who participated in the resistance across the country, and an official statement declaring that there will be no further investigation into them.
- The abolition of all bans on meetings and demonstrations in all of our squares and public areas, and the removal of all the de facto blockades and barriers to freedom of expression—starting with Taksim and Kızılay squares.

The TDP's declaration finally made a call to the public: "Being supported from all corners of our country and the world, our demands are incontestably legitimate...We call on the citizens of Turkey to gather in Gezi Park, Taksim Square at 7 p.m. in order to claim their demands with us. We are waiting for you in Gezi Park. We are here and we are not leaving" (JadaliyyaReports 2013). The Socialist International published a declaration a week later to officially endorse the platform's demands, highlighting that "the Gezi Park protests marked a turning point in Turkish politics...in favor of democracy and fundamental freedoms" (SocialistInternational 2013). In response to the Solidarity Platform, the AKP government took a pre-concerted action by calling for a negotiation committee formed of its own organic intellectuals, which would meet with PM Erdoğan so as to undermine the genuine leadership of TDP. However, this attempt dramatically backfired following the post-meeting statements of pro-AKP committee members, especially those of Necati Şaşmaz, a Turkish actor, who tried to delegitimize the participating actors of Gezi protests with a poor Turkish that turned into a widespread mocking subject in social media (HürriyetDailyNews 2013g). Upon severe criticism widely expressed by protesters, social media, and critical media actors, PM Erdoğan had to receive the committee formed by the TDP leadership. However, many accounts revealed that the negotiation process between the TDP leadership and PM Erdoğan was not carried out in a constructive manner, during which PM Erdoğan menacingly bore down on the committee members and left the meeting without handshake (SolNews 2013a, HürriyetDailyNews 2013b).

Feminist and LGBT groups constituted one of the main strongholds of the GPPs that require particular attention. Against the ultraconservative social interventionism of the AKP government that involves various misogynist and homophobic advances discussed in the previous chapter, the militant participation of women and LGBT organizations gave the GPPs indispensible vitality and dynamism. A statement published by the Socialist Feminist Collective on June 1, 2013 titled "Women are also Resisting!" represents some of the claims and grievances voiced by women against the AKP government. The statement highlighted that PM Erdoğan and his circle have enabled lynching and killing of women, stigmatized raped women and pressured them to give birth, equalized abortion and murder, made women dependent on men and family life, and "condemned us to poverty, to work in precarious, insecure jobs, to live in slavery conditions." The statement ended with the following message: "We call all women to go out to streets, and resist for our liberation!" (SocialistFeministCollective 2013). Similarly, Women's Coalition underlined the PM Erdoğan's "disrespect for the universal human rights and related laws," and urged the government to refrain "from using terminology that continually criminalizes peaceful demonstrators" (KadınKoalisyonu 2013).

Unsurprisingly, women came to symbolize the movement in images that represented their will and agency against patriarchal aggressors. The emblematic photos of the "woman in red" frantically teargassed by a police officer and the "woman in black" attacked from a police vehicle with pressurized water both embodied the central theme of the protests: firmly standing one's ground and protecting social space against authoritarian intrusions. This was also valid for the "protesters' moms," who, in response to the governor of Istanbul's patronizing call to mothers "to come and take their kids back home," raided into Taksim to create a human chain for the purpose of blocking police violence against their sons and daughters (GoodMorningTurkey 2013). Moreover, LGBT communities, whose efforts to include gender identity and sexual identity into the equality clause of the constitution and other laws have been systematically rejected by the AKP, forcefully participated in the GPPs and voiced their concerns in solidarity with other groups. A press release by Kaos GL, for instance, stated that "it is time to say that Gezi Park belongs also to gay and trans individuals. It is time to say all together that 'we are here, and we are not leaving!'" LGBT Block, likewise, made a call to the general public to support the pride march, declaring that "for us, beyond these barricades…life continues with male violence, state oppression and police cruelty…We invite you to join us in solidarity in our struggle for rights" (EverywhereTaksim 2013, KaosGL 2013). Their invitations were not left unanswered, as the Pride March of June 30, 2013 became the largest one ever held in Turkey thanks to the participation of Gezi Park protesters in solidarity (Bianet 2013c).

4c. Cultivating Resistance Repertoires

The spontaneous participation of large masses in the GPPs quickly fused with a rich and diverse set of collective leadership mechanisms to enable the mobilization and effective utilization of various internal resources, and contributed to the organizational strength of the movement in articulating collective action repertoires. As mentioned in the introduction, we use the term "repertoire cultivation" to explicate the emergence and development of collective action repertoires, which can be categorized into (a) repertoire refinement, (b) repertoire transfer, (c) repertoire expansion, and (d) repertoire generation. In the coming paragraphs, we elaborate on each category of repertoire cultivation except for "repertoire expansion" for it is implicitly addressed in each category within the context of our repertoire examples, expanding and spreading all over the country. One significant aspect of that expansion in the GPPs has been the previously mentioned dialog and solidarity created among diverse and uncompromising groups and organizations. We believe that such unlikely interactions potentially create a larger dynamic than a mere increase in the popularity of resistance tools.

A characteristic instance of repertoire refinement during the GPPs can be found in online networking and activism. As iterated earlier, Facebook and Twitter activism has proved vital for news sharing, raising consciousness, and organizational strategies. Throughout the protest cycle in June 2013, more participants and (potential) leaders have learned utilizing these sites as alternative news and information networks as well as platforms to call people to demonstrations. More significantly, through Facebook and Twitter on smart phones, protesters in action learned informing each other on the practical strategies to follow. These include information such as which neighborhood is under police attack, which streets are blocked and which back alleys should be taken, what kind of gas is being used by the police, which venues open their doors to wounded protesters, what are the wireless Internet codes in certain locations, and so on. These sites served, as it were, like "walkie-talkies" for tens of thousands of people trying to protect themselves from relentless police violence. The refinement of social networking repertoires in this context has been invaluable for the organizational capabilities of the movement.

Repertoire refinement was further consolidated by the spontaneous mobilization of such leadership groups as health personnel, lawyers, and journalists who provided the protesters with technical knowledge and expertise. Health personnel established mobile popular health tents in order to treat injured people and educate the protesters online and on the streets regarding how to minimize the detrimental effects of gas bombs. They were also arrested or threatened to be prosecuted by government officials for aiding the "illegal" protesters (SolNews 2013d). Lawyers, who volunteered to offer free legal consultancy and representation to protesters and shared legal tips online, shared the same fate with health personnel, and they were subjected to police violence (HürriyetDailyNews 2013g). The contact information of lawyers and health personnel was widely shared on social media in solidarity. Professionals with journalism, publishing, or technological background provided the protesters with recommendations on how to validate the authenticity of information that circulates in social media in order to distinguish between police disinformation (and/or provocation) and genuine knowledge. Methods of validating the authenticity of information and photos were widely shared on social media (EkşiSözlük 2013d). Deniz Utku, a former Google employee and the founder of *Teknokrasi Ajans*, revealed on his Twitter account how to avoid social media disinformation as follows: "Do not share anything that you are unsure about its validity! Do not ever share anything if no photo or link is provided! Beware of the people who circulate falsified information just to get credit" (Utku 2013). RedHack, on its part, circulated a list of tips to avoid prosecution for tweeting. The hacktivist group suggested that when taken under police custody, protesters should never admit ownership of the Twitter account in question, and that they should delete electronic traces of their accounts (such as automatic passwords, etc.) from their computer or mobile devices (MilliyetDailyNews 2013b).

Repertoire transfer occurred in two distinct ways: emulation and redeployment. People emulated what they observed in such waves of mass mobilization as the Occupy Movement and the Arab Spring (emulative repertoire transfer). They also redeployed the sets of repertoires that were employed in previous collective action processes such as soccer fan mobilization, May Day Demonstrations since 2007, TEKEL Resistance of 2010, Republic Demonstrations of 2007, and the protests that occurred in the wake of the 1997 military memorandum on February 28 (redeployed repertoire transfer). Emulative repertoire transfer strongly expressed itself in close parallelisms with the repertoire of the Arab Spring movement. As is well known, starting in Tunisia in December of 2010, the "Arab Spring" is a name coined to describe the spread of a series of popular uprisings through several countries ruled by dictatorial leaders in Northern Africa and the Middle East. As Alenius Boserup argues, the originality of the Arab Spring repertoire consisted of co-occurrence of a number of factors: the occupation of post-colonial urban spaces that symbolize postcolonial dictatorial regimes such as Avenue Bourguiba in Tunis, on Tahrir Square in Cairo; extensive use of social media and online networks for social mobilization; emphasis on peaceful mobilization (with the exception of Libya and Syria); and claim-making against what is perceived as "sultanistic" regimes (Boserup 2012). Indeed, such repertoires found broad echo in the Turkish public opinion, given geographical and cultural proximity. It is thus no coincidence to see the Gezi protesters reclaimed Taksim Square and Gezi Park by mobilizing through social media and online networks with peaceful claims that mainly target the authoritarian rule of PM Erdoğan. As discussed in the previous chapter, Taksim Square, just as Avenue Bourguiba in Tunis and Tahrir Square in Cairo, constitutes a historically, culturally, and politically important symbol in Turkey.

Aside from the case of the Arab Spring and the symbolic importance of the struggle for public spaces, another major articulation of emulative repertoire transfer drew on the Occupy movement, an international protest movement that erupted under the name of Occupy Wall Street in New York City's Zuccotti Park on September 17, 2011. Also inspired by the Arab Spring, the Occupy movement made extensive use of social media for social mobilization and adopted the repertoire of occupying public spaces and/or urban spaces that are sym-bolic of social and economic inequality (Juris 2012). As such, the Gezi protesters heavily relied on social media mobilization and referred to the motto of "#Occupy" (#İşgal et) as an under-lying repertoire of action. "#OccupyGezi," "OccupyIstanbul," and "OccupyTurkey" were among the trending topics on Twitter throughout the protests. In turn, it is possible to argue that such emulation greatly contributed to repertoire refinement with reference to online activism. The use of symbolism by some of the protesters, likewise, consciously drew on the Occupy movement and construed the GPPs as the Turkish counterpart of that global initiative. "Signs among the protesters read, 'Occupy from Zuccotti to Gezi,'" and Justin Wedes, one of the earliest organizers of the Occupy Wall Street movement who joined the resistance in Istanbul, stated in an interview that Gezi Park "has elements of both Tahrir Square and Zuccotti Park," and added: "There was the beautiful solidarity and unity I felt in Zuccotti Park, but also the righteous anger and intensity fueled by police violence that was evident in Tahrir Square" (World 2013, Occupy.com 2013). The GPPs built on these external experiences in different ways.

One of the popular instances of redeployed repertoire transfer occurred with the collective leadership of soccer fan clubs (Çarşı, Vamos Bien, ultrAslan) to the protests. Their active involvement led to an extensive and more efficient use of such repertoires as cheering, whistling, chanting, and protection from police attacks. It is reported that in Gezi Park as well as in Dolmabahçe, Akaretler, and Köyiçi (all in Istanbul), Çarşı took initiative to organize the masses against advances of the police so much so that a popular tweet read, "if it were not for Çarşı, so many people would have been harmed in Gezi Park" (DumanFanPage 2013, Bianet 2013a). Fans of soccer clubs such as those of Göztepe, Karşıyaka, and Ankaragücü performed comparable roles in İzmir and Ankara. These fan clubs in the GPPs constitute an example to the redeployment of extra-political collective action strategies and tactics for direct political mobilization.

The GPPs were also marked by the repertoires that drew on past political experiences of civil and working-class resistance in Turkey. Since 2007, police clampdown on May Day Demonstrations in Taksim witnessed scenes of struggle comparable to those of June 2013, during which organized labor organizations and other leftwing parties and groups gained considerable experience in collectively resisting the AKP's "disproportionate violence" (HürriyetDailyNews 2013i). Similarly, the historic TEKEL resistance of 2009–2010 is another example of repertoire redeployment that added to the GPPs. As TEKEL, a former state enterprise of tobacco and alcoholic beverages, was privatized, thousands were laid off and the remaining workers were imposed lower wages and precarious temporary contracts. For 78 days in freezing cold, TEKEL workers occupied the streets of one of Ankara's central squares, Sakarya, and they were joined by activists from socialist parties, students, artists, and so on turning their tents into a "commune" of solidarity (Özugurlu 2011). TEKEL, which was endorsed by a general strike in February 2010, was regarded by many as the rebirth of working-class struggles in Turkey (Yeldan 2010), and the tents of TEKEL, as well as the repertoires of street protest and sit-ins that it refined, can be seen as among the forerunners of what built up to the GPPs.[3]

In addition to May Days and the TEKEL resistance, certain repertoires of the secularly oriented Republic Demonstrations of 2007, and the protests that occurred in the wake of the 1997 military memorandum in reaction to the Susurluk Scandal and Islamic fundamentalism were also redeployed in the GPPs. The Republic Demonstrations of 2007, which is among the largest political mobilization initiatives in the history of Turkey (Gürcan 2010), consolidated the repertoire of peaceful mass rallies as an expression of spontaneous social reaction. Likewise, flashing lights at houses at specific times of the day and pot-banging in balconies and in the streets were actively used in the protests of 1997. These past repertoires flashing lights and pot banging, although not employed for the same political purpose, were so widely redeployed in the GPPs that police had to resort to unprecedented violent measures to stop them. Several cases were reported and documented where the police climbed up to windows and balconies to drop gas bombs inside apartments (NTVMSNBC 2013a). PM Erdoğan himself warned of the "crime of banging pots and pans," and urged his followers to report and sue the "perpetrators": "Are there people banging pots and bans in your building? You immediately take them to the courts" (Today'sZaman 2013). Furthermore, it must be mentioned that between 2007 and 2013, several mass protests such as those against Internet bans, against the imprisonment of journalists and politicians, against the injustices regarding the Hrant Dink case, against police clampdown on national holiday celebrations (such as the Republic Day), against anti-abortion legislation, against hydroelectric centrals, various strikes (such as in Turkish Airlines) and so on contributed to the resistance repertoires that were redeployed with vigor in the GPPs.

Finally, with regard to the creation of new strategies and tactics of resistance, what the media called "standing man" emerged as an innovative form of passive resistance illustrative of how repertoire generation works. As a reaction to violent police repression, this action was initiated by Erdem Gündüz, a performance artist who protested the government by standing still silently at Taksim Square for hours on end. As Richard Seymour, from *The Guardian*, forcefully portrays, Gündüz's action put the violent Turkish police into a dilemma: "Gündüz's protest was both an affront and a question for the authorities: beat him? Why? He's just standing there. Leave him alone? Then he wins, doesn't he?" (TheGuardian 2013e). The crowds were not delayed in emulating Gündüz's action, and the repertoire of "standing men/women" was soon spread all over the country via conventional and social media's powerful influence. Across Turkey, the police detained people who simply stood in public places in solidarity. The repertoire of standing, therefore, is already inscribed in the culture of resistance in Turkey, and received considerable international attention and support (DemocracyNOW 2013).

As was noted in *The Independent*, however, standing man did not mean that the protest cycle was standing still: another significant instance of repertoire generation was the development of community organizations through the emergence and spread of people's forums held at public parks and neighborhoods (TheIndependent 2013). Sparked with the initiative of

TDP, and partly emulated from the Occupy Movement, spheres of collective grassroots leadership and direct democratic participation were established to decide on the course of popular resistance (SolNews 2013c). Although the longer-term implications of people's forums remain to be seen, one could assert that the forum repertoire tremendously helped the GPPs to go beyond a mere temporal enterprise of spontaneous protesting and resistance. The forums initiated a protracted process of everyday life transformation in a political-cultural fashion, along with the articulation of a myriad of claims ranging from everyday life necessities and public projects concerning the neighborhood residents to political issues, problems of institutionalization, and movement alliances. As far as neighborhood residents' everyday issues are concerned, Yeniköy Forum objected to a mosque construction project that would harm the green environment of the neighborhood, by also claiming that there already is a sufficient number of mosques in the area. Üsküdar Doğancılar Forum decided to take action against the AKP's neoliberal urban transformation projects. As for movement institutionalization and alliances, many forums such as Bebek Parkı Forum, Üsküdar Doğancılar Forum, and Yoğurtcu Forum discussed the questions of how to ensure permanent participation, how to use social media (Facebook, e-mail lists, etc.) to organize forum activities, what kind of new repertoires can be developed, what kind of working groups, workshops, and committees are to be established and how to forge closer ties with other forums, neighborhood movements, local shopkeepers, and artists. Bebek Parkı Forum decided to join the march organized by the LGBT movement, and expressed the need to also appeal to the AKP electorate. When it comes to political issues, Bakırköy Forum emphasized that the resistance should not forget about the Uludere and Reyhanlı massacres, arguing that the government is responsible. The Chamber of Architects of Turkey Forum pointed to the necessity of countering person-centered and over-centralized authoritarian forms of leadership by creating a new organizational language. In a similar fashion,

Göztepe Özgürlük Parkı Forum underlined the importance of eliminating all kinds of oppressive language that do not respect differences and promotes racist, homophobic, sexist statements in the course of people's resistance to the hegemonic discourse of the government (BirgünDailyNewspaper 2013, SendikaNews 2013b). Overall, the practice of people's forums is new in Turkey, and the generation of this repertoire to be practiced by large groups could only be made possible through the process of collective resistance and solidarity that emerged in the GPPs.

Reprise and Review

This chapter sought to demonstrate that despite the arguments presented by mainstream accounts, spontaneous mobilization and collective leadership formation were not mutually exclusive in the GPPs, but they were rather mutually enabling in enhancing the political capacity of the movement. The chapter has presented "leadership" as neither a mere collection of leading individuals nor a single center leading the totality of a given social movement, but as a collective process composed of several social and political organizations to form counter-hegemonic alliances in mass mobilization. We have revealed that the membership base of the Gezi movement presents a highly diversified profile, and draws its strength from a myriad of networks, including social media as well as friend and neighborhood connections. When it comes to membership integration and involvement, a major factor has been the presence and participation of previously organized left-wing political parties, activists, social movements, professional organizations, soccer fan clubs, and trade unions, the resources of which facilitated the sustainability of the GPP.

In the second section of this chapter, we have provided further details on the profile and involvement of the leading organizational actors during the GPPs. Our discussion of such groups of collective leadership, of course, cannot claim to be exhaustive due to space limitations. In turn, the final section elaborated on how the fusion of spontaneity and leadership in the GPPs, as well as the national and international experiences of past mobilizations, impacted the organizational forms and collective action repertoires of the movement. A major and influential ideational resistance factor generated and consolidated in the GPPs, however, was not touched upon in this chapter. That factor came to be known as the practice of "disproportionate intelligence," which not only strengthened the political consciousness and membership integration processes of the movement, but also gave the GPPs its vitality, morale, and ethical high ground over movement antagonists. This will be the topic of the next chapter, where we focus on the ideational aspects of collective action in the GPPs.

5

Forging Political Consciousness at Gezi: The Case of "Disproportionate Intelligence"

A final factor in the emergence and spread of extra-parliamentary/ disruptive collective action is political consciousness. In Chapter 1, we discussed the inadequacy of culturalist perspectives that place the emphasis on a vaguely defined and shallowly operationalized concept of "identities" to explain political consciousness. In this chapter, we rather propose to elaborate on political consciousness from a Marxist standpoint, which brings us to Doug McAdam's notion of "cognitive liberation" as a transformative agent of social mobilization.

The term "cognitive liberation" first appeared in Doug McAdam's early work in which he challenged the pluralist and elitist political sociological approaches from a Marxian perspective (McAdam 1982). Over time, following the rise to prominence of Weberian perspectives and the growing popularity of symbolic-interactionist approaches, McAdam's notion of "cognitive liberation" ceded its place to "framing analysis." "Framing" refers to the ways in which social movements attach meanings to their situation, and it serves as a mediating factor that ignites, sustains, and develops social mobilization. Framing involves the transformation of people's perception so as to establish a shared awareness that their situation is unjust and needs to be changed through collective action, whereas the status quo is considered illegitimate and vulnerable (McAdam

1982, 48, 51, McAdam, McCarthy, and Zald 2008, 8, Benford and Snow 2000, 615). In light of these considerations, one could broadly conceptualize framing as "the conscious strategic efforts by groups of people to fashion shared understandings of the world and of themselves that legitimate and motivate collective action" (Doug McAdam, John D. McCarthy, and Mayer N. Zald quoted in Baud and Rutten 2004, 1).

Framing perspectives, however, have been criticized for reducing the essence of political consciousness almost exclusively to social interaction and claim making (Jasper 1997). Consequently, to the extent that "frames" are not thought in the context of the more enduring and politically charged structures of "ideology," they run the risk of voluntarism and being trapped in methodological individualism. As Oliver and Johnston (2000, 37) summarize, "frame theory is rooted in linguistic studies of interaction, and points to the way shared assumptions and meanings shape the interpretation of events." On the other hand, "ideology is rooted in politics and the study of politics, and points to coherent systems of ideas which provide theories of society...for promoting or resisting social change." Carragee and Roefs (2004, 215) touch upon a similar point by adding that framing alone tends to "evade a meaningful consideration of political and social power," neglecting that the "distribution of power shapes the construction and interpretation of those frames." Following that cue, we believe that the political expression of a social movement should be embedded in the larger politico-ideological structures and struggles prevalent in a given geography.

Reclaiming the Marxist essence of McAdam's earlier work, we thus revisit the notion of "cognitive liberation" to underscore the collective practice of engendering and acquiring critical political consciousness in the very process of collective action. In this sense, "cognitive liberation" highlights the transformative aspects of social movement subjectivity that reformulate the configuration of political consciousness through social disruption and frontal action. Taken as such, the concept refers to a partial break from pre-established cognitive structures promoted by dominant ideological frameworks. It therefore requires the development of a collective sense of injustice, an acknowledgment of the illegitimacy of the system, and a belief in the necessity and possibility for change (McAdam 1982). The significance of cognitive liberation emanates from the fact that "the overturning of repressive social hierarchies requires not just the organization of oppositional social forces but the development of new modes of understanding. Thus the striving for cognitive liberation will form a crucial dimension of the emancipatory process" (Mills 1990, 1). In the words of Gramsci, such liberation "must be a criticism of 'common sense,' basing itself initially, however, on common sense in order to demonstrate that 'everyone' is a philosopher and that it is not a question of introducing from scratch a scientific form of thought into everyone's individual life, but of renovating and making 'critical' an already existing activity" (Gramsci 1971, 330–331). It is our purpose in this chapter to demonstrate that through creative graffiti, street art, slogans, tweets, aphorisms, music, poems, photo captions, and other media, the GPPs embedded critically engaged "philosophy" in the structures of everyday life, which is in direct opposition to dominant ideological structures represented by "neoliberalism with Islamic characteristics."

More particularly, we argue that an original and underlying component of cognitive liberation during the GPPs in achieving political consciousness has been the widespread use of what we call "cognitive diversion." Deriving from Guy Debord's concept of "détournement" (diversion), cognitive diversion constitutes a counter-hegemonic technique for cognitive liberation, aiming to reverse and demystify the meanings and ideological efforts led by movement opponents through the active utilization of humor and "plagiarism" for propaganda purposes (Debord 2004b, a). This is explicitly stated in Debord's slogan: "plagiarism is necessary." By plagiarism, Debord understands the act of "an author's phrasing, exploits his expressions, deletes a false idea, replaces it with the right one" (Debord 2005, 113).

The technique of cognitive diversion is not peculiar to the Turkish case. The Occupy Movement, for instance, also heavily relied on humor and plagiarism to demystify and delegitimize neoliberalism. Some of the signs and slogans used in Occupy can better exemplify cognitive diversion: "Free tampons to stop economic bleeding," "Land of the fee, home of the slave," "It's one person, one vote. Not one dollar, one vote!" "Lost my job, found an Occupation," "Wall Street has the real weapons of mass destruction," "If only the war on poverty was a real war," "The People are too big to fail," "Did you lose your home or Wall Street stole it from you?" "United Slaves Arise," "Wall Street is our Street," "Yes we camp." Slogans such as these helped over-turn and critically engage with mainstream accounts that pro-vided explanations for the economic downturn. In the GPPs as well, the various expressions of the wage-earning class fractions were not confined to the voicing of grievances, but the very act and form of articulating those expressions became a tactical tool and membership building strategy in their own right.

Our further operationalization of cognitive diversion builds on Mikhail Bakhtin's conceptualization of the "carnivalesque," which can reveal how exactly plagiarism might work to humor-ously transform mainstream ideological rhetoric for militant purposes while generating a feeling of relief and solidarity. Drawing on Bakhtin's interpretation of medieval European car-nivals, the term refers to the subversion of dominant cognitive structures to build "a second world and a second life outside officialdom" (Bakhtin 1984, 6). Through the liberation from pre-established cognitive structures,[1] the carnivalesque turns the world upside down along with its inherent social hierarchies and power structures to redefine what is sacred and profane (Bakhtin 1984).

The carnivalistic sense of the world, according to Bakhtin, has four dimensions. First, it engenders (a) unity and free inter-action among the people in new and original ways, and relatedly (b) brings together "misalliances," that is, groups and percep-tions that would normally function separately, in an unlikely harmony. In the GPPs, these two dimensions were realized in the solidarity of unlikely sociopolitical groups against the AKP and its police violence. This improbable alliance and interaction created, though temporarily, a unique reality on the streets, where "life is subject only to its laws, that is, the laws of its own freedom. It has a universal spirit" (Bakhtin 1984, 7). (c) Eccentric (or unacceptable) behavior is encouraged, which, in the case of Turkey and many other protests elsewhere includes popular-democratic disruption, creativity, and the confrontation of the police via civil disobedience. Lastly, (d) the carnivalistic sense of the world involves the verbal discrediting of the ethical and normative impositions of predominant cognitive structures (branded as "sacriligeous" by Bakhtin), which was an easily discernible theme in the GPPs. What is more, in the generation of the carnivalistic sense of the world against pre-established cognitive structures, humor is central in enabling political agency and participation: "The people's...laughter...expresses the point of view of the whole world; he who is laughing also belongs to it" (Bakhtin 1984, 12). Used in this politically critical, transformative, and solidarity-building sense, humor/laughter was a central component of the GPPs (Eken 2014, 432). In brief, Bakhtin's operationalization of how the carnivalesque works can shed light on the ways in which the Debordian act of plagiarism delegitimizes and ridicules dominant ideological cognitive structures so as to bring about popular-democratic cognitive liberation. In the case of the GPPs, it was the Islamist-neoliberal ideology of the AKP government that was being "cognitively diverted."

In what follows, we analyze how the technique of cognitive diversion was used in the GPPs to constitute the basis of "disproportionate intelligence." In response to the "disproportionate violence" used by police forces, the concept "disproportionate intelligence" came to refer to the creative and humorous slogans, tweets, music, graffiti, photo captions, videos, and other forms of physical and online media that challenge and reverse the various manifestations of the repressive and Islamic neoliberal urban-cultural transformations in Turkey. The concept, which is the product of cognitive diversion itself,[2] has had a unifying influence on the protesters both in terms of morale and establishing "the psychological superiority" and "moral high ground" over the AKP government and to expand popular contention nationwide (Helvacıoğlu 2013, 7). It had a counter-hegemonic content and transformative potential to cultivate cognitively liberated political consciousness vis-à-vis "neoliberalism with Islamic characteristics" in Turkey. Disproportionate intelligence also became a popular tool to appropriate the streets and reclaim the public sphere against its invasion both by the police and neoliberal urban renewal projects. As Eken (2014, 432) describes: "amid the barricade wars with the police...İstiklal Street, which leads to Taksim Square and its expensive shops, art galleries, and bank offices, was covered with graffiti. The texts incorporated the language of video games, high poetry, popular culture, as well as the revolutionary epic in addressing whatever oppressive condition the author(s) might be suffering from, but the same comic spirit characterized all of them, without exception."

The chapter is organized as follows: the first section briefly lays out the AKP's response to and interpretation of the GPPs, which was not only based infamously on a rhetoric of patronizing slander and provocation, but also on a conspiracy-driven representation that quickly lost touch with reality. In this manner, we will argue in Chapter 6 that the GPPs signify a breaking point that created an insurmountable discrepancy between two cognitive universes in Turkey: one that revolves around Erdoğan and his party, and another that is centered on the collective resistance initiative—which all drifted further away from each other in the post-Gezi environment. We then turn our attention in the second section to our core task, namely to exemplifying the practice of "disproportionate intelligence" in the GPPs, which internalized the technique of cognitive diversion to reverse, undermine, ridicule, and expose the inconsistency of the Islamist-neoliberal ideology propagated by the government. In the final section, we touch upon the internal rhetorical/

ideological alliances as well as tensions within the GPPs that manifested themselves in diverse ways.

5a. The AKP's Interpretation of the Gpps: Marauders and Conspiracies

As demonstrated in previous chapters, the cognitive structures promoted by the AKP-imposed Islamist-neoliberal "political-cultural fix" envisage a world where the commons are privatized, nature is commodified, Sunni Islam dominates as an overarching worldview and source of symbolism, no public expression of affection is permitted, alcohol consumption is prohibited, homosexuality is stigmatized, women are subordinated, and dissent voices are silenced with disproportionate violence and imprisonment, and so on. These cognitive structures, which have consistently manifested themselves in the AKP's policies and rhetoric, propagate a culture of allegiance with unconditional loyalty to Islamist-neoliberal values personified in Erdoğan's authoritarian leadership. We argue that the GPPs enabled the crystallization of these ideologies in an intensified manner, which not only further exposed the aggressive authoritarianism and patronization inherent to the AKP government, but also revealed the incessant fabrication of falsehoods, propaganda, and provocation as ordinary features of its *modus operandi*. A focus on PM Erdoğan's speeches during the GPPs can be highly representative of those tendencies.

On May 28, 2013, in a speech that defended the government's alcohol restrictions, Erdoğan made the following statement that succinctly summarized his worldview: "Some people have referred to human beings as, god forbid, thinking beings." On the contrary, he added, "our party's view of humans is very clear: humans are the caliphs of Allah on earth." Erdoğan then defended the alcohol bans on religious grounds: "when two drunkards [referring to Atatürk and İnönü, founders of the Republic] make a law, you respect it. But when we make a law for something that religion orders, you reject it. Why?... Go drink alcohol at home if you want to drink" (HürriyetDailyNews 2013a). The statement can be considered as the last example of the government's condescending attitude toward the non-AKP population before the GPPs broke out. The next day, on May 29, Erdoğan commemorated the conquest of Istanbul in a grandiose ceremony that laid the foundations of the city's third bridge, where he directly targeted the Gezi Park Protesters for the first time: "Do whatever you want in Gezi Park. We have made our decision, and we will implement it" (SabahNews 2013b). As the protests took a nationwide character on the evening of May 31, 2013, instead of seeking to calm the tension, Erdoğan raised the stakes by declaring that the Atatürk Cultural Center (AKM) in Taksim would also be demolished, and a new mosque would be built in the area. He asserted: "I do not need permission for these from...a handful of marauders. Our voters have already given us that authority" (HürriyetDailyNews 2013d). As they passed by, official provocative statements escalated exponentially.

The central feature of the government's interpretation of the GPPs was to place the movement in the framework of various farfetched conspiracy theories, which feverishly rejected the existence of genuine popular grievances, let alone spontaneous mobilization. On the first day of June, Erdoğan quickly framed the events as led by the main opposition party, CHP: "Once again, we see the opposition party siding with illegal organizations to take part in these plots for the purpose of aggravating tension and provocation...I want my people...to clearly identify such schemes" (HaberTurkNews 2013a). By mid-June, Erdoğan's conspirators had become more diverse and numerous. As he put it: "Powerful ad agencies, some capital groups, interest rate lobby, internal and external organizations and collaborators were all prepared and equipped for the job. Tactics, messages, and tweets were accompanied by premade films and photos, where every step of the disinformation was calculated in advance" (MilliyetDailyNews 2013a). These were alongside "the CIA, Europeans jealous of...economic success, unspecified foreign forces in cahoots with terrorists, Twitter...and...the international Jewish conspiracy" (TheGuardian 2013b). Moreover, some AKP officials and intelligentsia pointed also to the airline company Lufthansa, Mossad, Serbian civil society organization Otpor!, a satirical theater play in Istanbul (*Mi Minör*), and other conspirators as collectively plotting the GPPs to realize a *coup d'état*. Perhaps the high point of such assertions was when Erdoğan's chief adviser argued that there were some hidden powers seeking to kill Erdoğan from afar through tele-kinesis. Finally, as renowned journalist Christiane Amanpour reported live from Taksim during the events, CNN International was also added to the list of conspirators, and a fake interview with Amanpour was published by the pro-government newspaper *Takvim*, where she allegedly "confessed" having "done it all for the money" (HuffingtonPost 2013).

Parallel with the irrational perception of the GPPs as plotted top-down by countless domestic and international conspirators, the AKP sought to respond to the events with government-organized mass rallies. As Erdoğan implied, the mentality behind the initiative was on their numerical superiority: "if this is about holding meetings, if this is a social movement, where they gather 20 thousand, I will get up and gather 200,000 people. Where they gather 100,000, I will bring together one million from my party" (Haaretz 2013). This was in line with his threatening statement before he left for North Africa on the third day of the GPPs, where "he hinted that his supporters could also take to the streets, saying he was 'hardly keeping the 50 percent [of voters] at home'" (Al-Monitor 2013b). Organized in five cities throughout June 2013, the "Respect to the National Will Rallies," subtitled "Let us halt the grand conspiracy," were meant precisely to serve the purpose of majoritarian intimidation, during each of which Erdoğan continued to stress the plotted nature of the GPPs, as well as various allegations about and insults toward the "marauders."

In the course of the first two weeks of June 2013 and after, Erdoğan and his party clung to Islamist-nationalist provocation to discredit the protesters, who were accused of a myriad of deeds among which were attacking and sexually assaulting a woman with headscarf, drinking beer in mosques, and burning Turkish flags—which were all subsequently proven to be fabricated (Al-Monitor 2013d, TheDailyStar 2014). At one point, Erdoğan went as far as asserting that "Gezi Park smells like urine. Most of the protesters defecate in the park" (AlJazeera 2013). Following the PM's lead, pro-government media joined in with even more creative scenarios: *Akit,* for instance, talked of an orgy inside the Dolmabahçe Mosque and at Gezi Park, *Yeni Şafak* claimed that protesters received orders through a Houston-based smart phone application, *Haber7* "discovered" coup plots to overthrow the AKP, *BeyazTV* purported that protesters drank cat blood, and national public broadcaster TRT used images of protesters burning Turkish flags—which turned out to be footage from 2010 unrelated to the GPPs.[3] As for police violence, Erdoğan stated on several occasions that he was proud of his police forces for "writing a heroic saga," and that he gave them the orders to fight the "forces of occupation." He also referred to an officer who lost his life as "a martyr," and awarded the police with generous bonuses at the end of June 2013 (HürriyetDailyNews 2013k, Today'sZaman 2013).

In all these reactions to the GPPs given by government circles, Islamic symbolism was implicitly and explicitly utilized to disrepute the protesters as immoral deviant subjects devoid of compliance and belief. A transatlantic message that came from Fethullah Gülen endorsed a similar perspective on June 6, 2013: "A generation that is rotten and in ruins...must be exposed to restoration...If we do not begin with the rehabilitation of these generations...if their brains are not modified...such unruliness continues" (HürriyetDailyNews 2013e). To counteract the "rotten generation," Erdoğan declared in his notorious "airport speech" on the morning of June 7, 2013 that "nobody can stop Turkey's rise but Allah," to which his followers responded with the slogans: *"ya allah bismillah allahu ekber"* (in the name of Allah, Allah is great"), "those who raise their hands against the police should have their hands broken," and "show us the road and we will crush Taksim!" Building on past ideological polarizations, therefore, the government's response to the GPPs consolidated a cognitive universe clearly separated not only from that of the movement, but also from plausible confines of reality, where every critic became an evil conspirator. The next section deals with the second universe, which was born and consolidated in the dynamism of the GPPs to divert the government's physical and psychological advances via humor, plagiarism, and various manifestations of creativity.

5b. Cognitive Diversion, or "Everyday I am Chapuling"

The political consciousness of the GPPs was expressed predominantly in humorous terms, yet as Dağtaş (2013) underlines, "humor...proved to be more than creative enjoyment during the Gezi Park protests," for it "served as an alternative medium for political communication about the 'serious world' that it emanates from yet refuses to accept at face value." Regarding the refusal to accept the government-imposed ideological structures, "cognitive diversion" stood out as the leading ideational tool of the GPPs, the most prominent example of which was the coining of an entirely new notion of "*çapulcu*." After the PM branded the Gezi Park protesters as "a handful of marauders" ("*çapulcu*" in Turkish), the protesters reclaimed the word "*çapulcu*" and fused it with various English grammatical forms (as verb, adjective, noun, etc.) to create new meanings. "Everyday I'm chapuling" was a popular slogan deriving from this understanding (plagiarized from the lyrics "Everyday I'm shuffling," by the American rapper duo LMFAO), where the verb "chapuling/çapuling" came to signify taking part in the protests and resisting police violence. The sign "I am chapuling Istanbul, my eyes closed" plagiarized from the famous Turkish poet Orhan Veli, replacing the word "listening." "Chapuller was here" showed the same word as a noun. Using Descartes's famous aphorism, "I'm chapuling, therefore I am" implied that the people began to exist only in resistance. One graffiti said: "Liberté, Egalité, Fraternité, *Chapulité*," whereas another declared, "*Hamdolsun* (Thank God) I am a *çapulcu*." Erdoğan's dismissive statement thus backfired, as *çapulcu* quickly became the uncontested collective character embraced by the masses that invoked unity and solidarity despite ideological and other differences. For instance, in an online survey that involved more than 1,000 participants, 88 percent of the protesters stated that they saw themselves "as a typical *çapulcu*." The study also revealed that the collective identity of *çapulcu* created a positive sense of belonging that encouraged and motivated people's partaking in the protests (RadikalDailyNews 2013c). Thousands of people added "*çapulcu*" before their names on Facebook and Twitter. A classic folksong readapted by the Boğaziçi Jazz Choir on the spot, titled, "Are you a *çapulcu*?" (*Çapulcu musun vay vay*) was widely incorporated and sung by the masses.[4] As a result, the concept of "chapuling" spread across the borders so much so that Noam Chomsky published a video message to support the resistance with a banner that said "I am also a '*çapulcu*' in solidarity."

Most Gezi participants claimed "freedoms" and "democracy" as underlying concepts in direct opposition to "oppression," "dictatorship," "fascism," or "Islamism" identified with the AKP government and the personal figure of PM Erdoğan. In one word, the commonly shared demand of the GPPs was "to become a democratic, equal, free, and enlightened society" (Helvacıoğlu 2013, 6). Thereby, such slogans as "shoulder to shoulder against fascism," "united against fascism," "we will win through resistance!" and "down with the AKP dictatorship" were among the most popular ones. "Everywhere is Taksim, everywhere is resistance!" underscored the sociospatial dimension of the protests as well as its spread, thus turning Taksim into a nationally recognized and acted out symbol for the movement across the country. Other slogans were addressed directly at the PM: "Tayyip, go away!" "Government Resign!" and "Hey Tayyip look here, count how many we are!" Another popular motivational and humorous slogan goes as follows: "Jump, jump, you're Tayyip/fascist if you don't jump" (accompanied by jumping).

The plunder of social space and nature through neoliberal urban practices constituted one of the most discernible concerns of the protesters. Another popular song that came to symbolize the movement, "Tencere Tava Havası" (Sound of Pots and Pans) by *Kardeş Türküler*, voiced that concern powerfully with the following lyrics: "They couldn't sell their shadows so they sold the forests/They knocked down and closed cinemas and squares/I'm surrounded by shopping malls, I don't feel like crossing this bridge/What happened to our city? It's now full of inflated buildings."[5] One famous placard said, "Let's demolish the government, and build a shopping mall instead!" whereas another warned, "don't touch my neighborhood, my square, my tree, my water, my land, my home, my seed, my forest, my village, my city, my park!" On a vandalized police car, the words "Security for the People" were changed by crossing out "people" and replacing with "shopping mall." The concept "urban renewal" was replaced with "revolutionary renewal" in one bill, and graffiti such as "all the trees of the world, unite!" "Long live our ecological revolution," and "Government kills, nature gives life!" all underscored the green tones of Gezi against the authoritarian market logic. Moreover, in response to the neoliberal plunder of cities, taking up the streets and claiming the material and cultural ownership of urban space through public initiative were brought forward in many slogans, bills, and graffiti. "Poetry is in the streets," "hope is in the streets," "The barricade blocks the road, but it paves our way," "Police out, Gezi Park is ours" were some examples that invoked that claim to the city. Rebelling against authority, in this sense, was encouraged: "Peace is in insurgency," "You look so beautiful when you're angry, Turkey!" "Don't thank God, rebel!" "I went to resist, I'll be back."

In the face of police brutality, most protesters kept on peaceful mobilization and improvized alternative ways to delegitimize state repression via humor-driven frame diversion. The police's extensive use of tear gas and pressurized water (blended with chemical substances) was among the central themes in this process: "Peaceful protests and humor are the only thing that they don't know how to handle" was a sign that was plagiarized from John Lennon's similar aphorism: "I think our opposition, whoever they may be…don't know how to handle humor." One other bill, "We haven't taken a bath for three days; please send a TOMA," humorously signified that the protesters were not intimidated by pressurized water fired by TOMAs. "We've been together with TOMA for eight days, and we're serious about our relationship" was along the same lines. "TOMAcracy is people's self-watering" played around the concept of "democracy" as people's "self-governing." A song by the popular rock band *Duman* touched upon police violence and called on to the protesters to not give up: "To your pepper, to your gas/To your batons and your sticks/And to your harsh kicks/I say bring it on, bring it on!/Attack me shamelessly, tirelessly/My eyes may burn/ But I don't bow, nor diminish in numbers."[6]

Other street signs read, "Let them eat pepper gas if they cannot not afford bread—Recep Tayyip Antoinette," "No Recep no Cry," and "Welcome to the First Traditional Gas Festival," all making fun of the extensive use of gas bombs by the police. "Chemical Tayyip," "Let's get chemical," "Hey brother, have you run out of gas?" "Do you have one with strawberry flavor?" also referred to the extensive use of gas by the government against the people. Examples can be multiplied: "Our national drink is now pepper gas" (plagiarized from the PM's speeches), "Pepper gas embellishes the skin," "I'm addicted to this gas, man," "I'm lovin' it" (plagiarized from McDonald's commercials), "Hey bro, is your pepper gas from Mexico?" "Sir, you didn't have to fire tear gas on us, we are already sentimental boys." Government-led police violence was further ridiculed by slogans such as "That's enough, I'm calling the police," "If you call the cops, the kid dies," "Police, help, they're destroying the state!" "Too many policemen, too little justice," "You've attacked the generation who beats up cops in *Grand Theft Auto!*" (a popular computer game), and "Even Tampax could have stopped bloodshed better than you."

The protestors' cognitive diversion efforts deliberately directed at the PM's personal characteristics as well as his authoritarian, antagonistic, and conservative style. In this sense, as Dağtaş (2013) notes, "expanding the range of the "publicly express-ible" in times of fear, despair, and dissatisfaction with the exist-ing order, humor during the Gezi events formed a language that was unexpected yet ordinary, entertaining yet deeply political." "Tayyip, winter is coming" plagiarized from the popular TV series *Game of Thrones* to imply that the PM's days are num-bered. "Welcome to Fight Club, Tayyip!" "Don't fight, make love with me, Tayyip," "Tayyip oppresses his own people," "We are going to overthrow your Sultanate!" and "Everyone can come except you, Tayyip" are some examples that demon-strate the public's reaction to Erdoğan's overbearing conduct. Soccer fans also joined in humorously criticizing the PM: "Even Alex is gone, you think you can stay, Tayyip?" referred to the former captain of Fenerbahçe whose departure from the club was controversial, whereas "Drogba is the cure/Drogba for Prime Minister" amusingly called on to the Galatasaray striker to take political power. In Istanbul, life-size stencil graffiti of Erdoğan was painted on a wall, under the heading "Resistance Souvenir," and protesters stood next to it to get their photos taken with the PM. In other imagery, the AKP's official sym-bol, the light bulb, was painted on walls with captions such as "turn off if unnecessary" and "Even Edison is regretful." Finally, when Erdoğan went to a North African diplomatic tour on the first few days of the GPPs, "please don't come back" was found on numerous walls, and "#resistAfrica" became a humorous trending topic on Twitter. The word "resist/diren," which was originally used with hash tags such as #resistanbul or #direngezi, was used comically to refer to a number of things such as #direnaklım ("resist my mind") or, in #direniphoneşarjı ("resist iPhone battery").

Signs and graffitti such as "We are all kissing incessantly, Tayyip," or "Cheers Tayyip" made fun of the government's socially interventionist and stigmatizing attitude on public demonstration of affection and alcohol consumption. "We do not want a prime minister who is fascist day and night" overturned the PM's controversial statement, "we don't want a generation who is drunk day and night." On alcohol restrictions, several other signs could be found: "You banned alcohol and sobered up the nation," "We the drunkards gathered here," and "You should not have forbidden that last beer" were among the popular ones. "I am the third drunkard" was a response to the PM's not-so implicit reference to the founders of the Republic as "two drunkards." "This is *ayran*'s stupor" also ridiculed the PM's assertion that *ayran* should be the national drink, as opposed to *rakı*. The government's interventions on reproduction and public morality (including abortion, C-section, etc.) were also the target of the protesters: "Public morality, whose morality?" "We resisted and aborted the dead citizen within us." Regarding Erdoğan's insistence that each family should have "at least three kids," there were numerous signs: "Are you sure you want three kids like us?" "I'll make three kids and get them to attack you Tayyip!" "Don't make 3 kids, plant 3 trees instead." Other women and LGBT groups, moreover, protested with signs that said, "Run Tayyip, women are coming!" "if morality is about force and violence, then we're immoral!" "I'm not interested in you Tayyip!" "so what we're gay!" ("velev ki ibneyiz") "Oh dear, it's a revolution!" ("Ay resmen devrim!").

Indeed, mainstream media and pro-government media organization got their share from the Gezi protesters, who were also attacked through cognitive diversion. Bills such as "Revolution will not be televised—it will be tweeted," or "and they ask me why I don't read the papers!" speak to the mainstream media's refusal to cover the early phase of the protests. Instead, the media resorted to auto-censure and aired irrelevant programs, which turned into a major controversy in the public opinion. "Media for sale," "Henchman media," Inglorious, sell-out media," "TVs didn't show it but we were here," "coward media," "Turkish Media: 'our consciousness is silent due to technical problems,', "Turn off the TV and take the streets for democracy," and "how much did you sell your honesty for?" were written on walls by protesters. Following the media blackout of the first few days, hundreds of protesters gathered in front of the headquarters of NTV, a major private news network, demanding them to cover the developments and inform the public (EuroNews 2013). Also, an NTV news van was vandalized in Taksim and covered with graffiti such as "Tayyip loves NTV," "Sellout!" "coward," and "fabricated news." Yet none of this took as much attention as penguins. Interestingly, penguins became the uncontested symbol of the media blackout among the protesters, due to CNN Turk airing (and not interrupting) a documentary on penguins on the first night of the events as hundreds of thousands of people were out in the streets, and the country was literally burning. Accordingly, street walls, bills, and tweets were decorated with penguin images (usually wearing gas masks) along with some protesters dressing up as penguins. References such as "Antarctica is resisting!" were abundant, and later in 2013, a smart phone game titled "Chapulling" was created, which involves penguins as main characters defending themselves against police forces in Taksim.

AKP's aggressive promotion of the Ottoman Empire as a glorious memory (and a model to abide by) also received considerable reaction from the protesters. "Claim your future, not your past!" said one bill, which was accompanied by another that held that "our history is not for sale." The latter bill refers to the commercialization of Ottoman history by the government. One placard picked on the government's Ottomanism: "you're at the age when Fatih conquered Gezi!" which makes fun of a conservative poem that warns the youth against complacency, for the Ottoman Emperor Fatih the Conqueror had done great things at their age. "Another head is possible," uttered one other bill (echoing the slogan "another world is possible"), where "head" here refers to the conservative mentality of the government. The popular defiance against PM Erdoğan as the "Sultan" or "a poor excuse for a sultan" ("padişah bozuntusu") was in itself critical of the Ottomanist aspirations of the government.

Another original component of cognitive diversion during the GPPs involved what one could call "false plagiarism," namely the act of inventing quotes that are associated with well-known critical thinkers. For instance, "Capitalism will cut down the tree whose shadow it cannot sell" was associated to Karl Marx and was used as a critique of AKP's neoliberal urban policies. Another quote was adapted from Mikhail Bakunin: "I want that hurricane in Kızılay, which was caused by a butterfly in Gezi Park." Cognitive diversion during the GPPs was also built on particular references to texts, songs, poems, and movies/TV series, some of which have been exemplified earlier. "It's hard to die in June," and "To live! Like a tree alone and free; like a forest in brotherhood" were plagiarized from the poet Nazım Hikmet. "The people are Clark Kent during the day and Superman at night" used popular culture to indicate how the protesters led divided lives during the events. "Red Hot Chili Tayyip" made a play on words using the American rock band to hint at the pepper gas used by the government. The same was valid for the pun "Tayyip Bieber," where the pop star Justin Bieber's last name sounds like "biber" (pepper) in Turkish. "Where are you, Spartacus?" "We are making a revolution here, señorita!" "Down with certain things!" "Couldn't find a slogan!" "Can't find an empty wall!" "Don't worry mom, I stay in the back of the group" were some other humorous examples from the GPPs that demonstrate "disproportionate intelligence."

The widespread use of Guy Fawkes masks by the Gezi participants was another symbol of resistance through cognitive diversion. Guy Fawkes is a famous figure of the failed Gunpowder Plot of 1605, a member of a group of English Catholics planning to assassinate the Protestant King James. The mask became famous with a film adaptation of the dystopian *V for Vendetta* in 2005. It was worn by an anarchist revolutionary who was struggling against a totalitarian police regime in order to liberate society. The mask was later incorporated by social movement activists, especially by the online hacktivist group Anonymous, Arab Spring protestors, and the Occupy Movement. In Turkey, the Guy Fawkes mask was the most popular mask during the GPDs next to gas masks. The protestors who wore Guy Fawkes masks used them both as a means of anonymity and that for the expression of their aspiration for the necessity of social change in the face of the growing authoritarianism and social interventionism of the AKP government.

Unsurprisingly, the Uludere Massacre and Reyhanlı Bombings constituted a major target for Gezi protesters. Hence the wall slogans "Gezi is Reyhanlı/Uludere" and "Don't forget about Reyhanlı/Uludere." Gezi protesters named the trees at Gezi Park after the victims of the Uludere and Reyhanlı Bombings. They also appropriated the symbol of Reyhanlı Bombings, that is, the well-known photo of 71-year-old Döne Kuvvet with her arms wide open crying in the middle of the ruins. Some wall illustrations made by the protesters presented a similar woman with the sole difference that Döne Kuvvet's figure was raising her left fist and wearing a gas mask. Finally, in every possible occasion, Gezi Park protesters honored the people who were killed by police violence during the GPPs. In the aftermath of the events, public squares, streets, parks, and other social spaces were named, officially or unofficially, after figures such as Ali İsmail Korkmaz, Abdullah Cömert, Mehmet Ayvalıtaş, and Ethem Sarısülük, and Berkin Elvan. Deeply inscribed in public memory, their names are still being written on walls and photos shared in various social media, and they remain inspirational symbols that give the GPPs its spirit and unending youthful energy.

Besides the streets, the social media, particularly Twitter and Facebook, was another space that was claimed by the Gezi Park protesters as a site of resistance and cognitive diversion. The role of social media in the GPPs was not confined to sharing the various news, graffiti, slogans, songs, videos, and other artwork that captured the momentum on the streets. In addition, pro-movement activity on social media created its own language and

tools of disproportionate intelligence that further contributed
to the political consciousness of the GPPs. Humor was again
a central component. For instance, the publicly contributed
satirical online news network, *Zaytung*, was actively used and
read during the GPPs. Ridiculing the AKP's conspiracy theories around the protests, one news item shared photos of "Gezi
Park Protesters Building Atomic Bomb in the Park." Another
article declared that in their search for the international conspiracy behind the events, the AKP "has inadvertently found
the perpetrators of the Kennedy assassination." In yet another
news, it was reported that "the people of Myanmar, which is the
only country not accused by the government to have plotted the
GPPs, have taken the streets in anger" (ZaytungNews 2013c,
b, a). *EkşiSözlük*, on its part, collectively brainstormed on possible bumper sticker suggestions for police TOMAs, some of
which were "the fountain of fascism," "pressurized and furious" (plagiarized from the American movie *Fast and Furious*),
and "Whatever Tayyip says" (EkşiSözlük 2013e). İnciSözlük,
another user-based online dictionary, joined in with a bright
idea to "hide the country away" before Erdoğan returns from
his North African visit, so that he would be lost on the way
back and the people would be saved from him. Long amusing
debates were held, using moving metaphors, to relocate the
country "without breaking it" (İnciSözlük 2013). Photo, video,
and GIF generation through plagiarism was another online
tool dynamically used by the protesters. These involved using
images or videos that relate to the AKP's declarations and/or
actions, and then editing them in entertaining ways using captions, music, pastiche, and other techniques. One widely shared
item took the original music video of "Everyday I'm Shuffling,"
and replaced the artists' faces with PM Erdoğan and deputy
Prime Minister Bülent Arınç, and made them dance with the
"chapullers" (YouTube 2013). Concerning media blackout,
another video used footage of NTV reporters in Taksim, and
edited it in such a way that they remain completely silent as
opposed to informing the people (Böbiler 2013). Examples

such as these demonstrated the pace with which the protesters responded to the rhetoric and advances of the government to cognitively divert them in creative ways.

5c. Inter-Movement Alliances and Intra-Movement Conflicts

It is noteworthy to mention that cognitive diversion efforts generated both inter-movement alliances and intra-movement contestation. By building a "good sense" of humor and social criticism, the GPPs helped bring together previously antagonistic groups such as republicans/populists, socialists, Turkish and Kurdish nationalists, gender justice movements, soccer fans, and so on. Nabi Avcı, the AKP's Minister of education, admitted that unlikely alliance in the following words: "We have succeeded in five days in doing something that the opposition wouldn't have been able to do in years...We have made very different segments, groups and fractions meet each other under the dust who would never have gotten together under normal conditions" (HürriyetDailyNews 2013f). For many groups, one outcome of such an amalgamation enabled the process of getting introduced to and empathizing with what used to be regarded as their opponents. Three such examples will be briefly touched upon here, which are crucial for the transformative political consciousness of the GPPs: the meeting of some Kurdish and Turkish nationalist groups, the meeting of secular and Muslim people, and the meeting of feminist/LGBT and heterosexual communities. We then exemplify some intra-movement contestation regarding symbols and slogans.

As for the first one, although the Kurdish movement in Turkey restrained from officially participating in the GPPs, some elements of it joined the ranks of Gezi protesters, particularly Kurdish students and individual figures of BDP such as Sırrı Süreyya Önder and Gültan Kışanak. Most other Kurdish participants joined the protests by expressing themselves with victory signs and *poşu*s (traditional scarves), and despite some tensions between those who carried PKK leader Abdullah Öcalan's posters and those who carry Atatürk posters, there were no major clashes reported. Instead, the symbolic photo of a couple running away from police attacks hand in hand, one carrying a Turkish flag (decorated with the image of Atatürk) and the other holding a BDP flag, was widely shared on social media sites, and became one of the symbols of the movement underlining the alliance of nations. With regard to the media blackout, moreover, many Turks shared remorseful tweets online saying, "In the last thirty years, we've been learning about the Kurdish issue from this media," and "I apologize my Kurdish brother," which indicated a realization in the population, especially after being branded as terrorists by Erdoğan, that the Kurdish issue may not have been as one-sided as they had been told in the previous decades (EkşiSözlük 2013b, c).

In the aftermath of June 16, 2013, after the police recaptured Gezi Park to end the first phase of the protest cycle, these achievements produced more concrete instances of inter-movement alliances thanks to the collective mobilization led by the Taksim Solidarity Platform and some Kurdish groups. The alliance was particularly in reaction to the government repression in the town of Lice, Diyarbakır, where the gendarmerie forces shot a villager dead on June 29, 2013 during the protests against the construction of a police station. Across the country in numerous cities, protests were organized in support of Lice (RadikalDailyNews 2013g). The inter-movement alliances were expressed via slogans such as "together against fascism," "long live the brotherhood of peoples," "Resist Lice, [name of city] is with you," "Turks and Kurds are brothers, don't lay hand on my brother," and "The AKP wants war, peoples want peace."

The inter-movement alliance between secular and Muslim protesters was another significant instance of solidarity during the GPPs. "During the protests, when the Anti-Capitalist Muslims [as well as the Revolutionary Muslims] started to pray, a human chain was formed around them [by secular groups] to protect against disturbance from the crowds. The Gezi Park protests witnessed many such examples of religious-secular collaboration" (Majalla 2013). For instance, as the ninth of the protests coincided with *Miraç Kandili*, a religious celebration of significance, many protesters distributed the traditional bagels associated with the event (*kandil simidi*) in and around the park in Istanbul and in other cities. In the immediate aftermath of the protests' first cycle, moreover, the month of Ramadan witnessed "public *iftars*" (breaking of the fast) in July 2013, where hundreds of secular and religious groups joined together on Istiklal Street to dine over long floor tables. These were in particular opposition to the "official *iftar*" events held by the government that took place in luxurious settings or by the endorsement of municipalities (WorldBulletin 2013). It is moments of solidarity like these that "have dented ... Erdogan's efforts to paint the protests as part of a long battle between coup-addicted, dissolute, secular 'white Turks' and downtrodden pious 'Black Turks'" (TheEconomist 2013b). The common ground between secular and Muslim groups was the GPPs' anti-neoliberal thrust and search for social justice.

For many protesters, a similar pattern of "meeting" was with various LGBT movements, whose active involvement in the GPPs created an unprecedented environment of support and solidarity. As mentioned in the previous chapter, the synergy between the LGBT movements and other Gezi participants yielded its fruits on June 30, 2013, when the eleventh LGBT Pride March witnessed the largest recorded participation in the country. The massive march included slogans such as "everywhere is Taksim, everywhere is resistance," "shoulder to shoulder against fascism," "no emancipation alone, it's all of us or none," "this is just the beginning, keep up the struggle," and "resist Lice, homosexuals are with you." The unity was present throughout the protests. The US-based LGBT organization GLAAD (2013), for instance, reported that "in the midst of the tear gas and rubber bullets," heterosexual and LGBT groups "have united in ways they never have before," as the latter "have become deeply entrenched in the movement." Such solidarity—in a predominantly homophobic society—is explained by the fact that "when people tasted firsthand the experience of what it is like to be pushed to become the 'other,' they better understood the challenges of these suppressed people, and the heterosexual community has earned a sincere empathy for them" (Al-Monitor 2013c). Political consciousness of the GPPs was built on alliances such as these against the conservative interventionism and police repression of the AKP government.

Besides these instances of recognition and empathy, the GPPs also created alliances and contestations within leftward groups, particularly regarding the use of slogans and symbolism. An example of alliance was the collective organization of the "First Gasman Festival" in Istanbul on July 7, 2013 with the participation of around 15,000 people (HürriyetDailyNews 2013c). The naming of the festival itself was an instance of cognitive diversion, laughing off the extensive use of gas bombs by the police. The festival included a "chapuller fashion show," music performances, and took as its symbol the scale model of a police TOMA. A unique element of the festival was its collective organization by a variety of political movements ranging from communists/socialists to nationalists and populists under the lead of numerous media organizations (including *Odatv, Sol Gazetesi, Ulusal Kanal, Cem TV, Halk TV, Cem Radyo, Yön Radyo, Yurt Gazetesi, Aydınlık Gazetesi, BirGün, and Cumhuriyet*). The festival helped bridging and extending various perspectives, where slogans such as "Long live the brotherhood of the peoples," "We are the soldiers of Mustafa Kemal," "This is just the beginning, keep up the struggle," and "Everywhere is Taksim, everywhere is resistance" were chanted. The popularity of the festival was furthered thanks to the participation of a large number of publicly known music bands, artists, and intellectuals. Following the Gasman Festival, the newspapers and networks that organized the festival held a panel named the "Independent Media Panel" in Kadıköy.

Within the GPPs, an important intra-movement contestation was on the use of national symbols and slogans. It was common

among many Gezi participants to carry Turkish flags decorated with a portrait of Mustafa Kemal Atatürk. The decora-
tion served to distinguish oneself from the supporters of AKP,
while still using the Turkish flag as a symbol. For many groups
within the Turkish left (with the exception of İP, which consid-
ers the Turkish flag as a symbol of anti-imperialist and revolutionary symbol), the Turkish flag was a taboo in that the idea
of marching under the Turkish flag was unacceptable in the era
preceding the GPPs. The TKP, for instance, who had actively
refused to join movements involving the Turkish flag (such as
the Republican Demonstrations of 2007), argued in the GPPs
for the pertinence and legitimacy of appropriating the flag by
the left, particularly to liberate it from the monopoly of right-
wing movements. What is more, the meaning of the Turkish flag
itself became a larger site of contention between supporters and
opponents of the AKP, where the protesters' active utilization
of the flag as a modern Republican symbol was met with the
hanging of flags over police panzers, and the PM's accusing of
protesters as "flag burners." To differentiate between the "two
flags," Erdoğan urged his followers to hang "undecorated"
Turkish flags in their balconies, and encouraged them to also
use Ottoman flags (with three crescents).

Some other leftist, anti-militarist, and anti-nationalist groups
strongly rejected and criticized the use of Turkish flags and of
Kemalist slogans, and expressed their discontent through cognitive diversion against such national symbols. Some slogans
that refer to national values such as "Neither USA nor EU,
Fully Independent Turkey" and "We are Mustafa Kemal's soldiers" took their share from the contesters' humorous initiatives of cognitive diversion: "Long Live Fully Independent Kuru
Kahveci Mehmet Efendi," "We are Mustafa Keser's [a folk music
singer] soldiers," "We are Freddy Mercury's Soldiers," "and
we are no one's soldier." A similar challenge was promoted by
feminist and LGBT movements who reacted against the use of
sexist/homophobic slogans and swear words by painting over
such graffiti with purple paint and by chanting such slogans

as: "insurgency with obstinacy, not with swear words," "swearing is an act of violation, resist with obstinacy," and, "put an end to sexism." Their voices were not left unheard. As one observer notes, "The Gezi resistance has given way to a process of learning and understanding between the Çarşı football fans on the one hand and the LGBT and women's rights organizations on the other. The latter has been endeavoring to cleanse the language of protest from sexist and homophobic expressions, and the former has been quite attentive to such warning" (Demirsu 2013). Lastly, the dichotomy between peaceful and violent protesters was noted when an online banner "you're not welcome, oaf!" was widely circulated, which was a call against the use of violence in the GPPs.

Reprise and Review

The multifaceted mechanisms of collective leadership, organization, and action repertoires employed in the GPPs generated a unique communal subjectivity and cognitive structures that translated into the political consciousness of the movement. The political consciousness of the GPPs, however, was far from being homogeneous. Yet the identification of a common threat, solidified in the neoliberal-authoritarian advances of PM Erdoğan and his government, created the conditions of possibility for the "carnivalesque" throughout the events. It was this carnivalesque atmosphere that brought together diverse and previously discordant groups, and gave them a chance to know and empathize with rival groups—be it in the form of opposing nationalisms, religiosity/secularity, perceptions of gender, and so on. It remains to be seen whether such instances of communication will generate more permanent bonds and unity. The immediate impact of these alliances, however, was reflected in the transformative political consciousness of the GPPs and its cognitively liberating forms of expression.

Revolving around the label of "chapulling," the consciousness of the movement found its strength and vitality in the active exercise of cognitive diversion, which was based on turning upside down the dominant political-ideological perspectives via creative humor and plagiarism; and throwing them back at their propagators. This way, the movement found itself largely immune from the government's consistent slanders and other psychological advances, and managed to preserve the ethical high ground through the collective practices of disproportionate intelligence. The unique political consciousness engendered during the events crafted a participatory framework where everybody was encouraged to be a "philosopher" on their own right and to challenge "commonsensical" assumptions, while still being a part of mass mobilization. In this process, the Gezi Park protesters across the country developed a high level of counter-hegemonic responsiveness, that is to say, a quick rate of reaction to halt and divert official propaganda both on the streets and on online platforms, which is an enduring influence, a learned reflex that lives on well beyond the GPPs. The final chapter will elaborate further on "life after Gezi" and its various other legacies.

6

Looking Ahead: "Gezi Spirit" and Its Aftermath

Neoliberal globalization as a class project is based on dynamics of unequal and combined development that not only present themselves in distinct geographical patterns of capital accumulation, but also in dissimilar configurations of political power and cultural/ideological transformations (Peck and Theodore 2012). Correspondingly, a fuller understanding of the sociospatial struggles against different manifestations of the neoliberal offensive requires a detailed knowledge of the geographical specificities in question. Despite their differences, in such processes of anti-neoliberal mobilization around the world, "the most obvious tangible struggles are over access to land and living space," which go hand in hand with "struggles over dignity, recognition, self-expression, and acknowledgement of... rights" (Harvey 2005b, 84). As a nationwide, spontaneous, and disruptive protest cycle facing "neoliberalism with Islamic characteristics" in the particularity of Turkey, the Gezi Park Protests constitute a rich, diverse, and versatile example of an extra-parliamentary uprising, carried out by an alliance of wage-earning class fractions for the preservation of communal space and social rights. Using ample evidence on the case analyzed through a Marxist political sociological perspective, it was the dual purpose of this book to recount the story of this exceptional mass initiative and to offer a critical contribution to the social movements literature based on empirical findings. This concluding chapter summarizes the main arguments and theoretical contributions of the book, discusses the post-Gezi developments in Turkey, and underlines the significance of the GPPs as a disruptive/extra-parliamentary mass mobilization initiative in the neoliberal era.

Influenced by the work of James Petras and Henry Veltmeyer, our central arguments were constructed on a four-pillar model of Marxist collective action analysis. More precisely, the model we utilized identified four different yet interrelated constituents of a social process that transformed the "private discontent" of the previously fragmented masses into "collective action" through extra-parliamentary/disruptive strategies and frontal tactics. These elements were (a) the structural social class base, (b) conjunctural conditions and "opportunities," (c) organizational forms and strategies/tactics, and (d) articulation of political consciousness (Petras and Veltmeyer 2013, 204, 216–217). After providing in Chapter 1 a general Marxist critique of new social movement theories, their reflections on the (neo)-liberal left thought in Turkey, and the latter's inadequate interpretation of the GPPs, we have shifted our attention in the rest of the book to respectively deal with each of the four analytical pillars in our investigation of the events. Criticizing civil society centrism, cultural reductionism, post-Marxist pluralism, poststructuralism, and/or postmodernism associated with the "classless" approaches of the New Left, our analysis sought to shed light on the political-economic and cultural-ideological foundations of Turkish neoliberalism as they pertained to the GPPs.

Contesting the mainstream perspectives that hastily branded the movement as a "middle-class" undertaking, Chapter 2 demonstrated, through Poulantzas and Wright's structural theories of class, that the GPPs brought together an alliance of various wage-earning class fractions sharing the common destiny of decreased class capacities and life-chances as well as increased precariousness and proletarianization under the AKP-led neoliberalism. The argument that Gezi was not a class movement

because it did not immediately voice concerns regarding processes of surplus value production (such as wages, contracts,
bargaining, or work hours) is undoubtedly based on a very narrow understanding of class politics, which neglects the larger
framework of the struggle that involves "the active defense of
environments, of social relations, of processes of social reproduction, of collective memories and cultural traditions...against the
destructive consequences of commodification" (Harvey 2005b,
87). In this sense, to recap the words of Boratav, Gezi was rather
a "matured class reaction" that disruptively confronted the various manifestations of neoliberalization in Turkey. Consequently,
the chapter also held that the cultural-ideological configurations
particular to the case of Turkish neoliberalism brought forward
the secularly oriented class fractions in the protests, due to the
AKP's Islamically legitimated subordination of a large segment
of the working population through paternalistic labor relations,
conservative trade unionism, and religious social aid networks.
Relatively free from these influences, the AKP's authoritarian
social and spatial interventionism based on an Islamic worldview made secular class fractions more sensitive to the perils of
neoliberalism, and robustly mobilized their organizational class
capacities.

Chapter 3 elaborated further on "neoliberalism with Islamic
characteristics" in Turkey to explain the socio-spatial conjunctural opportunities that triggered secularly oriented wage-
earning class fractions to take the lead in the GPPs. We thus
supplemented Harvey's political-economic notion of "spatial
fix" with what we call the "political-cultural fix" to underline
neoliberalism's need to extensively rely on the political-cultural
readjustment of society and space in parallel with the market-
based transformation of the economy and accumulation processes. Political-cultural fix, as a form of social control and
political legitimation, is by definition geographically specific,
which, in the case of Turkey, amalgamated the AKP's neoliberal plunder of urban space through rent-seeking investment
schemes with the lavish imposition of an Islamic discourse, and

neo-Ottomanist symbolism and *Weltanschauung* along with ultra-conservative social interventionism. For the Gezi protesters, therefore, protection of urban social and natural space against neoliberal commodification was firmly intertwined with resisting the AKP's Islamically driven authoritarian moral impositions and limitations as to how they should and they should not live their lives in the public sphere. As Moudouros (2014, 191) notes, "in the case of Gezi Park and Taksim Square, the protesters claimed to maintain the wider space as a field for social life and activity. Therefore, they placed barriers to prevent its commercialization and submission to the AKP's ideological vision." In addition to these political opportunities that brought forward the secularly oriented class fractions, the rising judicial arbitrariness and repressive authoritarianism inherent to the AKP government was another major factor that went hand in hand with sociospatial interventionism, which was exacerbated further with the government's warmongering Syrian policy that began claiming lives at home. Our examination showed that a combination of these internal and external factors proved influential in creating the immediate conjunctural environment for the massive protest cycle.

Continuing with our Petras and Weltmeyer-influenced model, Chapter 4 brought us to the organizational forms and resistance strategies and tactics employed by the participants of the GPPs. With regard to organizational forms, our analysis strongly rejected the false dichotomy between "spontaneity" and "leadership," which was promoted widely by the (neo-)liberal left to depoliticize the movement by glorifying the former while demonizing the latter. Instead, the empirical data suggested that spontaneity and leadership were not mutually exclusive, but mutually enabling during the GPPs in enhancing the political capacity of the movement. Our understanding of leadership here did not refer to a single center leading the totality of a given movement, but instead, to a collective initiative involving multiple sociopolitical organizations forming counter-hegemonic alliances. It is based on this conception that we closely studied

various political parties, trade unions, occupational associations, civil society platforms, mass organizations, online groups,
gender/LGBT movements, soccer fans, and so on that not only
took part in the GPPs, but also fused with the masses to join
the mechanisms of collective leadership that gave the movement its grassroots/democratic character. The dynamism of this
participatory framework gave birth to the practice of what we
call "repertoire cultivation." In the rest of the chapter, we went
on to illustrate that the multiple alliances and mass mobilization present in the GPPs enabled the "refinement," "transfer,"
"expansion," and "generation" of movement strategies and tactics, which developed the communal capabilities and know-how
of disruptive actions as well as a collective culture of resistance
widely internalized and practiced by the masses. We believe that
repertoire cultivation constitutes one of the enduring aspects of
the GPPs in Turkey.

Finally, in relation to the organizational forms and strategies/
tactics of the movement, Chapter 5 elaborated on the various
indicators of political consciousness in the GPPs, expressed in
the form of "disproportionate intelligence." Here, we introduced
our concept of "cognitive diversion" as a vital ideational tool
for the political consciousness of mass mobilization. The GPPs
provided plentiful evidence to exemplify the operational logic of
cognitive diversion. Against the various advances of the repressive and Islamic neoliberal urban-cultural transformations in
Turkey, and in response to the violent, dismissive, slandering,
and conspiracy-driven reaction of the government against the
protests, cognitive diversion served as a collectively developed
mechanism to reverse, demystify, undermine, and ridicule such
ideational assaults through humor and plagiarism. Expressed in
creative slogans, tweets, music, graffiti, photo captions, videos,
and other forms of physical and online media, disproportionate
intelligence thus became a unifying instrument. Embodied in
the common practice of "chapulling," it contributed to the creation of the carnivalesque that connected diverse and previously
discordant groups in an environment of relative understanding

and empathy. This is not to say that the meeting process was all rosy. It was subject to various disagreements, contestations, challenges, and negotiations regarding various symbols and slogans, which however enriched rather than weakened the political consciousness of the GPPs as long as the unity was present. Overall, the GPPs left a valuable heritage of cognitively liberating practices whose effects cannot be easily undone in Turkey's political-ideational realm in Turkey.

Having scrutinized the complex process that transformed private discontent into collective action in the GPPs, the aftermath of the events should be elaborated on to better assess Gezi's implications for Turkey. Our objective here is not to provide a comprehensive list of what happened in the country during the year that followed the GPPs, but to conceptually approach the period drawing on accumulated evidence. It is our contention that the sociopolitical developments that took place during the 12 months that followed May 2013 have crystallized certain tendencies that would justify qualifying the GPPs as having instigated a "critical juncture" in Turkish politics, whose conclusions cannot yet be determined due to the ongoing nature of the process. "Critical junctures" in political/historical sociology refer to contingent, yet significant historical intervals that end up creating novel trajectories through "the adoption of a particular institutional arrangement from among...alternatives" (Mahoney 2000, 513). Contingency here does not mean that "the event is truly random and without antecedent causes," but that the particular transpiring of a momentous phenomenon, such as a massive disruptive protest cycle in our case, opens an unexpected and critical window of opportunity for relatively rapid transformations, although with no definite outcome. It is based on this understanding that we refer to the GPPs as having prompted a contingent and unstable period in the AKP rule since 2002, whose most discernible novel characteristic is virtually ceaseless street protests met with aggravated police violence to protect an increasingly personal regime. In the narrowest sense of the term, the GPPs were over on June 16, 2013 as the police recaptured the park by force. Yet once identified as inau-gurating a critical juncture in the countrywide sociopolitical scene, it can be concluded that the historical process originated in Gezi has in fact never come to an end. On the contrary, the GPPs were only the primary markers of a new period in Turkey, the outcome of which will be determined by the playing out of social forces.

Theoretically, we know that as a critical juncture comes to an end, the result is the creation of "path dependencies," namely, historical trajectories "in which contingent events set into motion institutional patterns or event chains that have deterministic properties" (Mahoney 2000, 507). That is to say, the closure of a critical juncture, by definition, is expected to generate par-ticular restrictions that subject sociopolitical actors to a certain course of action based on pathways they have followed during the contingent period. Returning from that path becomes all the more costly and increasingly impossible in positive correlation with the passing of time, as actions that have been undertaken in the contingent period give way to institutional configura-tions, practices, and ideational structures. Writing in May 2014, although the critical juncture set off by the GPPs in Turkey are ongoing, the year that followed the events has produced palpable tendencies that seem to be solidifying particular path dependen-cies for all actors involved—the AKP government in particular. More precisely, we argue that the reaction the AKP gave to the mass mobilization, which was based on extreme police violence, conspiracy theories, lies, and patronizing slander (as exempli-fied in Chapter 5), has gradually locked the government in a political path that necessitates further centralization of power to be able to hold on to its rule. In other words, one of the unintentional consequences of the GPPs was to subject the AKP toward a path dependency to constantly deepen, extend, and intensify its repressive-authoritarian rule for the continuation of the class project called "neoliberalism Islamic characteristics" in Turkey. By shaking the material and ideational foundations of this regime and placing it on the defensive, the GPPs have fully exposed and aggravated the dictatorial tendencies inherent in this political-economic and cultural-ideological bloc.[1]

6.1 The AKP's Longest Year and Its Path Dependencies

The year following the GPPs has provided abundant evidence in support of this argument, where all the grievances that triggered the events were further exacerbated as Erdoğan's government took an even more pronounced, reckless, and unapologetic authoritarian turn. With regard to ultra-conservative social interventionism, for instance, Erdoğan personally imposed a controversial regulation in November 2013 to ban co-ed university dorms where "boys and girls...are living together," and sought to extend that further to prevent male and female students from sharing private homes. With such a move, as noted in Al-Monitor (2013a), "it is not hard to foresee that the self-styled morality guardians of neighborhoods and apartment buildings will now feel emboldened to harass unmarried couples or men and women sharing homes." In the city of Edirne, the unconstitutional yet *de facto* policy bore its fruits when a twenty year-old male university student fell from his girlfriend's balcony and died as he was trying to escape police harassment regarding the two of them being in the same apartment (CumhuriyetNews 2013). Moreover, abortion, which had been limited to 10 weeks in 2012 and was another controversial issue leading to the GPPs, has been effectively banned—or made virtually impossible—in state hospitals by March 2014. In a declaration issued by the Turkish Society of Obstetrics and Gynecology, it was revealed that "abortion has been removed from the online appointment system without any legal basis," and that all services regarding "abortion were automatically stopped" (HürriyetDailyNews 2014a).

Concerning the neoliberal transformation of urban space, the AKP also intensified its efforts to open cities to capitalist plunder. In August 2013, the government undertook demolishing a forest in the Middle East Technical University (Ankara) for a road construction project, which was met with strong resistance from the students and sparked movements across the country in solidarity (Bianet 2013b). Meanwhile, the "Taksim Pedestrianization Project" along with the plans for the third bridge, third airport, TOKI projects, and so on are still being enforced, which is despite court decisions and various reports by environmental, professional, and urban planning organizations underlining their illegality and potential to cause severe socio-natural hazards (RadikalDailyNews 2014a, e). In addition to the already existing plans for "accumulation by construction," a new colossal construction project titled "Yenişehir İstanbul" was introduced in early 2014, according to which a virtual city within Istanbul will be constructed to house 2.5 million residents (RadikalDailyNews 2014c).

As for the immediate impacts of the GPPs that created an increasingly authoritarian path dependency for Erdoğan and his party, the mass initiative's contribution to revealing and escalating the internal power struggles within the Islamic-neoliberal power bloc stands out as its most disruptive consequence. Only months after the massive June uprising, which continued in smaller-scale and intermittent organizational forms in the fall, the decade-long alliance between the AKP government and the Gülen Movement came to a spectacular end by the end of 2013. Although Gezi was not the only factor in this divorce, which came to a point of no return in December with the eruption of major corruption scandals, its destabilizing influence against the *modus operandi* of "neoliberalism with Islamic characteristics" cannot be overlooked. For our present analysis, instead of the intricate dealings between the AKP and the Gülen Movement and the details of their break-up, we are more interested in how the fallout, in which Gezi was a catalyst and accelerator, further exposed, factored in, and strengthened the AKP's authoritarian trajectory in multifaceted ways.

On December 17, 2013, through orchestrated raids at dawn, the Gülenist faction within the Turkish police detained the sons of three AKP ministers and more than 30 other AKP-related officials and businessmen on charges of corruption, bribery, and tender rigging. In the raids, millions of dollars and euros in cash, gold, bill counters, and several safe vaults were found in private homes (FinancialPost 2014). State housing agency TOKI, which lies at the heart of the government's neoliberal spatial fix (as discussed in Chapter 3), proved to be central in the corruption scheme that embezzled massive public funds (along with Halkbank, which is Turkey's main intermediary with Iran). Three construction sector tycoons in close association with TOKI (Ali Ağaoğlu, Osman Ağca, and Emrullah Turanlı) were among the detainees, who are in addition to Murat Kurum, the head of TOKI's commercial arm, and the son of Erdoğan Bayraktar, the Minister of Environment and Urban Planning and the ex-president of TOKI. The Gülen Movement, a close ally of the AKP since the beginning and known to have increased its "influence inside the judicial and security apparatus" with the help of this party to play a key role in the controversial *Ergenekon*, *Sledgehammer*, and *KCK* cases, is suspected to have exposed the corruption as their partnership came to an end (TheGuardian 2014c).

Not surprisingly, "like the Gezi protests, the prime minister has brushed off this corruption as an international conspiracy as well," more particularly the US and "Israel in a plot against Turkey" (Haaretz 2014). Erdoğan asserted that these "were 'traps' set up by 'dark forces' at home and abroad," and AKP circles from then on referred to the December 17 events as a "coup attempt" (FinancialTimes 2014a, Reuters 2014b). To cover up for the corruption through spoliation of evidence, the AKP responded immediately with an exceptional anti-Gülenist purge within the police force, judiciary, and national intelligence, while the Ministries of Interiors and Justice changed their regulations to tighten control over these institutions. In the course of a few months, "the government has reassigned or dismissed thousands of police officers and hundreds of judges and prosecutors in what was widely seen as retaliation and a bid to impede investigations" (Reuters 2014c). Moreover, two significant laws have passed in the post-December context: one on the Supreme Board of Judges and Prosecutors (HSYK), and another on the National Intelligence Organization (MIT), both of which substantially institutionalized the AKP's monopolization of power. The HSYK law gave the Minister of Justice unprecedented power over the judiciary, thus completely undermining the separation of powers, whereas the MIT law bestowed the intelligence service with widely expanded authority in surveillance, violation of privacy, and unaccountability that go against any definition of the rule of law (Al-Monitor 2014b). Human Rights Watch declared that the HSYK law would "increase the likelihood of judges and prosecutors being disciplined or reassigned at the behest of the government" by enabling "politically motivated decisions and a form of entrenched government pressure on the council." Regarding the MIT law, the group further stated that it would give immunity to secret service personnel "who violate human rights in the course of their duties," as well as allowing "the intelligence agency unfettered access to private data without a court order" (HumanRightsWatch 2014b, a). These laws speak to the consolidation of the extremely authoritarian path the AKP has been following after the GPPs, to which they are increasingly dependent on so as to preserve their power.

In response to the AKP's purge within the security forces, the Gülen Movement's retaliation began in early 2014 by publicly sharing incriminating tapped phone conversations of various high-profile AKP members, including PM Erdoğan and numerous ministers, which proved their involvement in countless corruption and malpractice schemes. The significance of the recordings—and the government's reaction to them—was that they essentially confirmed every single suspicion and grievance against the government that had originally caused the masses to take to the streets in June 2013. Four of those themes will be discussed here: personalized rule and use of public of funds, employment of religion for social control, government crackdown on media/Internet, and the AKP's aggressive involvement in the Middle East. Erdoğan's conversation with his son on

December 17, 2013, recorded in the immediate aftermath of the corruption scandal, came to be the most sensational and outrageous of the tapes. In the dialog, Erdoğan informs his son about the police operation toward other ministers' sons that morning, and gives him detailed instructions to "dissolve" the money they keep in their home through relocation. After a series of talks throughout the day, Erdoğan's son finally tells him that he "zeroed" all the money except for 30 million euros, which leaves to the imagination the amount of cash they have been illegally hiding at home. In the talks, the names of businessmen with close ties to Erdoğan come up, including the Kalyoncu family, the contractor for the Taksim construction project (Today'sZaman 2014a). The conversation caused nationwide indignation, while Erdoğan defended himself with contradicting statements, simultaneously arguing that his phone was "tapped" and that the recording was "fabricated" by conspirators (BBCNews 2014). Sound analysts and engineers, on the other hand, validated the authenticity of the tape (RadikalDailyNews 2014f).

AKP's instrumental use of Islam as a pacifying political tool was also exemplified in the process. To defend the PM in the face of the major corruption scandal, several religiously justified arguments were presented by pro-government circles. One author, for instance, held that Erdoğan was keeping the fortune at home for the purpose of giving it away as *zekat*—Islamic charity based on wealth, and one of the five pillars of Islam (VatanDailyNews 2014). Likewise, AKP deputy Metin Külünk implied that the PM might have embezzled public funds, yet claimed that investigating into that would be to violate the boundaries of Allah, because "the concept of intervening in the lives of individuals, in a sense taking that right to commit sins" is against Islamic law (Today'sZaman 2014b). In yet another leaked telephone conversation, the AKP's Minister for EU and Chief Negotiator Egemen Bağış said to a journalist friend that he "'tosses' verses from the Quran onto Twitter every Friday," thus admitting his populist exploitation of religious citations. In the conversation, the two men laugh over the Arabic pronunciation of verses, and Bağış describes his process of citing religious material on Twitter as follows: "you can just go on Google, type a word like jealousy or ungratefulness then Baqarah [name of *surah*/chapter] and there you go, you have it" (RussiaToday 2014). Bağış's remarks incited anger in the Muslim community, while a pro-AKP Muslim cleric declared that "listening to, believing in, and disseminating these recordings is *haram*, forbidden by Islam (RadikalDailyNews 2014b).

About political control of the media, several tapes exposed the government's direct intervention to television channels. Leaked phone calls of Erdoğan revealed him giving direct orders to Fatih Saraç of Ciner Media Group on the particular contents of the Habertürk News Network, with which Saraç complied and promised to make the changes immediately (Al-Monitor 2014c). In another recording, Erdoğan personally calls Ferit Şahenk, owner of the Doğuş Media Group, and tells him that he wants certain pro-AKP commentators to be given air time on NTV to influence public opinion (SolNews 2014). The leaked conversations also expose a chain of command within the media corporations, where the instructions coming from the government are communicated to the lower strata within the network. Far from being exceptions, these incidents demonstrated "business as usual" in AKP's relationship with corporate media, where the latter is given detailed orders on every important news item (HürriyetDailyNews 2014b). Concerning restrictions on the Internet, another major law was introduced in February 2014, which allows the government "to block websites without first obtaining a court order…within four hours," and "creates a legal basis to sweep news reports and other online information under the carpet" (AlJazeera 2014). The law, which provoked a wave of mass demonstrations, also allows the government to monitor the private traffic data of individuals without a court order, thus giving them unlimited access to people's lives and communications. According to one cyber law expert, "these are the first steps toward the creation of surveillance society in Turkey" (HürriyetDailyNews 2014c).

Lastly, the adventurous Middle Eastern policy, which we recounted as among the triggers of the GPPs, was unmistakably documented in this period. With the police raid of December 17, 2013, for instance, it was revealed that the state owned bank Halkbank had been in a $13 billion worth "Gas-For-Gold Scheme" with Iran despite trade restrictions Turkey agreed to be a part of (InternationalBusinessTimes 2014). With regard to Syria, however, the evidence is more frightening as they may amount to war crimes. In an article published by the Pulitzer Prize winner journalist Seymour M. Hersh in the *London Review of Books*, it was argued that Turkey (along with Saudi Arabia) was responsible for supplying chemical weapons to the rebels. The article also emphasized that Erdoğan had been "supporting the al-Nusra Front, a jihadist faction among the rebel opposition, as well as other Islamist rebel groups," and seeking to get US endorsement to spark off a war (Hersh 2014). On March 28, 2014, just five days after Turkey shot down a Syrian military plane that was allegedly in airspace violation, a leaked recording of top Turkish officials discussing a military incursion into Syria indisputably confirmed worries of warmongering (BloombergNews 2014). In the recording, top officials[2] are considering organizing false flag attacks on the Tomb of Suleiman Shah (exclave of Turkey landlocked in Syria) so as to create a pretext for invading Syria. It is also disclosed in the conversation that Turkey has transported at least 2,000 trucks of weapons and ammunition to the insurgents in Syria (GlobalResearch 2014, IslamTimes 2014).

All in the course of less than a year, therefore, these internal and external developments suggest that the AKP has been tightening its grip on society after the GPPs to perpetuate its rule. We hold that the path dependency created in the post-Gezi context has practically locked the government in this irreversibly authoritarian trajectory, where such blatant domination over society can only be expected to exacerbate. Especially given the abundance of incriminating evidence and public indignation, loss of power at this stage would unquestionably lead to indictment for Erdoğan and his circle, which is why the AKP regime is aggressively utilizing legal/illegal resources at its disposal to stay in government at all costs. Based on the new Internet law, Twitter, YouTube, and SoundCloud bans in March 2014 to stop the dissemination of the inculpating evidence was only one example of that practice (TheGuardian 2014b). All in all, it was the disruptive mobilization of the GPPs that triggered this process, which has increasingly forced "neoliberalism with Islamic characteristics" to its extremes—that is, to an "all or nothing" path.

6.2 Disruptive Mobilization against Ballot-Box Reductionism

In reaction to the government's unconcealed authoritarian advances during that year, the disruptive resistance repertoires cultivated in the GPPs as well as the humorous cognitive diversion processes have been actively used in intermittent protest initiatives and online platforms, proving that they have consolidated themselves beyond the initial mobilization cycle. In the fall of 2013, as universities were opened and the soccer season began, the mass initiative was reignited in many cities, although sporadically, with graffiti such as "Where were we?" "Gezi Season 2," "We miss the pepper!" "So tell the cops we are back in town" (plagiarizing from a song by Jay-Jay Johanson), and "Hey police did you miss us?" From Gezi onwards, based on different reasons such as the destruction of the METU forest, anti-war initiatives, government restrictions on co-ed apartments, corruption scandal, Internet censorship law, and so on, street protests—coupled with violent police intervention—became rather commonplace in the country.

For instance, as a pro-AKP Islamist lawyer declared that it is a "disgrace" for pregnant women to stroll in public because of "aesthetic" reasons, protests were held where people were dressed up like pregnant women to accompany actually pregnant women (HürriyetDailyNews 2013j). Government's Internet bans, moreover, were protested with graffiti and slogans such as "all browsers of the world, unite!" "No to censorship!" "404 Tayyip not found," "let's shut down the government if the government shuts down the Internet." President Abdullah Gül, who hastily ratified the bill, was subject to an "#unfollowAbdullah-Gul" campaign on Twitter, causing him to lose about 100,000 followers. The massive corruption scandal also found strong resonance on the streets. "Tayyip the Thief!" was written on walls everywhere, along with signs such as "our underwear is cleaner than politics," "Bilal sell your father, live with your honor," and "you have *tarikat* (religious brotherhoods), we have *barikat* (barricades)." Billboards of Erdoğan in subways, which featured his photo with the caption "Strong Will," were vandalized, where the word "Will" was crossed over and replaced with several other adjectives such as "thief," "fascist," "public enemy," and "censorship." Interestingly, shoeboxes came to symbolize the corruption scandal due to the fact that millions of cash was found hidden in shoeboxes in the home of one government official. Protesters with shoeboxes were detained in many cities as part of the government's attempt to cover up for the embezzlement (AlArabiya 2013). The fallout between the AKP and the Gülen Movement, as well as the contents of the various leaked recordings were widely ridiculed on social media sites, where the phenomenon of photo captions using countless popular cultural references became a particularly popular way of providing humorous commentary on the developments as well as a feeling of solidarity (Listelist.com 2014, Onedio.com 2013).

On March 11, 2014, the biggest mass protest cycle since the GPPs took place upon the death of Berkin Elvan, a 15-year-old, who was hit by a tear gas canister during the Gezi events while out to buy bread for his family. Elvan had been in a coma for 269 days, whose condition was closely followed by Gezi protesters in support of the family. Elvan's death created unparalleled exasperation among the people, creating immense mobilization across the country before, during, and after his funeral (TheGuardian 2014a). "Murderer Tayyip!" "Your kids stole, our kids died!" "Natural born killer Tayyip!" "Happy birthday Berkin," "Berkin Elvan is immortal," and "Wake up Berkin, we'll get you that bread" were among the slogans and graffiti during protests, which were also countered by uncontrolled police attacks. Not sharing the grief, PM Erdoğan referred to Elvan as a "terrorist," had his followers boo his mother in a public rally, while Egemen Bağış held that the mourners of the dead teen are suffering from "necrophilia" (HuffingtonPost 2014).

The 12 months following the GPPs definitely felt more than a year for every actor in the Turkish sociopolitical scene, which makes it all the more difficult to recount the period in a chapter. Certain conclusions, however, can be drawn based on the present data. One such conclusion is that a culture of mass mobilization, despite its weaknesses and limited capacity to create immediate change, has been firmly consolidated in Turkey, which goes parallel with the fixed authoritarian trajectory of the government discussed earlier. Various resistance repertoires and tools of cognitive diversion have been collectively internalized in the process, and they proved to be easily reenergized when the political opportunity presented itself. Secondly, in the same extent as the polarization between the government and the mass initiative in Turkey, the two separate cognitive universes inhabited by the AKP and non-AKP groups, which we saw to be created in the GPPs, drifted further away from each other in the post-GPP context in an irreconcilable manner. In the cognitive universe of the people's opposition, although there is not a clear-cut politico-ideological direction, the many faces of the AKP's authoritarianism are identified and quickly reacted against, where the legitimacy and credibility of the government is completely nonexistent after the collective experience during and after the GPPs. The disruptive, humorous, and anti-authoritarian quality of the Gezi spirit lives on in this universe, although there persist significant internal challenges. In the cognitive universe dwelled by the AKP circles, nevertheless, there is much less self-doubt, as there seems to be nothing that cannot be explained by domestic or foreign conspiracy theories, or justified by electoral majoritarianism.

Electoral majoritarianism became all the more visible as the AKP won the municipal elections of March 30, 2014 by receiving 43 percent of the votes. For the AKP, the elections, although shadowed by suspicious power outages and thousands of reports on fraudulent practices that was met with mass protests across the country (SendikaNews 2014, Reuters 2014a), was interpreted as a clear vindication of its authoritarian "neoliberalism with Islamic characteristics." AKP officials had declared on several occasions since the GPPs that the "ballot box" would be the answer to claims of corruption, police violence, and any other unlawful practices. During the "Respect for the National Will" rallies in June 2013, for instance, Erdoğan had uttered: "Gezi is an excuse. The real intention is to plunder. The people will spoil this game, and the finale will be written by the ballot box. If you dare and believe in democracy, wait for the coming elections" (YeniŞafak 2013). Predictably, on the night of the elections in March 2014, Erdoğan declared that the victory was "a full Ottoman slap by the nation" against adversaries, and continued: "The message our precious people gave is very clear…What did they say? They said…'The Turkish people are impassable'…They said, 'we are the owners of this country'…One nation, one country, one flag, one state" (HürriyetDailyNews 2014d). As one commentator noted, Erdoğan's statement represents an aggressive "mentality that translates" the election results "into a one-man rule" in a "narrow-minded and majoritarian manner" (Al-Monitor 2014a). The AKP's interpretation of the electoral success as a license for arbitrariness was further demonstrated by the fact that virtually all charges regarding the corruption scandal were dropped and the confiscated assets were returned to the detained suspects in the post-election context. Another rather tragic outburst of this electorally reductionist logic was witnessed in the aftermath of the Soma mining explosion on May 13, 2014, where more than 300 hundred mineworkers were killed as a result of the extremist neoliberal policies in the Turkish mining sector.[3] Met with strong mass reaction in Soma, Erdoğan called some

protesting families "rascals," and added: "March 30th [the election date] has already given these people the necessary answer.
Particularly in Soma, they have lost [the elections] disastrously"
(DeutscheWell 2014). The clear implication here was that people
did not have the right to voice their concerns, because they lost
the elections.

Turkey's case of "ballot-box reductionism" provides theoretical implications for struggles against the authoritarian
essence of neoliberalism across the globe. More particularly,
the authoritarian nature of the neoliberal state puts into question the limits of parliamentarianism as an agent of progressive social change, and highlights the significance of disruptive
mass initiatives as a popular-democratic alternative to various
faces of neoliberalization. These questions closely resonate with
Frances Fox Piven's notion of disruptive politics. In her classic *Challenging Authority*, Piven (2008) forcefully argues that
genuine democratic change in capitalist societies can only be
achieved through extra-parliamentary "disruptive power" exercised by popular-democratic movements. Refuting the belief
that collective action is "noisy, disorderly, or violent," she
argues that disruptive power finds its fullest expression in the
"breakdown of institutionally regulated cooperation" and the
withdrawing of cooperation by contending groups so as to create new and alternative cooperation networks (Piven 2008, 21,
23). Disruptive power emerges once people's grievances serve
as a means to create new networks of social interdependence or
cooperation by generating new forms of political action outside
of electoral-representative procedures.

As such, Piven's notion of disruptive power seems to fully and
accurately capture what has happened during the GPPs. As a dis-
ruptive/extra-parliamentary, yet inherently political mobilization
of various wage-earning class fractions against "neoliberalism
with Islamic characteristics," the GPPs negated mainstream
accounts that view the essence of democracy exclusively in voting. Underlined in the words of Ellen Meiksins Wood (1998,
196–197), the transition to democratic alternatives "requires

organization and coordination," which would ensure social mobilization beyond promoting the mere act of voting. Using a Marxist framework that amalgamated political-economic and cultural-ideological realities, it was the core task of this book to provide an account of one such instance in the age of neoliberal globalization in view of the particularity of Turkey. Although the outcome of that process, the "critical juncture," may still be uncertain, what is certain is that the GPPs have made, and continue to make, a powerful contribution to popular-democratic initiatives both in Turkey and around the world. As the popularly chanted Gezi slogan goes: "this is just the beginning, keep up the struggle."

Notes

Introduction: Neoliberal Globalization, State Intervention, and Collective Action

1. In a misplaced comparison in September 2013, Egemen Bağış, AKP's Minister for EU Affairs and Chief Negotiator at the time, declared that the number of deaths in the GPPs was "negligible" (*devede kulak*) compared to those in Syria (RadikalDailyNews 2013a).
2. Accordingly, it must be stressed that "neoliberalism with Islamic characteristics" is not intended to be a comprehensive concept to denote the "Muslim world" (Muslim-majority geographies) as a whole in the neoliberal era. Instead, expanding on Karaman's (2013) conceptualization that deals particularly with urban transformations, the term is used here to refer to the multifaceted ways in which the AKP government articulates and embeds Sunni Islam within an aggressive neoliberal agenda in the specificity of Turkey since 2002. The following chapters will demonstrate the various manifestations of "neoliberalism with Islamic characteristics" especially as they pertain to the GPPs.

1   New Social Movement Theories and Their Discontents

1. These figures include, but are not limited to, intellectuals such as Murat Belge, Ahmet İnsel, Baskın Oran, Halil Berktay, Ufuk Uras, Etyen Mahçupyan, Mehmet Altan, Mete Tunçay, Nabi Yağcı, Ferhat Kentel, Taner Akçam, Oral Çalışlar, Hasan Cemal, Fuat Keyman, Oya Baydar, Roni Marguiles, Doğan Tarkan, Nilüfer Göle, etc.
2. The liberal Left *Weltanschauung* rests primarily on the premises of the "center-periphery" approaches that have dominated mainstream social sciences in Turkey since at least the last quarter of the twentieth century (Heper 1980, Mardin 1973). Accordingly, the late Ottoman-Turkish history is interpreted uniformly as a cleavage

between a relatively secular minority bureaucratic elite controlling the state apparatus to dominate the traditional Muslim masses. As an offshoot of this paradigm, the AKP is seen as intrinsically democratic and progressive due to being the representative of the "periphery" against the "center."

3   "Neoliberalism with Islamic Characteristics": Political Economic and Cultural Conjuncture of the GPPs

1. The rise in the construction sector's contribution to Gross Domestic Product, in comparison with agriculture and manufacturing, demonstrates the spectacular influence of the construction sector under AKP. The share of construction grew by 14.1 percent, 9.3 percent, 18.5 percent in 2004, 2005, and 2006 and 18.3 percent and 11.5 percent in 2010 and 2011. The rise in the GDP share of agriculture and manufacture is considerably lower than that of construction: in agriculture, the growth was recorded only as 2.7 percent, 6.6 percent, 1.3 percent, 2.4 percent, and 6.2 percent for the same time period. As for manufacture, the growth amounted to 11.9 percent, 8.2 percent, 8.4 percent, 13.6 percent, and 10 percent (TurkStat 2013d).
2. In January 2014, PM Erdoğan participated in the wedding ceremony of Orhan Cemal Kalyoncu's son to serve as the witness for the marriage. Moreover, in a leaked phone conversation recorded on the first day of the GPPs, the Minister of the Interior Muammer Güler personally assured Orhan Cemal Kalyoncu that he was going to clear the protesters off Taksim (his exact words were "I will fuck them all up"). Leaked phone conversations of AKP officials will be further discussed in Chapter 6.
3. Külliye refers to a Seljuk-Ottoman conception of Islamic architecture that involves a complex of buildings centered around a mosque including religious schools, kitchens, baths, and so on.
4. The choice of Ottoman-Islamic names are not limited to construction projects. A major initiative to introduce tablets in elementary schools, for instance, was named the "Fatih Project," after Fatih the Conqueror. Relatedly, the increase of Islamic-Ottomanist symbolism has been accompanied in early 2013 by the removal of the initials "T.C." (Republic of Turkey) from the signs of certain state institutions/buildings. The latter caused strong reaction especially among the nationalist population, where thousands of people added the initials "T.C." before their names on Facebook.
5. The massive government corruption scandal exposed in December 2013 revealed the centrality of TOKI in the embezzlement of public funds, which will be touched upon in Chapter 6.

6. As we use Freedom House data together with other sources, our disagreement with Freedom House's conceptualization of democracy is immaterial to the present discussion.
7. In March 2014, after years of imprisonment, several of the *Ergenekon* and *KCK* suspects were released.
8. Erdoğan said on International Women's Day 2011 that violence against women is being exaggerated by the main opposition and the media. Fatma Şahin, similarly, declared in May 2013 that violence against women appears to be high due to "selective perception." Other AKP officials did not refrain from blaming the victim in cases of women murders. For instance, as an 18-year-old high school student Münevver Karabulut was decapitated by her boyfriend in 2009, AKP's chief of police in Istanbul accused the Karabulut family, for "they should have kept an eye on their daughter".

4 Organizational-Strategic Aspects of the Gpps: Leadership and Resistance Repertoires

1. The concept of "repertoires" for collective action was introduced to the social movements literature by Charles Tilly in the 1970s. Repertoires (such as sit-ins, strikes, boycotts, public meetings, street protests, online activism, pamphleteering, etc.) refer to resistance "routines that are learned, shared, and acted out" in collective mobilization (Tilly 1995, 26), They emerge from mass initiative, and show variations according to different historical periods, geographies, and types of struggle.
2. The number of people interviewed in each study, as well as the date and location of the interviews are as follows: KONDA: 4.411 people, June 6–7, Taksim. GENAR: 489 people, June 8–9, Taksim. MetroPoll: 500 people, June 11–13, Taksim. Bilgi University: 3,008 people, June 3–4, Online (73.2 percent of the respondents were from Istanbul).
3. TEKEL's association with Gezi was also confirmed in the leaked phone conversation of Muammer Güler, the Minister of Interior. In the conversation recorded during the GPPs, Güler voiced the government's fear that Gezi may turn into another TEKEL, where the protesters "would not leave the premises." Erdoğan, similarly, said in a television interview during the GPPs that in Turkey, "there are some groups who refuse to leave a space when they settle there...We have seen the same thing in Ankara during the issue of TEKEL workers" (BugünNews 2013).

5 Forging Political Consciousness at Gezi: The Case of "Disproportionate Intelligence"

1. Cognitive structures can be simply understood as "interpreted situations and perceived social/collective experiences" (Ingwersen and

Järvelin 2005, 27), or more precisely, "representation[s] of the environment through which people receive and organize information" (White 2001, 309). In more precise terms, cognitive structures refer to the ways in which people process and make sense of information via a combination of comparative thinking (metaphors, classification, etc.), symbolic representation (language, visuals, arts, etc.) and logical reasoning (deductive/inductive reasoning, analogical/hypothetical thinking, cause–effect relationships, etc.) (Garner 2007, 2). They are inscribed by predominant ideological/educational apparatuses in society rather than pure individual choice and interaction.

2. The term "disproportionate violence" became commonplace in the past few years before the GPPs to refer to the excessive police advances, especially during the May Day incidents since 2007. It was through the diversion of this concept that the GPPs referred to their own humorous and creative activities as "disproportionate intelligence." As summarized by one tweet addressing the government: "You may use disproportionate violence. But we have disproportionate intelligence!" The latter concept was used in previous social movements, the first of which was probably the student resistance in the Middle East Technical University upon Erdoğan's visit in December 2010. The concept took a nationwide character in the GPPs.

3. For an extensive list of such allegations along with references to the news sources mentioned, see: http://en.wikipedia.org/wiki/Media_censorship_and_disinformation_during_the_2013_protests_in_Turkey.

4. The lyrics of the song went: "We will find a way, the people are on their feet now/They are behind barricades on the way to Taksim/Are you a çapulcu, a demonstrator?"

5. "Satamayınca gölgelerini sattılar ormanları/Devirdiler kapadılar sinemaları meydanları/Her taraf AVM'den, geçesim yok bu köprüden/Ne oldu bizim şehre ne oldu? Hormonlu bina doldu."

6. "Biberine gazına, copuna sopasına/tekmelerin hasına/eyvallah eyvallah/Saldır bana utanmadan, sıkılmadan/gözlerim yanar/ama ezilmedim, azalmadım."

6   Looking Ahead: "Gezi Spirit" and Its Aftermath

1. This converges with Harvey's argument that by definition, "the neoliberal state is profoundly anti-democratic, even if it frequently seeks to disguise this fact. Governance by elites is favored and a strong preference for government by executive order and by judicial decision arises." That is because the authoritarian nature of the neoliberal

state is "embedded in dominant class relations whose reproduction is fundamental to the social order" (Harvey 2005, 20–21). In the case of Turkey, the GPPs have crystallized these realities in their most visible form.

2. The tape features the Minister of Foreign Affairs Ahmet Davutoğlu, Director of MIT Hakan Fidan, Foreign Ministry Undersecretary Feridun Sinirlioğlu, and Deputy Chief of General Staff General Yaşar Gürel.

3. In many ways, the Soma mining tragedy and its aftermath fully encapsulated the AKP's authoritarian "neoliberalism with Islamic characteristics." It has been unquestionably documented that the neoliberal practices of privatization, deregulation, and subcontracting in the Turkish mining industry since 2005 has made the accident inevitable (Buğlalılar 2014, Yeldan 2014). Moreover, in response to the mass protests in Soma, police used copious amounts of tear gas and pressurized water against the mourning families. Coming to Soma, Erdoğan and his advisor personally beat up some of the protesting citizens, while Erdoğan called one of them "Israeli spawn." Soma was blockaded for weeks by the police, and the government sent in hundreds of Islamic clerics to the town to appease tensions, who advised people that "they could not go to heaven" if they protested. Deeply traumatizing the people, Soma incited huge mass mobilization cycles across the country, where the greedy neoliberal policies and the accompanying police violence and Islamic justifications were strongly protested (FinancialTimes 2014b, TheEconomist 2014).

Bibliography

AkşamDailyNews. *Hedef Yeni Osmanlılık Olmalı* 2012 [cited October 7, 2013]. Available from http://www.aksam.com.tr/roportaj/hedef-yeni -osmanlilik-olmali--155869h/haber-155869.

Akser, Murat and Banu Baybars-Hawks. 2012. "Media and Democracy in Turkey: Toward a Model of Neoliberal Media Autocracy." *Middle East Journal of Culture and Communication* no. 5(3):302–321.

Aladağ, Aras. 2013. *Hegemonya Yeniden Kurulurken Sol Liberalizm ve Taraf.* Istanbul: Patika Kitap.

AlArabiya. *Turkish Woman Detained over Shoebox Protest* 2013 [cited May 2, 2014]. Available from http://english.alarabiya.net/en/News /middle-east/2013/12/30/Turkish-woman-detained-over-shoebox -protest.html.

AlJazeera. *The Odour of Gezi: On the Dangers of Crass Populism* 2013 [cited March 11, 2014]. Available from http://www.aljazeera .com/indepth/opinion/2013/06/201362495929920667.html.

AlJazeera. *New Internet Law in Turkey Sparks Outrage* 2014 [cited May 2, 2014]. Available from http://www.aljazeera.com/indepth/features/2014 /02/new-internet-law-turkey-sparks-outrage-201422312144687859 .html.

Al-Monitor. *Erdogan's "Morality Police" Assume Duty* 2013a [cited May 20, 2014]. Available from http://www.al-monitor.com/pulse/originals /2013/11/turkey-morality-police-erdogan.html.

Al-Monitor. *Is Turkey Heading Toward Civil War?* 2013b [cited March 11, 2014]. Available from http://www.al-monitor.com/pulse/originals/2013 /06/turkey-headed-civil-war-erdogan-protests.html.

Al-Monitor. *LGBT Turks Seek to Capitalize on Gezi Good Will* 2013c [cited May 19, 2014]. Available from http://www.al-monitor.com /pulse/originals/2013/07/turkey-lgbt-gezi.html.

Al-Monitor. *Turkish Muezzin Who Couldn't Lie Is Exiled* 2013d [cited March 10, 2014]. Available from http://www.al-monitor.com/pulse /originals/2013/09/gezi-mosque-alcohol-lie-muezzin-exile.html.

Al-Monitor. *What is Turkey's Role in Syria's Islamic Opposition?* 2013e [cited April 8, 2014]. Available from http://www.al-monitor.com/pulse /originals/2013/09/turkey-syria-islamic-opposition-role.html.

Al-Monitor. *Erdogan: Political Enemies will "Pay the Price"* 2014a [cited May 10, 2014]. Available from http://www.al-monitor.com/pulse /originals/2014/03/turkey-akp-elections.html.

Al-Monitor. *Is Turkey Reverting to a "Muhaberat" State?* 2014b [cited May 10, 2014]. Available from http://www.al-monitor.com/pulse /originals/2014/04/erdogan-mit-interference-authoritarian.html.

Al-Monitor. *Shared Blame for State of Turkish Media* 2014c [cited March 10, 2014]. Available from http://www.al-monitor.com/pulse/originals/2014 /02/erdogan-censors-news.html.

AnadoluAjans. *STK'lardan Gazete İlanıyla Sağduyu Çağrısı* 2013 [cited July 11, 2013]. Available from http://www.aa.com.tr/tr/turkiye/194627 — stklardan-sagduyu-cagrisi.

Andy-Ar. *Türkiye Siyasi Gündem Araştırması: Gezi Parkı Eylemleri* 2013. Available from http://andy-ar.com/wp-content/uploads/2013/06/Gezi -Park%C4%B1-Ara%C5%9Ft%C4%B1rmas%C4%B1.pdf.

Aybet, Gülnur and Filiz Başkan. 2011. "Constitutional Overhaul?" *The World Today* no. 67(6):19–21.

Aydin, Zülküf. 2013. "Global Crisis, Turkey and the Regulation of Economic Crisis." *Capital & Class* no. 37(1):95–109.

BağımsızSosyalBilimciler. 2009. *Türkiye'de ve Dünyada Ekonomik Bunalım, 2008–2009.* Istanbul: Yordam.

Bakhtin, Mikhail Mikhaïlovich. 1984. *Rabelais and His World.* Bloomington: Indiana University Press.

Balaban, Osman. 2011. "İnşaat Sektörü Neyin Lokomotifi?" *Birikim* no. 270:19–26.

Başkan, Filiz. 2010. "The Rising Islamic Business Elite and Democratization in Turkey." *Journal of Balkan and Near Eastern Studies* no. 12(4):399–416.

Baud, Michiel and Rosanne Rutten. 2004. "Introduction." In *Popular Intellectuals and Social Movements: Framing Protest in Asia, Africa, and Latin America*, edited by Michiel Baud and Rosanne Rutten, 1–18. Cambridge: Cambridge University Press.

Baykan, Aysegul and Tali Hatuka. 2010. "Politics and Culture in the Making of Public Space: Taksim Square, 1 May 1977, Istanbul." *Planning Perspectives* no. 25(1):49–68.

BBCNews. *Turkey PM Erdogan Says "Tapped" Phone Call to Son "Fabricated"* 2014 [cited May 20, 2014]. Available from http://www.bbc .com/news/world-europe-26336354.

BBCTurkish. *Erdoğan: Polise Talimatı Veren Benim* 2013 [cited July 4, 2013]. Available from http://www.bbc.co.uk/turkce/haberler/2013/06 /130623_erdogan_erzurum.shtml.

Bedirhanoğlu, Pınar and Galip L. Yalman. 2010. "Neoliberal Transformation in Turkey: State, Class and Discourse." In *Economic Transitions to Neoliberalism in Middle-Income Countries Policy Dilemmas, Crises, Mass Resistance*, edited by Alfredo Saad-Filho and Galip Yalman, 107–127. London: Routledge.

Belge, Murat. Turkey—Normal at Last? 2002 [cited October 7, 2013]. Available from http://www.opendemocracy.net/democracy-europefuture /article_735.jsp.

Belge, Murat. Hangi "İttifak"? 2008 [cited October 7, 2013]. Available from http://www.taraf.com.tr/murat-belge/makale-hangi-ittifak.htm.

Belge, Murat. 2009. "Nationalism, Democracy and the Left in Turkey." *Journal of Intercultural Studies* no. 30 (1):7–20.

Benford, Robert D. and David A. Snow. 2000. "Framing Processes and Social Movements: An Overview and Assessment." *Annual Review of Sociology* no. 26(1):611–639.

Bennett, John T. Cyberspace: Pentagon Declares the Internet a "War Domain" 2011 [cited October 05, 2012]. Available from http://www .globalresearch.ca/cyberspace-pentagon-declares-the-internet-a-war -domain/.

Berberoglu, Berch. 2003. *Globalization of Capital and the Nation-State.* Oxford: Rowman & Littlefield Publishers.

Berberoglu, Berch. 2010. "Global Capitalism in Crisis: Globalization, Imperialism, and Class Struggle." In *Globalization in the 21st Century: Labor, Capital, and the State on a World Scale,* edited by Berch Berberoglu, 113–132. New York: Palgrave Macmillan.

Berktay, Halil. 16 Haziran 2013, Pazar 2013 [cited October 7, 2013]. Available from http://kuyerel.org/yazarlarimizYaziGoster. aspx?id=1318&yazarId=101 - .Ub6YVJivFDA.gmail.

Bianet. *Çarşı'nın Tepkisi Sosyolojiktir* 2013a [cited March 12, 2014]. Available from http://www.bianet.org/biamag/yasam/148057-carsi-nin -tepkisi-sosyolojiktir.

Bianet. *METU Resists to Road Construction* 2013b [cited May 20, 2014]. Available from http://www.bianet.org/english/local-goverment /149434-metu-resists-to-road-construction.

Bianet. *Thousands Rally for LGBT Pride Parade in Istanbul* 2013c [cited March 17, 2014]. Available from http://www.bianet.org/english /gender/139480-thousands-rally-for-lgbt-pride-parade-in-istanbul.

Bilgiç, Esra Ercan and Zehra Kafkaslı. *Gencim, Özgürlükçüyüm, Ne İstiyorum?* Bilgi University 2013. Available from http://www.bilgiyay .com/Content/files/DIRENGEZI.pdf.

BirgünDailyNewspaper. *Halk Geleceğine Sahip Çıkıyor* 2013 [cited June 22, 2013]. Available from http://www.birgun.net/actuels _index.php?news_code=1371802523&year=2013&month=06&day =21.

BirgünDailyNewspaper. *Yıldönümünde BirGün'den 'Gezi' manşetleri* 2014 [cited May 31, 2014]. Available from http://birgun.net/haber /yildonumunde-birgunden-gezi-mansetleri-15076.html.

Blad, Corey and Banu Koçer. 2012. "Political Islam and State Legitimacy in Turkey: The Role of National Culture in Neoliberal State-Building." *International Political Sociology* 6 no. 6:36–56.

BloombergNews. *Turkey Religious Authority Rules Abortion Is Murder* 2012 [cited December 15, 2013]. Available from http://www .bloomberg.com/news/2012-06-04/turkey-religious-authority-rules -abortion-is-murder-ntv-says.html.

BloombergNews. *Turkey's Alevis Outraged by "Executioner" Name for Bridge* 2013 [cited March 14, 2014]. Available from http://www .bloomberg.com/news/2013-05-30/turkey-s-alevis-outraged-by -executioner-name-for-bridge.html.

BloombergNews. *Turkey Blocks YouTube After Syria Incursion Plans Leaked* 2014 [cited May 10, 2014]. Available from http://www .bloomberg.com/news/2014-03-27/turkey-blocks-youtube-after-leak -of-syria-incursion-planning.html.

Böbiler. *Orantısız Basın* 2013 [cited April 1, 2014]. Available from http:// www.bobiler.org/orantisiz_basin_m269383n.

Bohn, Lauren E. and Elmira Bayrasli. *Why Gezi Park Isn't Resonating in the Rest of Turkey* 2013 [cited July 4, 2013]. Available from http:// online.wsj.com/article/SB1000142412788732341960457857383422 5336270.html.

Bonzon, Ariane. Did the Turkish Liberal Intellectuals act as the Islamists' "Useful Idiots"? 2013 [cited February 18, 2014]. Available from http:// arianebonzon.fr/did-the-liberal-intellectuals-act-as-the-islamists -useful-idiots/.

Boratav, Korkut. 2011. *Türkiye İktisat Tarihi 1908–2009*. Ankara: Imge.

Borras Jr, S. M., Marc Edelman, and Cristobal Kay. 2008. "Transnational Agrarian Movements: Origins and Politics, Campaigns and Impact." In *Transnational Agrarian Movements: Confronting Globalization*, edited by S. M. Borras Jr, Marc Edelman, and Cristobal Kay, 1–36. Chichester: Wiley & Sons.

Boserup, Alenius. *Bringing Society Back In: The Arab Spring and the Challenge to State- and Regime-Based Models of Arab Politics* 2012 [cited June 22, 2013]. Available from http://brismes2012.files .wordpress.com/2012/03/alenius-boserup-bringing-society-back-in .pdf.

Buechler, Steven M. 1995. "New Social Movement Theories." *The Sociological Quarterly* no. 36(3):441–464.

Buğlalılar, Eren. *The Prisoners of Democracy AKP Style in Turkey* 2012 [cited July 12, 2013]. Available from http://mrzine.monthlyreview .org/2012/buglalilar030812p.html.

Buğlalılar, Eren. *Unity in Diversity: The June Uprising (a.k.a. Gezi Uprising) of Turkey* 2013 [cited March 2, 2014]. Available from http:// teachingthecrisis.net/wp-content/uploads/2014/03/Unity_in_diversity _Turkey.pdf.

Buğlalılar, Eren. 2014. "Low-Cost Mass Graves for the Working Class: Miners Massacre in Turkey." *Socialist Project*.

Buğra, Ayşe. 1998. "Class, Culture, and State: An Analysis of Interest Representation by Two Turkish Business Associations." *International Journal of Middle East Studies* no. 30(4):521–539.

Buğra, Ayşe. 2002. "Labour, Capital and Religion: Harmony and Conflict among the Constituency of Political Islam in Turkey." *Middle Eastern Studies* no. 38(2):187–204.

BugünNews. *Erdoğan'ın Teke Tek'teki Konuşmasının Tam Metni* 2013 [cited September 21, 2013]. Available from http://gundem. bugun.com.tr/erdoganin-teke-tekteki-konusmasinin-tam-metni -haberi/649842?epeixuojqgtkegmp.

Burkev, Yalcin. *The Gezi Park Resistance and Social Class: A Revolt of the "Middle Class"* 2013 [cited August 5, 2013]. Available from http:// www.socialistproject.ca/bullet/857.php - continue.

BusinessTurkeyToday. *2023 Vision of The Republic of Turkey* 2013 [cited March 15, 2014]. Available from http://www.businessturkeytoday.com /2023-vision-of-the-republic-of-turkey.html.

CanliTV. *Tv Reytingleri* 2013 [cited June 24, 2013]. Available from http:// www.canlitv.com/rating/bilgi.php?tur=tv&tarih=2013-06.

Carragee, Kevin M. and Wim Roefs. 2004. "The Neglect of Power in Recent Framing Research." *Journal of Communication* no. 54(2):214–233.

Castells, Manuel. 2010. *The Power of Identity*. Malden: Wiley-Blackwell.

Çavdar, Tevfik. 2013. *Neoliberalizmin Türkiye Seyir Defteri*. Istanbul: Yazılama.

CNN-TURK. *Gezi Parkı Tweet'lerinin Linguistiği!* 2013 [cited June 15, 2013]. Available from http://www4.cnnturk.com/2013/bilim .teknoloji/06/15/gezi.parki.tweetlerinin.linguistigi/711774.0/index .html.

CNNWorld. *Turkish-Armenian Blogger Sentenced to Turkish Prison for Blasphemy* 2013 [cited March 14, 2014]. Available from http://www .cnn.com/2013/05/23/world/meast/turkey-blasphemy-sentence/.

Çolak, Yılmaz. 2006. "Ottomanism vs. Kemalism: Collective Memory and Cultural Pluralism in 1990s Turkey." *Middle Eastern Studies* no. 42(4):587–602.

Cook, Steven and Michael Koplow. *How Democratic Is Turkey?* 2013 [cited April 10, 2014]. Available from http://www.foreignpolicy .com/articles/2013/06/02/how_democratic_is_turkey.

Cosar, Simten and Gamze Yucesan-Ozdemir. 2012. *Silent Violence: Neoliberalism, Islamist Politics and the AKP Years in Turkey*. Ottawa: Red Quill Books.

CumhuriyetNews. *Kızlı Erkekli Ev İhbarı Üniversiteli Gencin Ölümüne Neden Oldu* 2013 [cited May 20, 2014]. Available from http://www .cumhuriyet.com.tr/haber/22883/Kizli_erkekli_ev_ihbari_universiteli _gencin_olumune_neden_oldu.html?lnrzpcesiaynzahy.

Dağtaş, Seçil. *The Politics of Humor and Humor as Politics During Turkey's Gezi Park Protests* 2013 [cited March 10, 2014]. Available from

http://www.culanth.org/fieldsights/397-the-politics-of-humor-and
-humor-as-politics-during-turkey-s-gezi-park-protests.

Damon, Andre. Domestic Spying and Social Media: Google, Facebook "Back Doors" for Government Wiretaps 2013 [cited October 7, 2013]. Available from http://www.globalresearch.ca/domestic-spying -and-social-media-google-facebook-back-doors-for-government -wiretaps/5334449.

Debord, Guy. 2004a. "Définitions." In *Œuvres*, edited by Jean-Louis Rancon and Alice Debord, 358–359. Paris: Gallimard.

Debord, Guy. 2004b. "Mode d'Emploi du Détournement." In *Œuvres*, edited by Jean-Louis Rancon and Alice Debord, 221–229. Paris: Gallimard.

Debord, Guy. 2005. *Society of the Spectacle*. London: Rebel Press.

Demirsu, İpek. 2013. Times of Hope and Despair: Lessons of Democracy Gezi Resistance Has Taught Us. *Critical Legal Thinking*, http://criticallegalthinking.com/2013/06/12/times-of-hope-and-despair -lessons-of-democracy-gezi-resistance/.

DemocracyNOW. *Defiant Turkish Demonstrators 'Finding New Ways to Protest' in Face of Relentless State Crackdown* 2013 [cited April 11, 2014]. Available from http://www.democracynow.org/2013/6/19 /defiant_turkish_demonstrators_finding_new_ways.

DeutscheWell. *Acı, Gözyaşı ve Protesto* 2014 [cited May 25, 2014]. Available from http://www.dw.de/ac%C4%B1-g%C3%B6zya%C5 %9F%C4%B1-ve-protesto/a-17635594.

DigitalTrends. *Arrested for Tweeting in Turkey* 2013 [cited October 7, 2013. Available from http://www.digitaltrends.com/social-media/the -invaluable-role-of-social-media-in-occupygezi-and-protest-culture/.

Diyanet. *Cami Sayısı* 2012 [cited March 14, 2014]. Available from http:// www.diyanet.gov.tr/UserFiles/CKUpload/Upload/2_1_cami_sayisi. xls.

Doğan, Ali Ekber. 2010. "İslamcı Sermayenin Gelişme Dinamikleri ve 28 Şubat Süreci." In *AKP Kitabı*, edited by İlhan Uzgel and Bülent Duru, 283–306. Ankara: Phoenix.

Dorsay, Atilla. 2013. *Quo Vadis Istanbul?* Istanbul: Remzi.

DumanFanPage. *Duman Fan Page Twitter Message* 2013 [cited March 12, 2014]. Available from https://twitter.com/dumanistminik/status /449995579796361216.

DünyaNews. *Biggest Mosque on Asian Side of Istanbul Symbolizes Power of AKP* 2013 [cited August 11, 2013]. Available from http://www .dunya.com/biggest-mosque-on-asian-side-of-istanbul-symbolizes -power-of-akp-176681h.htm.

Durak, Yasin. 2011. *Emeğin Tevekkülü: Konya'da İşçi-İşveren İlişkileri ve Dindarlık*. İstanbul: İletişim.

Eken, Bülent. 2014. "The Politics of the Gezi Park Resistance: Against Memory and Identity." *The South Atlantic Quarterly* no. 113(2):427–436.

EkşiSözlük. *7 Ağustos 2013 Halk TV RedHack Konuşması Tam Metni* 2013a [cited April 22, 2014]. Available from https://eksisozluk.com/7 -agustos-2013-halk-tv-redhack-konusmasi-tam-metni--3961404.

EkşiSözlük. *30 Yıldır Kürt Olayını Bize bu Medya Anlattı* 2013b [cited April 21, 2014]. Available from https://eksisozluk.com/30-yildir-kurt -olayini-bize-bu-medya-anlatti--3858338?focusto=34272396.

EkşiSözlük. *Özür Dilerim Senden Kürt Kardeşim* 2013c [cited April 1, 2014]. Available from https://eksisozluk.com/ozur-dilerim-senden-kurt -kardesim--3878838.

EkşiSözlük. *Paylaşılan Resimleri Doğrulama Yöntemi* 2013d [cited June 22, 2013]. Available from https://eksisozluk.com/paylasilan-resimleri -dogrulama-yontemi—3881388.

EkşiSözlük. *Toma Arkası Yazıları* 2013e [cited April 1, 2014]. Available from https://eksisozluk.com/toma-arkasi-yazilari--3869422?p=1.

Engel-Di Mauro, Salvatore. 2006. *The European's Burden: Global Imperialism in EU Expansion.* New York: Peter Lang.

EngelliWeb. *Engelli Web: İstatistikler* 2014 [cited April 10, 2014]. Available from http://engelliweb.com/istatistikler/.

Erandaç, Bülent. *Yeni Orta Sınıf'ın (Orta Direk) Ruhu ve Ufku* 2013 [cited July 1, 2013]. Available from http://www.takvim.com.tr/Yazarlar /erandac/2013/06/30/yeni-orta-sinifin-orta-direk-ruhu-ve-ufku.

Ercan, Fuat and Şebnem Oğuz. 2006. "Rescaling as a Class Relationship and Process: The case of Public Procurement Law in Turkey." *Political Geography* no. 25(6):641–656.

Erkip, Feyzan. 2005. "The Rise of the Shopping Mall in Turkey: The Use and Appeal of a Mall in Ankara." *Cities* no. 22(2):89–108.

EuroNews. *Turkey's Media Under Fire: Protests at NTV* 2013 [cited April 11, 2014]. Available from http://www.euronews.com/2013/06/03 /turkey-s-media-under-fire-protests-at-ntv/.

EverywhereTaksim. *LGBT Blok Basın Açıklaması* 2013 [cited March 21, 2014]. Available from http://everywheretaksim.net/tr/lgbt-blok-basin -aciklamasi/.

EvrenselNews. *Ayşenur Arslan Uludere Sansürünü Anlattı* 2013 [cited February 12, 2014]. Available from http://www.evrensel.net/haber/70796 /aysenur-arslan-uludere-sansurunu-anlatti.html—.U0l_reZdW80.

Faiola, Anthony and Paula Moura. *Middle-Class Rage Sparks Protest Movements in Turkey, Brazil, Bulgaria and Beyond* 2013 [cited July 1, 2013]. Available from http://articles.washingtonpost.com/2013-06 -28/world/40250885_1_turkey-new-government-arab-spring.

FinancialPost. *Police Probing Corruption in Turkey Seize Millions Stashed in Shoe Boxes* 2014 [cited May 10, 2014]. Available from http:// business.financialpost.com/2013/12/18/police-probing-corruption -seize-millions-stashed-in-shoe-boxes-in-turkish-bank-chiefs-home/.

FinancialTimes. *Business Figures Questioned in Turkey Anti-Corruption Probe* 2014a [cited May 10, 2014]. Available from http://www

.ft.com/intl/cms/s/0/51f07524-66f6-11e3-8d3e-00144feabdc0.html
- axzz32kCytOxD.

FinancialTimes. *Unruly Erdogan Will Preside over a Divided Turkey*
2014b [cited May 25, 2014]. Available from http://www.ft.com/cms/s
/0/74732b02-e025-11e3-b709-00144feabdc0.html - axzz32qtmv6P9.

ForzaBeşiktaş. *Çarşı'dan Açıklama* 2013 [cited March 15, 2014]. Available
from https://http://www.facebook.com/Forzabesiktas/photos/a.14334
5769034289.13384.143288092373390/538328949535967/?type=1&t
heater.

FoxNews. *Istanbul's Bitterly Rival Soccer Fans United for Now by
Turkey's Anti-Government Protests* 2013 [cited June 22, 2013].
Available from http://www.foxnews.com/world/2013/06/10/istanbul
-bitterly-rival-soccer-fans-united-for-now-by-turkey-anti-government/.

FreedomHouse. *Erdoğan's Ambiguous Decade* 2012a [cited September
10, 2013]. Available from http://www.freedomhouse.org/blog/erdo
%C4%9Fan%E2%80%99s-ambiguous-decade—.U4ueQJRdX6w.

FreedomHouse. *The Ergenekon Case and Turkey's Democratic Aspirations*
2012b [cited September 10, 2013]. Available from http://www
.freedomhouse.org/blog/ergenekon-case-and-turkey%E2%80%99s
-democratic-aspirations—.U4uej5RdX6w.

FreedomHouse. *Turkey* 2013 [cited July 3, 2013]. Available from http://
www.freedomhouse.org/report/freedom-world/2013/turkey.

Garner, Betty K. 2007. *Getting to "Got It!"* Alexandria, Virginia:
Association for Supervision and Curriculum Development.

GENAR. *Gezi Parkı Profili* 2013 [cited February 15, 2014]. Available
from http://www.genar.com.tr/files/GEZIPARKI_PROFIL-SON.pdf.

Gill, Stephen. 2011. *Global Crises and the Crisis of Global Leadership.*
New York: Cambridge University Press.

GLAAD. *LGBT Organizations in Turkey Participate (and Are Accepted)
in Gezi Park Protests* 2013 [cited March 11, 2014]. Available from
http://www.glaad.org/blog/lgbt-organizations-turkey-participate
-and-are-accepted-gezi-park-protests.

GlobalResearch. *Intelligence and Social Media: CIA is Monitoring
Twitter and Facebook* 2011 [cited October 7, 2013]. Available from
http://www.globalresearch.ca/intelligence-and-social-media-cia-is
-monitoring-twitter-and-facebook/27480.

GlobalResearch. *Turkey Wages War on Syria: Leaked Recording
Confirms Turkish "False Flag" Attack* 2014 [cited May 10, 2014].
Available from http://www.globalresearch.ca/turkey-wages-war-on
-syria-leaked-recording-confirms-turkish-false-flag-attack/5375807.

Göker, Emrah. *İzlenimler II: Wacquant'a Göre Gezi İsyanı* 2014 [cited
February 18, 2014]. Available from http://istifhanem.com/2014/01/18
/17ocakwacquantizlenim/.

Göle, Nilüfer. 1997. "Secularism and Islamism in Turkey: The Making of
Elites and Counter-Elites." *The Middle East Journal* no. 51(1):46–58.

Göle, Nilüfer. 2002. "Islam in Public: New Visibilities and New Imaginaries." *Public Culture* no. 14 (1):173–190.

Göle, Nilüfer. 2003. "Contemporary Islamist Movements and New Sources for Religious Tolerance." *Journal of Human Rights* no. 2(1): 17–30.

Göle, Nilüfer. *Gezi: Anatomy of a Public Square Movement* 2013a [cited October 7, 2013]. Available from http://www.todayszaman.com/news -317643-gezi-anatomy-of-public-square-movementby-nilufer-gole -.html.

Göle, Nilüfer. Public Space Democracy 2013b [cited October 7, 2013]. Available from http://www.eurozine.com/articles/2013-07-29-gole-en .html.

GoodMorningTurkey. *Mothers of Protesters Join Demos By Forming Human Chain in Gezi Park* 2013 [cited April 25, 2014]. Available from http://www.goodmorningturkey.com/mothers-of-protesters-join -demos-by-forming-human-chain-in-gezi-park/.

Gramsci, Antonio. 1971. *Selections from the Prison Notebooks.* New York: International Publishers.

Gramsci, Antonio. 2000. *The Gramsci Reader: Selected Writings (1916– 1935).* New York: NYU Press.

Gramsci, Antonio. 2012. *Selections from the Prison Notebooks.* New York: International Publishers.

Gümüşcü, Şebnem. 2010. "Class, Status, and Party: The Changing Face of Political Islam in Turkey and Egypt." *Comparative Political Studies* no. 43(7):835–861.

Gürcan, Efe Can. 2010. "The Evolution of Turkish Nationalism: an Unconventional Approach Based on a Comparative and International Perspective." In *Beyond Imagined Uniqueness: Nationalisms in Contemporary Perspectives* edited by Joan Burbick and William Glass, 141–168. Cambridge Scholars Publishing: Newcastle.

Haaretz. *Erdogan: For every 100,000 Protesters, I will Bring out a Million from my Party* 2013 [cited March 11, 2014]. Available from http://www.haaretz.com/news/middle-east/1.527188.

Haaretz. *Erdogan in the Headlights: Crimes, Corruption and Conspiracies* 2014 [cited May 10, 2014]. Available from http://www.haaretz.com/ opinion/.premium-1.565912.

HaberTurkNews. *Başbakan'dan Önemli Açıklamalar* 2013a [cited March 10, 2014]. Available from http://www.haberturk.com/gundem /haber/849277-basbakandan-onemli-aciklamalar.

HaberTurkNews. *"Kendiliğinden Oluşmuş, Planı Yok"* 2013b [cited October 7, 2013]. Available from http://m.haberturk.com/polemik /haber/850716-kendiliginden-olusmus-plani-yok.

HaberlerNews. *Memurun Sendika Tercihi* 2013c [cited July 6, 2013]. Available from http://www.haberler.com/memurun-sendika-tercihi -4803948-haberi/.

Haber7News. *Barbar Beyaz Türk Baharı!* 2013a [cited July 5, 2013]. Available from http://www.haber7.com/yazarlar/hacer-aydin/1034545 -barbar-beyaz-turk-bahari.

Haber7News. *İşte Çamlıca Camii Gerçekleri* 2013b [cited March 27, 2014]. Available from http://www.haber7.com/guncel/haber/1098815 -iste-camlica-camii-gercekleri.

Hallsworth, Simon and John Lea. 2011. "Reconstructing Leviathan: Emerging Contours of the Security State." *Theoretical Criminology* no. 15(2):141–157.

Harvey, David. 2003. *The New Imperialism.* Oxford: Oxford University Press.

Harvey, David. 2005a. *A Brief History of Neoliberalism.* Oxford: Oxford University Press.

Harvey, David. 2005b. *Spaces of Neoliberalization: Towards a Theory of Uneven Geographical Development.* Munich: Franz Steiner Verlag.

Helvacıoğlu, Ender. 2013. "Yeni Türkiye [The New Turkey]." *Bilim ve Gelecek* (114):6–8.

Heper, Metin. 1980. "Center and Periphery in the Ottoman Empire: With Special Reference to the Nineteenth Century." *International Political Science Review* no. 1(1):81–105.

Hersh, Seymour M. *The Red Line and the Rat Line* 2014 [cited May 10, 2014]. Available from http://www.lrb.co.uk/v36/n08/seymour-m-hersh /the-red-line-and-the-rat-line.

HuffingtonPost. *Turkish Newspaper Takvim Publishes Fake Christiane Amanpour Interview* 2013 [cited March 14, 2014]. Available from http://www.huffingtonpost.com/2013/06/18/christiane-amanpour -takvim-turkish-newspaper_n_3460023.html.

HuffingtonPost. *Turkish Politician Accused of Insensitivity Toward Mourners for Dead Teen* 2014 [cited May 2, 2014]. Available from http://www.huffingtonpost.com/2014/03/13/egemen-bagis-necrophiliac -tweet-turkey-protest_n_4952315.html.

HumanRightsWatch. *Turkey: Backward Step for Women's Rights* 2011a [cited September 21, 2013]. Available from http://www.hrw.org /news/2011/06/09/turkey-backward-step-women-s-rights.

HumanRightsWatch. *Turkey: Kurdish Party Members' Trial Violates Rights* 2011b [cited September 15, 2013]. Available from http:// www.hrw.org/news/2011/04/18/turkey-kurdish-party-members-trial -violates-rights.

HumanRightsWatch. *Turkey: President Should Veto Judiciary Law* 2014a [cited May 10, 2014]. Available from http://www.hrw.org /news/2014/02/21/turkey-president-should-veto-judiciary-law.

HumanRightsWatch. *Turkey: Spy Agency Law Opens Door to Abuse* 2014b [cited May 10, 2014]. Available from http://www.hrw.org /news/2014/04/29/turkey-spy-agency-law-opens-door-abuse.

HürriyetDailyNews. *2014 Yılında Türkiye'de 347 AVM Olacak* 2012a [cited July 3, 2013]. Available from http://www.hurriyet.com.tr /ekonomi/20034610.asp.

HürriyetDailyNews. *Barış Şehri Tedirgin* 2012b [cited September 10, 2013]. Available from http://www.hurriyet.com.tr/gundem/21302803.asp.

HürriyetDailyNews. *Turkish PM Insistent on Giant Mosque on Istanbul Hill* 2012c [cited March 14, 2014]. Available from http://www .hurriyetdailynews.com/turkish-pm-insistent-on-giant-mosque-on -istanbul-hill.aspx?pageID=238&nid=35714.

HürriyetDailyNews. *Başbakan: İçeceksen Git Evinde İç* 2013a [cited May 7, 2014]. Available from http://hurarsiv.hurriyet.com.tr/goster/haber.a spx?id=23382843&tarih=2013-05-28.

HürriyetDailyNews. *Başbakan'ın 'Aşırı sendikacı' Dediği Arzu Çerkezoğlu Konuştu* 2013b [cited June 22, 2013]. Available from http://www.hurriyet.com.tr/gundem/23510391.asp.

HürriyetDailyNews. *Crowds Denounce Police Crackdowns in "Man Made of Tear Gas" Festival on Istanbul's Asian Shore* 2013c [cited August 11, 2013]. Available from http://www.hurriyetdailynews.com /crowds-denounce-police-crackdowns-in-man-made-of-tear-gas-festival -on-istanbuls-asian-shore.aspx?pageID=238&nID=50236&NewsCat ID=341.

HürriyetDailyNews. *Erdoğan: "Taksim'e Cami de Yapacağız"* 2013d [cited September 11, 2013]. Available from http://www.hurriyet.com .tr/gundem/23419723.asp.

HürriyetDailyNews. *Fethullah Gülen'den Gezi Parkı Değerlendirmesi* 2013e [cited March 10, 2014]. Available from http://www.hurriyet .com.tr/gundem/23446001.asp.

HürriyetDailyNews. *Gezi Park Protests May Turn 2014 Election Calculations Upside Down* 2013f [cited September 21, 2013]. Available from http://www.hurriyetdailynews.com/gezi-park-protests-may-turn -2014-election-calculations-upside-down.aspx?pageID=238&nID=48 512&NewsCatID=338.

HürriyetDailyNews. *Hasan Kaçan ve Necati Şaşmaz Twitter'ı Salladı* 2013g [cited June 22, 2013]. Available from http://www.hurriyet.com .tr/gundem/23493686.asp.

HürriyetDailyNews. *PM Erdoğan Repeats Previously Denied Reports of Protesters Entering Mosque with Shoes On* 2013h [cited July 5, 2013]. Available from http://www.hurriyetdailynews.com/pm-erdogan -repeats-previously-denied-reports-of-protesters-entering-mosque -with-shoes-on-.aspx?pageID=238&nid=48520.

HürriyetDailyNews. *Police Stage Crackdown on May Day Protesters in Istanbul* 2013i [cited April 12, 2014]. Available from http://www .hurriyetdailynews.com/police-stage-crackdown-on-may-day-protesters -in-istanbul.aspx?pageID=238&nID=45996&NewsCatID=341.

HürriyetDailyNews. *Pregnant Women Gather to Protest Sufi Thinker who Urged Them Not To "Stroll in Public"* 2013j [cited May 2, 2014]. Available from http://www.hurriyetdailynews.com/pregnant-women-gather-to-protest-sufi-thinker-who-urged-them-not-to-stroll-in-public.aspx?pageID=238&nID=51442&NewsCatID=341.

HürriyetDailyNews. *Prime Minister Erdoğan Blesses Turkish Police for "Heroic" Action During Gezi Unrest* 2013k [cited February 10, 2014]. Available from http://www.hurriyetdailynews.com/turkish-prime-minister-erdogan-praises-polices-intervention-in-gezi-protests-as-heroic.aspx?pageID=238&nid=49356.

HürriyetDailyNews. *Ruling Party Member Calls for the "Annihilation of Atheists" on Twitter, Sparking Controversy* 2013l [cited April 21, 2014]. Available from http://www.hurriyetdailynews.com/ruling-party-member-calls-for-the-annihilation-of-atheists-on-twitter-sparking-controversy--.aspx?pageID=238&nID=47441&NewsCatID=341.

HürriyetDailyNews. *Supporter Groups of Istanbul's Three Major Teams Join Forces for Gezi Park* 2013m [cited June 22, 2013]. Available from http://www.hurriyetdailynews.com/supporter-groups-of-istanbuls-three-major-teams-join-forces-for-gezi-park.aspx?pageID=238&nid=48007.

HürriyetDailyNews. *Turkish Prosecutors File Indictment on Controversial Ergenekon Case* 2013n [cited July 3, 2013]. Available from http://www.hurriyet.com.tr/english/home/9430816.asp.

HürriyetDailyNews. *Abortion Banned in Turkish State Hospitals, Health Group Claims* 2014a [cited May 20, 2014]. Available from http://www.hurriyetdailynews.com/abortion-banned-in-turkish-state-hospitals-health-group-claims-.aspx?PageID=238&NID=63512&NewsCatID=341.

HürriyetDailyNews. *"Instructions Rain Down on Turkish Media Every Day," Days Prominent Editor-in-Chief* 2014b [cited March 10, 2014]. Available from http://www.hurriyetdailynews.com/instructions-rain-down-on-turkish-media-every-day-says-prominent-editor-in-chief-.aspx?pageID=238&nID=62306&NewsCatID=338.

HürriyetDailyNews. *"Turkey's New Internet Law Is the First Step toward Surveillance Society,' says Cyberlaw Expert* 2014c [cited May 2, 2014]. Available from http://www.hurriyetdailynews.com/turkeys-new-internet-law-is-the-first-step-toward-surveillance-society-says-cyberlaw-expert.aspx?pageID=238&nID=62815&NewsCatID=338.

HürriyetDailyNews. *Turkish PM Erdoğan's Post-Election "Balcony Speech"* 2014d [cited May 10, 2014]. Available from http://www.hurriyetdailynews.com/full-text-turkish-pm-erdogans-post-election-balcony-speech.aspx?pageID=238&nID=64341&NewsCatID=338.

ILO. *Unemployment Rates* 2013 [cited July 1, 2013]. Available from http://laborsta.ilo.org/sti/DATA_FILES/TABLE_XLS/EN/COU_TUR_UNE_DEAP_RT_EN.xls.

İnciSözlük. *Tayyib Dönmeden Ülkeyi Saklıyoruz Beyler* 2013 [cited April 1, 2014]. Available from http://inci.sozlukspot.com/w/tayyib-d %C3%B6nmeden-%C3%BClkeyi-sakl%C4%B1yoruz-beyler/.

Ingwersen, Peter and Kalervo Järvelin. 2005. *The Turn: Integration of Information Seeking and Retrieval in Context.* Dordrecht: Springer.

İnsel, Ahmet. 2003. "The AKP and Normalizing Democracy in Turkey." *The South Atlantic Quarterly* no. 102(2–3):293–308.

InternationalBusinessTimes. *Turkey's State-Owned Bank Accused of "Cash-for-Gold" Scheme with Iran* 2014 [cited May 10, 2014]. Available from http://www.ibtimes.com/turkish-courts-return-45 -million-cash-found-shoe-boxes-home-ex-head-turkeys-state-owned -bank-accused.

IslamTimes. *Turkey Picks Up on Syrian False Flags Where US-NATO Left Off* 2014 [cited May 10, 2014]. Available from http://www.islamtimes .org/vdcjovethuqea8z.92fu.html.

JadaliyyaReports. *Taksim Solidarity Statement: To the Press and Citizens of Turkey* 2013 [cited June 22, 2013]. Available from http://www .jadaliyya.com/pages/index/12192/taksim-solidarity-statement_to-the -press-and-citiz.

Jasper, James. 1997. *The Art of Moral Protest.* Chicago: Chicago University Press.

Jessop, Bob. *From Localities via the Spatial Turn to Spatial-Temporal Fixes: A Strategic Relational Odyssey* 2004a. Available from https:// http://www.hcu-hamburg.de/fileadmin/documents/Professoren_und _Mitarbeiter/Gernot_Grabher/secons_06_jessop.pdf.

Jessop, Bob. *Spatial Fixes, Temporal Fixes, and Spatio-Temporal Fixes* 2004b [cited September 22, 2013]. Available from http://www.lancaster .ac.uk/sociology/research/publications/papers/jessop-spatio-temporal -fixes.pdf.

Jessop, Bob. 2008. *State Power.* Cambridge: Polity Press.

Juris, Jeffrey S. 2012. "Reflections on #Occupy Everywhere: Social Media, Public Space, and Emerging Logics of Aggregation." *American Ethnologist* no. 39(2):259–279.

KadınKoalisyonu. *Declaration by Women's Coalition Turkey* 2013 [cited October 25, 2013]. Available from http://www.kadinkoalisyonu.org/en /node/177.

Kahraman, Tayfun. 2013. "Kent Hukukunun Yeni Yüzü." In *Istanbul: Müstesna Şehrin İstisna Hali*, edited by Ayse Cavdar and Pelin Tan, 17–50. Istanbul: Sel.

KaosGL. *LGBT'ler Bu Akşam Gezi Parkı'nda Çarka Çıkıyor* 2013 [cited March 28, 2014]. Available from http://kaosgl.org/sayfa.php? id=14262.

Karacimen, Elif. 2014. "Financialization in Turkey: The Case of Consumer Debt." *Journal of Balkan and Near Eastern Studies* no. 16(2): 161–180.

Karaman, Ozan. 2013. "Urban Neoliberalism with Islamic Characteristics." *Urban Studies* no. 50 (16):3412–3427.

Kaya, Yunus. 2008. "Proletarianization with Polarization: Industrialization, Globalization, and Social Class in Turkey, 1980–2005." *Research in Social Stratification and Mobility* no. 26:161–181.

Keller, Bill. *The Revolt of the Rising Class* 2013 [cited July 4, 2013]. Available from http://www.nytimes.com/2013/07/01/opinion/keller-the-revolt-of-the-rising-class.html?pagewanted=all&_r=0.

Kentel, Ferhat. 1998. "Recompositions du Religieux en Turquie: Pluralisme et Individualisation." *Cahiers d'Etudes sur la Méditerranée Orientale et le monde Turco-Iranie* no. 26(1):2–19.

Kentel, Ferhat. 2011. "'Nationalist' Reconstructions in the Light of Disappearing Borders." In *Nationalisms and Politics in Turkey: Political Islam, Kemalism and the Kurdish Issue*, edited by Marlies Casier and Joost Jongerden, 48–64. New York: Routledge.

KESK. *Özgürlüğün ve Demokrasinin Sesini Hiçbir Zorbalık Kesemez!* 2013 [cited June 24, 2013]. Available from http://www.kesk.org.tr/content/%C3%B6zg%C3%BCrl%C3%BC%C4%9F%C3%BCn-ve-demokrasinin-sesini-hi%C3%A7bir-zorbal%C4%B1k-kesemez-g%C3%B6zalt%C4%B1na-al%C4%B1nanlar-derhal-serbest.

Keyman, Fuat. Gezi Park Protests: Need for a Democratic Administration 2013a [cited October 7, 2013]. Available from http://www.turkishweekly.net/columnist/3773/gezi-park-protests-need-for-a-democratic-administration.html.

Keyman, Fuat. Gezi Parkı ve Gençleri Doğru Okumak 2013b [cited October 7, 2013]. Available from http://dunya.milliyet.com.tr/gezi-parki-ve-gencleri-dogru-okumak/dunya/ydetay/1721691/default.htm.

Kılıç, Cem. *1 Mayıs'ı Kutladık da Acaba Sendikalaşmada Neredeyiz?* 2013 [cited July 1, 2013]. Available from http://www.aksam.com.tr/yazarlar/1-mayisi-kutladik-da-acaba-sendikalasmada-neredeyiz/haber-201656.

Koç, Yıldırım. 2009. *İşçi Sınıfı ve Sendika Sorunlarına Ulusalcı Çözüm.* Istanbul: Kaynak.

Koç, Yıldırım. 2010. *Türkiye İşçi Sınıfı Tarihi.* Ankara: Epos.

KONDA. *Gezi Parkı Araştırması* 2013 [cited September 25, 2013]. Available from http://t24.com.tr/files/GeziPark%C4%B1Final.pdf.

Laclau, Ernesto. 1985. "New Social Movements and the Plurality of the Social." In *New Social Movements and the State in Latin America*, edited by David Slater, 27–42. Amsterdam: CEDLA.

Laclau, Ernesto and Chantal Mouffe. 2001. *Hegemony and Socialist strategy: Towards a Radical Democratic Politics.* London & New York: Verso.

LGBTNewsInTurkey. *AKP Dağoğlu's Rebuttal of CHP's Motion to Investigate LGBT Problems* 2013 [cited March 13, 2014]. Available from http://lgbtinewsturkey.com/2013/08/09/akp-rebuttal-lgbt-motion/ - more-13.

Listelist.com. *Telefon Konuşmasının 21 Mizahi Yorumu* 2014 [cited May 2, 2014]. Available from http://listelist.com/kritik-telefon-konusmasi/.

Lovering, John and Hade Türkmen. 2011. "Bulldozer Neo-liberalism in Istanbul: The State-led Construction of Property Markets, and the Displacement of the Urban Poor." *International Planning Studies* no. 16(1):73–96.

Mahoney, James. 2000. "Path Dependence in Historical Sociology." *Theory and Society* no. 29(4):507–548.

Majalla. *Meeting Halfway: Breaking Down the Religious-Secular Cleavage of the Gezi Protests* 2013 [cited April 20, 2014]. Available from http://www.majalla.com/eng/2013/07/article55243840.

Mardin, Şerif. 1973. "Center–Periphery Relations: A Key to Turkish Politics?" *Daedalus* no. 102(1):169–190.

Mason, Paul. *The Hopes that Blaze in Istanbul* 2013 [cited July 1, 2013]. Available from http://www.bbc.co.uk/news/world-europe-22752121.

Matlack, Carol and Steve Bryant. *Turkey's Credit-Card Crunch* 2011 [cited July 7, 2013]. Available from http://www.businessweek .com/magazine/turkeys-creditcard-crunch-10272011.html.

McAdam, Doug. 1982. *Political Process and the Development of Black Insurgency, 1930–1970*. Chicago and London: The University of Chicago Press.

McAdam, Doug, John. D. McCarthy, and Mayer N. Zald. 2008. "Introduction: Opportunities Mobilizing Structures and Framing Processes." In *Comparative Perspectives on Social Movements: Political Opportunities Mobilizing Structures and Cultural Framings*, edited by Doug McAdam, John. D. McCarthy and Mayer N. Zald, 1–22. Cambridge: Cambridge University Press.

MedyaTava. *Gazete Tirajları* 2013 [cited June 22, 2013]. Available from http://www.medyatava.com/tiraj/10.06.2013.

Melucci, Alberto. 1989. *Nomads of the Present: Social Movements and Individual Needs in Contemporary Society.* London: Hutchinson Radius.

Melucci, Alberto. 1996. *Challenging Codes: Collective Action in the Information Age.* New York: Cambridge University Press.

MetroPOLL. *Gezi Parkı Protestoları* 2013. Available from http://www .metropoll.com.tr/report/get/373/1.

MilliyetDailyNews. *Polisin Müdahale Gücünü Artıracağız* 2013a [cited March 12, 2014]. Available from http://siyaset.milliyet.com.tr/polisin-mudahale-gucunu-artiracagiz/siyaset/detay/1724771/default.htm.

MilliyetDailyNews. *RedHack Yol Gösterdi: Tweet'i Nasıl Atarsanız Suç Olmaz* 2013b [cited January 15, 2014]. Available from http://www .milliyet.com.tr/redhack-yol-gosterdi-tweet-i/gundem/detay/1718952 /default.htm.

MilliyetDailyNews. *RedHack'ten Reyhanlı Belgeleri* 2013c [cited June 24, 2013]. Available from http://gundem.milliyet.com.tr/redhack-ten -reyhanli-belgeleri/gundem/detay/1712586/default.htm.

Mills, Charles. 1990. "Getting out of the Cave: Tension Between Democracy and Elitism in Marx's Theory of Cognitive Liberation." *Social and Economic Studies* no. 39(1):1–50.

Morton, Adam David. 2007. *Unravelling Gramsci: Hegemony and Passive Revolution in the Global Political Economy, Reading Gramsci.* London: Plato Press.

Moudouros, Nikos. 2014. "Rethinking Islamic Hegemony in Turkey through Gezi Park." *Journal of Balkan and Near Eastern Studies* no. 16(2):181–195.

Nazemroaya, Mahdi Darius. *The Tale of a Turkish Summer: Is there a Link between "Occupy Gezi" and the IMF?* 2013 [cited March 21, 2014]. Available from http://www.globalresearch.ca/the-tale-of-a-turkish -summer-is-there-a-link-between-occupy-gezi-and-the-imf/5339942.

Nepstad, Sharon Erickson. 2011. *Nonviolent Revolutions: Civil Resistance in the Late 20th Century.* New York: Oxford University Press.

NewYorkTimes. *Mosque Dream Seen at Heart of Turkey Protests* 2013 [cited April 1, 2014]. Available from http://www.nytimes.com/2013/06/24 /world/europe/mosque-dream-seen-at-heart-of-turkey -protests.html?pagewanted=all&_r=0.

Nişancı, Ensar. 2013. "The New Intellectual Capital Of Turkey: Muslim Intellectuals." *Emerging Markets Journal* no. 3(2):127–135.

NTVMSNBC. August 21, 2013. *'Nefes Alamıyoruz Atmayın'* 2013a [August 21, 2013]. Available from http://video.ntvmsnbc.com/nefes -alamiyoruz-atmayin.html.

NTVMSNBC. *Sendikalardan 'Gezi' Grevi* 2013b [cited June 24, 2013]. Available from http://www.ntvmsnbc.com/id/25447157/.

Occupy.com. *Occupy Gezi through the Eyes of an Occupy Wall Street Organizer* 2013 [cited March 14, 2014]. Available from http://www .occupy.com/article/occupy-gezi-through-eyes-occupy-wall-street -organizer.

OECD. *Better Life Index: Turkey* 2013a [cited July 11, 2013]. Available from http://www.oecdbetterlifeindex.org/countries/turkey.

OECD. *Turkey Statistics* 2013b [cited July 7, 2013]. Available from http://www.oecd-ilibrary.org/economics/country-statistical-profile -turkey-2013_csp-tur-table-2013-1-en.

Oliver, Pamela E. and Hank Johnston. 2000. "What a Good Idea! Ideologies and Frames in Social Movement Research." *Mobilization: An International Journal* no. 4(1):37–54.

Onedio.com. *Yolsuzluk ve Rüşvet Operasyonu Sosyal Medyayı Salladı* 2013 [cited May 2, 2014]. Available from http://onedio.com/haber /yolsuzluk-ve-rusvet-operasyonu-sosyal-medyayi-salladi-221005.

Öngel, Serkan. 2013. "Fetih Algısının Karşı Emek Perspektifi." *Express* (136):71.

Öniş, Ziya. *Beyond the 2001 Financial Crisis: The Political Economy of the New Phase of Neo-Liberal Restructuring in Turkey* 2006 [cited September 29, 2013]. Available from http://papers.ssrn.com/sol3 /papers.cfm?abstract_id=924623.

Oran, Baskın. 2001. "Kemalism, Islamism and Globalization: A Study on the Focus of Supreme Loyalty in Globalizing Turkey." *Southeast European and Black Sea Studies* no. 1(3):20–50.

Oran, Baskın. Taksim-Gezi'nin Üç Halkası ve AKP 2013 [cited October 7, 2013]. Available from http://www.radikal.com.tr/radikal2/taksim _gezinin_uc_halkasi_ve_akp-1142041.

Otero, Gerardo. 1999. *Farewell to the Peasantry? Political Class Formation in Rural Mexico.* Oxford: Westview Press.

Özugurlu, Metin. 2011. "The TEKEL Resistance Movement: Reminiscences on Class Struggle." *Capital & Class* no. 35(2):179–187.

Panitch, Leo. 1994. "Globalization and the State." *Socialist Register* no. 30(1):61–93.

Panitch, Leo and Sam Gindin. 2012. *The Making of Global Capitalism: The Political Economy of American Empire.* London & New York: Verso.

Peck, Jamie and Nik Theodore. 2012. "Reanimating Neoliberalism: Process Geographies of Neoliberalisation." *Social Anthropology* no. 20(2):177–185.

Peker, Efe. *Laikliğin Ruhuna El Fatiha*, September 22, 2013 2013 [cited June 25, 2013]. Available from http://solgazetebakis.com/2013-nisan -mayis/islamci-hegemonya-ve-laiklik/laikligin-ruhuna-el-fatiha/.

Petras, James. *Intellectuals and the War: From Retreat to Surrender* 2001a [cited September 26, 2013]. Available from http://petras.lahaine .org/?p=91&print=1.

Petras, James. 2001b. "Left Intellectuals and Desperate Search for Respectability." *Economic and Political Weekly* no. 36 (7):540–544.

Petras, James. 2003. *The New Development Politics: The Age of Empire Building and New Social Movements.* Aldershot: Ashgate.

Petras, James and Henri Veltmeyer. 2011. *Social Movements in Latin America: Neoliberalism and Popular Resistance.* New York: Palgrave Macmillan.

Petras, James and Henri Veltmeyer. 2013. "Socialism or Barbarism?" In *21st Century Socialism: Reinventing the Project*, edited by Henry Veltmeyer, 204–221. Halifax & Winnipeg: Fernwood.

Piven, Frances Fox. 2008. *Challenging Authority: How Ordinary People Change America.* Lanham: Rowman & Littlefield Publishers.

PlazaEylemPlatformu. *PEP Kimdir?* 2013 [cited July 11, 2013]. Available from http://plazaeylemplatformu.wordpress.com/pep-hakkinda/.

Polletta, Francesca and James M. Jasper. 2001. "Collective Identity and Social Movements." *Annual Review of Sociology* no. 27:283–305.

Poulantzas, Nicos. 1975a. *Classes in Contemporary Capitalism*. London: NLB.

Poulantzas, Nicos. 1975b. *Political Power and Social Classes*. London: NLB.

Poulantzas, Nicos. 2008. *The Poulantzas Reader*. London: Verso.

RadikalDailyNews. *Halep'te 50 Türk Savaşıyor* 2012 [cited September 10, 2013]. Available from http://www.radikal.com.tr/dunya/halepte_50_turk_savasiyor-1098170.

RadikalDailyNews. *Bağış: Gezi'de Ölenler Suriye'dekilerin Yanında Devede Kulak* 2013a [cited March 26, 2014]. Available from http://www.radikal.com.tr/turkiye/bagis_gezide_olenler_suriyedekilerin_yaninda_devede_kulak-1150827.

RadikalDailyNews. *Başbakan Erdoğan: 'Twitter Denen bir Bela Var'* 2013b [cited June 22, 2013]. Available from http://www.radikal.com.tr/politika/basbakan_erdogan_twitter_denen_bir_bela_var-1135952.

RadikalDailyNews. *Gezi Araştırmasında İlginç Sonuçlar: Ben Tipik bir Çapulcuyum* 2013c [cited May 8, 2014]. Available from http://www.radikal.com.tr/turkiye/gezi_arastirmasinda_ilginc_sonuclar_ben_tipik_bir_capulcuyum-1160203.

RadikalDailyNews. *Gezi'den 'Yeniden Doğuş' Beklemek* 2013d [cited April 7, 2014]. Available from http://www.radikal.com.tr/yazarlar/oral_calislar/geziden_yeniden_dogus_beklemek-1151691.

RadikalDailyNews. *Gezi Parkı'nın Bileşenleri* 2013e [cited July 5, 2013]. Available from http://www.radikal.com.tr/radikal2/gezi_parkinin_bilesenleri-1139898.

RadikalDailyNews. *Haysiyet Ayaklanması* 2013f [cited March 15, 2014]. Available from http://www.radikal.com.tr/yazarlar/ahmet_insel/haysiyet_ayaklanmasi-1136174.

RadikalDailyNews. *Tüm Yurtta "Diren Lice" Yürüyüşleri* 2013g [cited March 10, 2014]. Available from http://www.radikal.com.tr/politika/taksimde_diren_lice_yuruyusleri-1139720.

RadikalDailyNews. *"3. Havalimanı için Tek bir Çivi bile Çakılamaz"* 2014a [cited May 20, 2014]. Available from http://www.radikal.com.tr/turkiye/3_havalimani_icin_tek_bir_civi_bile_cakilamaz-1176618.

RadikalDailyNews. *Demircan: Tapeleri Dinlemek, İnanmak ve Yaymak Haram* 2014b [cited May 2, 2014]. Available from http://blog.radikal.com.tr/Sayfa/demircan-tapeleri-dinlemek-inanmak-ve-yaymak-haram-57388.

RadikalDailyNews. *İstanbul'a Yeni bir Çılgın Proje* 2014c [cited May 20, 2014]. Available from http://www.radikal.com.tr/turkiye/istanbula_yeni_bir_cilgin_proje-1168931.

RadikalDailyNews. *İşte Kabataş Görüntüleri* 2014d [cited February 20, 2014]. Available from http://www.radikal.com.tr/turkiye/gezi_olaylarinda_kabatasda_saldiriya_ugradigi_iddia_edilen_kadinin_goruntuleri_ortaya_cikti-1176660.

RadikalDailyNews. *Taksim'de Topçu Kışlası Tarihe Gömüldü* 2014e [cited May 20, 2014]. Available from http://www.radikal.com.tr /turkiye/taksimde_topcu_kislasi_tarihe_gomuldu-1190840.

RadikalDailyNews. *Uzmanlar Ses Kayıtlarını Analiz Etti* 2014f [cited May 20, 2014]. Available from http://www.radikal.com.tr/turkiye /uzmanlar_ses_kayitlarini_analiz_etti_montaj_degil-1178411.

Reuters. *Turkey Passes School Reform Law Critics View as Islamic* 2012 [cited March 12, 2014]. Available from http://uk.reuters.com /article/2012/03/30/uk-turkey-education-idUKBRE82T12D20120330.

Reuters. *Election Protests in Turkey as Opposition Cries Foul* 2014a [cited May 10, 2014]. Available from http://www.reuters.com /article/2014/04/01/us-turkey-election-idUSBREA3017H20140401.

Reuters. *Turkish Minister Says Fending Off "Mini-Coup Attempt"* 2014b [cited May 10, 2014]. Available from http://www.reuters.com /article/2013/12/31/us-turkey-corruption-idUSBRE9BU0BC20131231.

Reuters. *Turkish PM Tightens Grip on Judiciary in Parliament Vote* 2014c [cited May 10, 2014]. Available from http://www.reuters.com/ article/2014/02/15/us-turkey-corruption-idUSBREA1E07C20140215.

Rodrik, Dani. 2011. Ergenekon and Sledgehammer: Building or Undermining the Rule of Law? *Turkish Policy Quarterly* Spring: 99–109, http://turkishpolicy.com/dosyalar/files/Dani Rodrik- Rule of Law in Turkey.pdf.

Russell, Bernard, H. and W. Ryan Gery. 1998. "Text analysis: Qualitative and Quantitative Methods." In *Handbook of Methods in Cultural Anthropology*, edited by H. Russell Bernard, 595–646.

RussiaToday. *The Art of Sinning: Turkey's AKP, December Fallout and the Religion of Islam* 2014 [cited May 20, 2014]. Available from http:// rt.com/op-edge/turkey-news-revelations-islam-361/.

SabahNews. *Beyaz Türkler'in Korkusu Gezi'yi Patlattı* 2013a [cited July 5, 2013]. Available from http://www.sabah.com.tr/Ekonomi/2013/06/24 /beyaz-turklerin-korkusu-geziyi-patlatti.

SabahNews. *3. Boğaz Köprüsü'nün Temeli Atıldı* 2013b [cited March 12, 2014]. Available from http://www.sabah.com.tr/Ekonomi/2013/05/29 /3-bogaz-koprusunun-temeli-atiliyor.

Saraçoğlu, Cenk. *Gezi Direnişi ve Müzmin Orta Sınıf Sorunu* 2014 [cited March 8, 2014]. Available from http://bilimsol.org/bilimsol/blog /kenar-notlari/gezi-direnisi-ve-muzmin-orta-sinif-sorunu.

SendikaNews. *DİSK'ten AKP Faşizmine Karşı İhtar Eylemleri Geliyor* 2013a [cited June 24, 2013]. Available from http://www.sendika .org/2013/06/diskten-akp-fasizmine-karsi-ihtar-eylemleri-geliyor -hukumet-durmazsa-hayati-durduracagiz/.

SendikaNews. *İstanbullular Parkta, Forumda, Mahallede eylemde* 2013b [cited June 22, 2013]. Available from http://www.sendika.org/2013/06 /istanbullular-parkta-forumda-mahallede-eylemde-guncelleniyor.

SendikaNews. *Korkut Boratav Evaluates the Gezi Resistance* 2013c [cited July 1, 2013]. Available from http://www.sendika.org/2013/06/her-yer-taksim-her-yer-direnis-bu-isci-sinifinin-tarihsel-ozlemi-olan-sinirsiz-dolaysiz-demokrasi-cagrisidir-korkut-boratav/, http://www.sendika.org/2013/06/korkut-boratav-1-evaluates-the-gezi-resistance-a-matured-class-based-contumacy/.

SendikaNews. *Sendika İstatistikleri Yayımlandı: AKP Taşeron İşçilere Sendika Hakkı Tanımadı* 2013d [cited July 6, 2013]. Available from http://www.sendika.org/2013/01/sendika-istatistikleri-yayimlandi-akp-taseron-iscilere-sendika-hakki-tanimadi/.

SendikaNews. *Turkey-Record Fraud Rate in Local Elections: 1418 Cases* 2014 [cited May 10, 2014]. Available from http://www.sendika.org/2014/03/turkey-local-elections-a-peoples-mobilisation-against-cheating-and-fraud-in-ballot-boxes/.

Senol, Selma and Esengül Metin. *AKP İktidarı Hak-İş ve Memur-Sen'e Yaradı* 2013 [cited July 6, 2013]. Available from http://www.milliyet.com.tr/Ekonomi/HaberDetay.aspx?aType=HaberDetayArsiv&KategoriID=3&ArticleID=1032833.

Sharon-Krespin, Rachel. 2009. "Fethullah Gülen's Grand Ambition Turkey's Islamist Danger." *Middle East Quarterly* (Winter):55–66.

Socialbakers. *The RedHack Twitter Statistics* 2013a [cited June 24, 2013]. Available from http://www.socialbakers.com/twitter/theredhack.

Socialbakers. *Turkey Facebook Statistics* 2013b [cited June 24, 2013]. Available from http://www.socialbakers.com/facebook-statistics/turkey.

SocialistFeministCollective. *Women Are Also Resisting!* 2013 [cited September 14, 2013]. Available from http://www.sosyalistfeministkolektif.org/english.html?start=5.

SocialistInternational. September 20, 2013. *Declaration on Gezi Park* 2013 [September 20, 2013]. Available from http://www.socialistinternational.org/images/dynamicImages/files/FINAL Gez%3F Park Decl-Engl%3Fsh.pdf.

SolNews. *Bu Gelenekle Araları Hiç iyi Olmadı* 2010 [cited October 7, 2013]. Available from http://haber.sol.org.tr/devlet-ve-siyaset/bu-gelenekle-aralari-hic-iyi-olmadi-haberi-36873.

SolNews. *Hatay'da neler oluyor?* 2012 [cited September 10, 2013]. Available from http://haber.sol.org.tr/kent-gundemleri/hatayda-neler-oluyor-haberi-58844.

SolNews. *Başbakan Gezi heyetinin Üzerine Yürümüş* 2013a [cited June 22, 2013]. Available from http://haber.sol.org.tr/devlet-ve-siyaset/basbakan-gezi-heyetinin-uzerine-yurumus-haberi-74737.

SolNews. *ÇARŞI Grubundan İkinci El 'Satılık TOMA' İlanı* 2013b [cited June 22, 2013]. Available from http://haber.sol.org.tr/devlet-ve-siyaset/carsi-grubundan-ikinci-el-satilik-toma-ilani-haberi-74188.

SolNews. *Taksim Dayanışması: Söz Gezi Parkı'nın* 2013c [cited June 22, 2013]. Available from http://haber.sol.org.tr/devlet-ve-siyaset/taksim-dayanismasi-soz-gezi-parkinin-haberi-74711.

SolNews. *TKP'den Gezi Parkı Açıklaması* 2013d [cited September 22, 2013]. Available from http://haber.sol.org.tr/soldakiler/tkpden-gezi -parki-aciklamasi-hep-birlikte-bu-zorbaliga-yeter-diyelim-haberi-73807.

SolNews. *Alo Ferit: Erdoğan'dan NTV'ye Müdahale* 2014 [cited May 20, 2014]. Available from http://haber.sol.org.tr/medya/alo-ferit -erdogandan-ntvye-mudahale-haberi-89156.

Sönmez, Mustafa. 2010. "2000'ler Türkiye'sinde Hâkim Sınıflar ve İç Çelişkileri." In *AKP Kitabı*, edited by İlhan Uzgel and Bülent Duru, 179–194. Ankara: Phoenix.

Sönmez, Mustafa. 2013. *Kent, Kapital ve Gezi Direnişi.* Ankara: Nota Bene.

SözcüDailyNews. *THY Hosteslerinden Gezi Parkı'na Destek* 2013 [cited August 12, 2013]. Available from http://video.sozcu.com.tr/2013 /video/haber/thy-hosteslerinden-gezi-parkina-destek.html.

StarNews. *İlk Günden Bugüne Hükümet Gezi Parkı Eylemleri İçin Neler Söyledi?* 2013 [cited July 4, 2013]. Available from http://www .stargundem.com/gundem/1324143-ilk-gunden-bugune-hukumet -gezi-parki-eylemleri-icin-neler-soyledi.html.

T24OnlineNews. *Abant Platformu'ndan 'Gezi Parkı' için Sağduyu Çağrısı* 2013a [cited October 7, 2013]. Available from http://t24.com.tr/haber /abant-platformundan-gezi-parki-icin-sagduyu-cagrisi/231377.

T24OnlineNews. April 10, 2014. *Babuşcu: Gelecek 10 yıl, Liberaller gibi Eski Paydaşlarımızın Arzuladığı gibi Olmayacak* 2013b [April 10, 2014]. Available from http://t24.com.tr/haber/babuscu-onumuzdeki -10-yil-liberaller-gibi-eski-paydaslarimizin-kabullenecegi-gibi -olmayacak/226892.

T24OnlineNews. *Devlet Dersinde Öldürülen ve Öldürülecek Çocuklara* 2013c [cited February 11, 2014]. Available from http://t24.com.tr/yazi /sos-hatay-sos-turkiye/7435.

T24OnlineNews. *Direniş Meşruiyetini ve Desteklerini Yitirmemeli* 2013d [cited February 17, 2014]. Available from http://t24.com.tr/yazi /direnis-mesruiyetini-ve-desteklerini-yitirmemeli/6900.

TaksimSolidarityPlatform. *Constituents* 2013 [cited June 22, 2013]. Available from http://taksimdayanisma.org/bilesenler?lang=en.

TGRTNews. *"Yükselen Güçler" Benzer Olaylar ile Yüz Yüze* 2013 [cited July 4, 2013]. Available from http://www.tgrthaber.com/news_viewng .aspx?newsid=850953.

TheDailyStar. *Video Casts Doubt over Alleged Attack on Headscarved Woman* 2014 [cited March 11, 2014]. Available from http:// www.dailystar.com.lb/News/Middle-East/2014/Feb-14/247358 -video-casts-doubt-over-alleged-attack-on-headscarved-woman .ashx – axzz31WjSTSY4.

TheEconomist. *Death from the Skies* 2012a [cited July 3, 2013]. Available from http://www.economist.com/node/21562922.

TheEconomist. *Massacre at Uludere* 2012b [cited July 14, 2013]. Available from http://www.economist.com/node/21556616.

TheEconomist. *Not so Good for You* 2013a [cited July 3, 2013]. Available from http://www.economist.com/news/europe/21578657-mildly-islamist -government-brings-tough-alcohol-restrictions-not-so-good-you.

TheEconomist. *The Anti-Capitalist Muslims* 2013b [cited March 14, 2014]. Available from http://www.economist.com/blogs/charlemagne /2013/07/turkish-politics.

TheEconomist. *The March of Protest* 2013c [cited July 1, 2013]. Available from http://www.economist.com/news/leaders/21580143-wave-anger -sweeping-cities-world-politicians-beware-march-protest.

TheEconomist. *The New Young Turks* 2013d [cited July 3, 2013]. Available from http://www.economist.com/news/briefing/21579005 -protests-against-recep-tayyip-erdogan-and-his-ham-fisted-response -have-shaken-his-rule-and.

TheEconomist. *Disillusioned and Divided* 2014 [cited May 25, 2014]. Available from http://www.economist.com/news/europe/21602728 -prime-ministers-popularity-taking-knock-his-bedrock-support -strong-and-his.

TheEconomistBlog. *Red No's day* 2013 [cited July 3, 2013]. Available from http://www.economist.com/blogs/gulliver/2013/05/turkish-airlines.

TheGuardian. *211 Journalists in World's Jails in 2013* 2013a [cited March 28, 2014]. Available from http://www.theguardian.com/media/ greenslade/2013/dec/18/journalist-safety-turkey.

TheGuardian. *Erdoğan's Chief Adviser Knows What's Behind Turkey's Protests—Telekinesis* 2013b [cited March 15, 2014]. Available from http://www.theguardian.com/commentisfree/2013/jul/13/erdogan -turkey-protests-telekinesis-conspiracy-theories.

TheGuardian. *Turkey Alcohol Laws could Pull the Plug on Istanbul Nightlife* 2013c [cited June 22, 2013]. Available from http://www .guardian.co.uk/world/2013/may/31/turkey-alcohol-laws-istanbul -nightlife.

TheGuardian. *Turkey's Protesters Proclaim Themselves the True Heirs of Their Nation's Founding Father* 2013d [cited April 9, 2014. Available from http://www.theguardian.com/world/2013/jun/08/turkey-protesters -proclaim-heirs-ataturk.

TheGuardian. *Turkey's "Standing Man" Shows How Passive Resistance Can Shake a State* 2013e [cited June 30, 2013]. Available from http:// www.theguardian.com/commentisfree/2013/jun/18/turkey-standing -man.

TheGuardian. *Turkish Police Arrest 25 People for Using Social Media to Call for Protest* 2013f [cited October 7, 2013]. Available from http:// www.theguardian.com/world/2013/jun/05/turkish-police-arrests -social-media-protest.

TheGuardian. *Berkin Elvan Protests in Turkey* 2014a [cited May 2, 2014]. Available from http://www.theguardian.com/world/gallery/2014/mar /13/berkin-elvan-funeral-protests-in-turkey-in-pictures.

TheGuardian. *Turkey's YouTube and Twitter Bans Show a Government in Serious Trouble* 2014b [cited May 10, 2014]. Available from http://www.theguardian.com/commentisfree/2014/mar/28/turkey-youtube-twitter-ban-government-trouble.

TheGuardian. *Turkish Police Caught in Middle of War between Erdoğan and Former Ally Gülen* 2014c [cited May 10, 2014]. Available from http://www.theguardian.com/world/2014/feb/09/turkish-police-fethullah-gulen-network.

TheIndependent. *Turkey's "Standing Man" Captured Attention, but Protest Doesn't Stand Still—It Forms Assemblies* 2013 [cited March 15, 2014]. Available from http://www.independent.co.uk/voices/comment/turkeys-standing-man-captured-attention-but-protest-doesnt-stand-still--it-forms-assemblies-8672456.html.

TheTelegraph. *Syrian Rebels say Turkey Is Arming and Training Them* 2012 [cited March 15, 2014]. Available from http://blogs.telegraph.co.uk/news/michaelweiss/100159613/syrian-rebels-say-turkey-is-arming-and-training-them/.

Tilly, Charles. 1995. "Contentious Repertoires in Great Britain, 1785–1834." In *Repertoires and Cycles of Collective Action*, edited by Mark Traugott. Durham: Duke University Press.

Tisdall, Simon. *Turkey's Sledgehammer Coup Verdict: Justice or Soviet-Style Show Trial?* 2012 [cited July 3, 2013]. Available from http://www.guardian.co.uk/world/2012/sep/25/turkey-sledgehammer-coup-trial-verdict.

TMMOB. *Yerel Yönetimler Seçim Bildirgesi* 2013 [cited March 14, 2014]. Available from http://www.tmmob.org.tr/resimler/ekler/b1c5bf541a24b23_ek.pdf?tipi=2&turu=X&sube=0.

Today'sZaman. *18 More Arrested for Engaging in Illegal Acts during Gezi Protests* 2013a [cited October 7, 2013]. Available from http://www.todayszaman.com/news-318843-18-more-arrested-for-engaging-in-illegal-acts-during-gezi-protests.html.

Today'sZaman. *Erdoğan Urges People to Sue Bangers of Pots and Pans* 2013b [cited July 12, 2013]. Available from http://www.todayszaman.com/news-321500-erdogan-urges-people-to-sue-bangers-of-pots-and-pans.html.

Today'sZaman. *From Gezi Park to Politics* 2013c [cited March 5, 2014]. Available from http://www.todayszaman.com/columnists/etyen-mahcupyan_317547-from-gezi-park-to-politics.html.

Today'sZaman. *Police Get Bonus for Gezi Park Crackdown* 2013d [cited February 10, 2014]. Available from http://www.todayszaman.com/news-319522-police-get-bonus-for-gezi-park-crackdown.html.

Today'sZaman. *Full Transcript of Voice Recording Purportedly of Erdoğan and His Son* 2014a [cited May 20, 2014]. Available from http://www.todayszaman.com/news-340552-full-transcript-of-voice-recording-purportedly-of-turkish-pm-erdogan-and-his-son.html.

Today'sZaman. *Ruling AK Party Deputy Defends Right to Commit Sins amid Corruption Woes* 2014b [cited May 20, 2014]. Available from http://www.todayszaman.com/news-341279-ruling-ak-party-deputy -defends-right-to-commit-sins-amid-corruption-woes.html.

TOKI. *TOKİ Konut Üretim Raporu* 2014 [cited 15 March, 2014]. Available from https://http://www.toki.gov.tr/TR/Genel/t.ashx?F6E1 0F8892433CFFAAF6AA849816B2EFDF36587C4B003136.

Touraine, Alain. 1988. *Return of the Actor*. Minneapolis: University of Minnesota Press.

Tuğal, Cihan. 2011. "Fight or Acquiesce? Religion and Political Process in Turkey's and Egypt's Neoliberalizations." *Development and Change* no. 43(1):23–51.

Tür, Özlem. 2011. "Economic Relations with the Middle East Under the AKP—Trade, Business Community and Reintegration with Neighboring Zones." *Turkish Studies* no. 12(4):589–602.

TurkStat. *İdari Sorumluluğu Olup Olmama Durumu ve Meslek Ana Grubuna Göre Ortalama Çalışma Süreleri ve Aylık Ortalama Brüt Ücret* 2010 [cited July 1, 2013]. Available from http://www.google .ca/url?sa=t&rct=j&q=TUIK%2B%22idari%2Bsorumlulugu%2Bolu p%2Bolmama%2Bdurumu%22&source=web&cd=1&ved=0CCwQ FjAA&url=http%3A%2F%2Fwww.tuik.gov.tr%2FPreIstatistikTablo .do%3Fistab_id%3D1056&ei=_0DSUeSYMuP9igK7zYGwDg&usg =AFQjCNE-lPQo_4kCCd8c59g2uCsEBNpPGQ&sig2=Mzj7c71Xt9 csr4OiPiAumw&bvm=bv.48705608,d.cGE.

TurkStat. *İstatistiklerle Gençlik* 2012 [cited July 1, 2013]. Available from http://www.tuik.gov.tr/PreHaberBultenleri.do?id=13509.

TurkStat. *15–24 Yaş Grubundaki Nüfusun Yıllar ve Cinsiyete Göre İşgücü Durumu* 2013a [cited December 20, 2013]. Available from http://www.tuik.gov.tr/PreIstatistikTablo.do?istab_id=1181.

TurkStat. *İstihdam Edilenlerin Yıllara Göre İktisadi Faaliyet Kolları* 2013b [cited July 1, 2013]. Available from http://www.tuik.gov.tr /UstMenu.do?metod=temelist.

TurkStat. *İstihdam Edilenlerin Yıllara Göre İşteki Durumu* 2013c [cited July 1, 2013]. Available from http://www.tuik.gov.tr/UstMenu.do? metod=temelist.

TurkStat. *National Accounts* 2013d [cited August 15, 2013]. Available from http://www.turkstat.gov.tr/UstMenu.do?metod=temelist.

TurkStat. *Sabit Telefon, Cep Telefonu ve İnternet Abone Sayısı* 2013e [cited June 25, 2013]. Available from http://www.tuik.gov.tr /PreIstatistikTablo.do?istab_id=1580.

TurkStat. *Construction Permit (1954–2003)* 2014a [cited April 12, 2014]. Available from http://www.tuik.gov.tr/PreIstatistikTablo.do? istab_id=2010.

TurkStat. *Construction Permit (2002–2013)* 2014b [cited April 12, 2014]. Available from http://www.tuik.gov.tr/PreIstatistikTablo.do?istab_id=609.

TurkishWeekly. *Turkish PM Erdogan Reiterates His Call for Three Children* 2013 [cited October 12, 2013]. Available from http://www.turkishweekly.net/news/146227/turkish-pm-erdo%EF%A3%BFan-reiterates-his-call-for-three-children.html.

USDepartmentofState. *Turkey 2012 Human Rights Report.* Bureau of Democracy, Human Rights and Labor 2012 [cited May 11, 2014]. Available from http://www.state.gov/documents/organization/204558.pdf.

Utku, Deniz. *Deniz Utku's Twitter Message* 2013 [cited June 22, 2013]. Available from https://twitter.com/denisutku/status/340891460817797120.

UyanmaSaati. *Uyanma Saati Nasıl Yürüyor?* 2013 [cited July 11, 2013]. Available from http://uyanmasaati.com/.

Uzgel, İlhan and Bülent Duru. 2010. *AKP Kitabı.* Ankara: Phoenix.

VatanDailyNews. *İşte Türkiye'nin Kredi Kartı Borcu* 2013 [cited July 7, 2013]. Available from http://haber.gazetevatan.com/iste-turkiyenin-kredi-karti-borcu/504710/2/ekonomi.

VatanDailyNews. *Kasetler Doğruysa Dindarlar Zekatını Vermiştir* 2014 [cited May 20, 2014]. Available from http://haber.gazetevatan.com/kasetler-dogruysa-dindarlar-zekatini-vermistir/612965/1/gundem.

VOANews. *Turkey's Murder Rate of Women Skyrockets* 2011 [cited February 15, 2014]. Available from http://www.voanews.com/content/turkeys-murder-rate-of-women-skyrockets-117093538/170517.html.

VOANews. *In Turkey, Religious Schools Gain a Foothold* 2012 [cited September 25, 2013]. Available from http://www.voanews.com/content/turkey-controversial-education-reform-imam-hatip-schools/1514915.html.

Vurucu, Ikbal. 2013. "Gezi Parki Olaylari." *2023* (147):10–23.

Washington'sBlog. *The Monitoring of Our Phone Calls? Government Spooks May Be Listening* 2013 [cited October 7, 2013]. Available from http://www.globalresearch.ca/the-monitoring-of-our-phone-calls-government-spooks-may-be-listening/5338103.

Webrazzi. *Türkiye'deki Twitter Kullanıcılarının Sayısı 9.6 Milyona Ulaştı* 2013 [cited June 23, 2013]. Available from http://www.webrazzi.com/2013/02/12/twitter-turkiye-istatistikleri-2013.

White, Susan O. 2001. "Reasoning and Justice." In *Handbook of Youth and Justice*, edited by Susan O. White. New York: Kluwer.

Wikipedia. *Ekşi Sözlük* 2013 [cited June 22, 2013]. Available from 4. Chapter 4 – Organization, Leadership, Repertoires.docx.

Wolf, Eric R. 2001. *Pathways of Power: Building an Anthropology of the Modern World.* Berkeley, Los Angeles & London: University of California Press.

Wood, Ellen Meiksins. 1998. *The Retreat from Class: A New "True" Socialism.* London & New York: Verso.

World, Worker's. *Occupy Wall Street "From Zuccotti to Gezi"* 2013 [cited March 12, 2014]. Available from http://www.workers.org /articles/2013/06/03/occupy-wall-street-from-zuccotti-to-gezi/.

WorldBank. *Turkey Statistics* 2013 [cited July 7, 2013]. Available from http://data.worldbank.org/country/turkey.

WorldBulletin. *Two Different Iftars in Taksim* 2013 [cited March 9, 2014]. Available from http://www.worldbulletin.net/haber/112792 /two-different-iftars-in-taksim.

Wright, Erik Olin. 1978. *Class, Crisis and the State.* London: Verso.

Wright, Erik Olin. 1997. *Class Counts: Comparative Studies in Class Analysis.* Cambridge: Cambridge University Press.

Wright, Erik Olin. 2005. "Foundations of a Neo-Marxist Class Analysis." In *Approaches to Class Analysis,* edited by Erik Olin Wright. Cambridge: Cambridge University Press.

Wright, Erik Olin and Joachim Singelmann. 1982. "Proletarianization in the Changing American Class Structure." *The American Journal of Sociology* no. 88:176–209.

Yalman, Galip. 2012. "Politics and Discourse under the AKP's Rule." In *Silent Violence: Neoliberalism, Islamist Politics and the AKP Years in Turkey,* edited by Simten Cosar and Gamze Yucesan-Ozdemir, 21–42. Ottawa: Red Quill Books.

Yaşlı, Fatih. 2013. "Hegemonya Krizi ve Karşı-Hegemonya: Öncesi ve Sonrasıyla Direnişe Bakmak." *Bilim ve Gelecek* (114):9–15.

Yeldan, A. Erinç. *Patterns of Adjustment in the Age of Finance: The Case of Turkey as a Peripheral Agent of Neoliberal Globalization* 2009 [cited July 11, 2013]. Available from http://ideaswebsite.org /workingpapers/01_2009.pdf.

Yeldan, A. Erinç. *TEKEL Workers' Resistance: Re-Awakening of the Proletariat in Turkey* 2010 [cited October 21, 2013]. Available from http://www.sendika.org/2010/01/tekel-workers-resistance-re -awakening-of-the-proletariat-in-turkey-erinc-yeldan/.

Yeldan, A. Erinç. 2014. "Don't Call Turkey Mine Disaster an Accident— Privatisation Made It Inevitable." *The Conversation.*

YeniŞafak. *Erdoğan: Gezi Yalan Hedef Talan* 2013 [cited July 14, 2013]. Available from http://yenisafak.com.tr/politika-haber/erdogan-gezi -yalan-hedef-talan-23.06.2013-534918.

YeniŞafakDailyNews. *Prof. Dr. Mete Tunçay: Günümüz Kemalistleri Geçmiştekilerden çok daha Doğmatik* 2007 [cited October 7, 2013]. Available from http://yenisafak.com.tr/roportaj-haber/prof-dr-mete -tuncay-gunumuz-kemalistleri-gecmistekilerd-30.04.2007-33056.

Yıldırım, Birge. *Transformation of Public Squares in Istanbul between 1938–1949* 2012 [cited June 22, 2013]. Available from http://www. fau.usp.br/iphs/abstractsAndPapersFiles/Sessions/10/YILDIRIM.pdf.. pdf.

Yıldırım, Deniz. 2010. "AKP ve Neoliberal Popülizm." In *AKP Kitabı*, edited by İlhan Uzgel and Bülent Duru, 66–107. Ankara: Phoenix.

YouTube. *Everyday I'm Chapulling—Tayyip feat. Bulent* 2013 [cited April 1, 2014]. Available from https://http://www.youtube.com /watch?v=CqxX40RibwE.

Yücesan-Ozdemir, Gamze. 2012. "The Social Policy Regime in the AKP Years: The Emperor's New Clothes." In *Silent Violence: Neoliberalism, Islamist Politics and the AKP Years in Turkey*, edited by Simten Cosar and Gamze Yücesan-Ozdemir, 125–152. Ottawa: Red Quill Books.

ZaytungNews. *Gezi Parkı Olayları Nedeniyle Hükümet Tarafından Suçlanmayan Tek Ülke Olan Myanmar'da Halkın Öfkesi Sokaklara Taştı* 2013a [cited April 1, 2014]. Available from http://www.zaytung. com/haberdetay.asp?newsid=217691.

ZaytungNews. *Gezi Parkı Olaylarının Arkasındaki Güçleri Ortaya Çıkarmaya Çalışan Melih Gökçek, Yanlışlıkla Kennedy Suikasti'nin Faillerini Buldu* 2013b [cited April 1, 2014]. Available from http:// www.zaytung.com/haberdetay.asp?newsid=215364.

ZaytungNews. *Gezi Parkı'ndaki Çadırlardan Çıkan Marjinal Örgütlere Ait Vahşet Planları* 2013c [cited April 1, 2014]. Available from http:// www.zaytung.com/fotohaberdetay.asp?newsid=215173.

Žižek, Slavoj. *Trouble in Paradise* 2013 [cited July 7, 2013]. Available from http://www.lrb.co.uk/2013/06/28/slavoj-zizek/trouble-in-paradise.

Index